ERASMUS

and the Age of Reformation

ER · ROT

TERMINVS

Pallas Apelleam nuper mirata tabellam,
Hanc ait, æternùm Bibliotheca colat.
Dædaleam monſtrat Muſis HOLBEINNIVS *artem*
Et ſummi Ingenii Magnus ERASMVS *opes.*

WOODCUT BY HANS HOLBEIN. 1535

ERASMUS

and the Age of Reformation

JOHAN HUIZINGA

*with a selection from
the letters of Erasmus*

⚡

HARPER TORCHBOOKS / The Cloister Library
HARPER & ROW, PUBLISHERS
NEW YORK

ERASMUS AND THE AGE OF REFORMATION

Printed in the United States of America

Huizinga's text was translated from the Dutch by F. Hopman and first published by Charles Scribner's Sons in 1924. The selection from the Letters of Erasmus was translated by Barbara Flower.

Reprinted by arrangement with Phaidon Press, Ltd., London
Originally published under the title: "Erasmus of Rotterdam"

First HARPER TORCHBOOK edition published 1957

Library of Congress catalogue card number: 57-10119

CONTENTS

PREFACE

by G. N. Clark, Provost of Oriel College, Oxford

RATHER more than twenty years ago, on a spring morning of alternate cloud and sunshine, I acted as guide to Johan Huizinga, the author of this book, when he was on a visit to Oxford. As it was not his first stay in the city, and he knew the principal buildings already, we looked at some of the less famous. Even with a man who was well known all over the world as a writer, I expected that these two or three hours would be much like the others I had spent in the same capacity with other visitors; but this proved to be a day to remember. He understood the purposes of these ancient buildings, the intentions of their founders and builders; but that was to be expected from an historian who had written upon the history of universities and learning. What surprised and delighted me was his seeing eye. He told me which of the decorative *motifs* on the Tower of the Four Orders were usual at the time when it was built, and which were less common. At All Souls he pointed out the seldom appreciated merits of Hawksmoor's twin towers. His eye was not merely informed but sensitive. I remembered that I had heard of his talent for drawing, and as we walked and talked I felt the influence of a strong, quiet personality deep down in which an artist's perceptiveness was fused with a determination to search for historical truth.

Huizinga's great success and reputation came suddenly when he was over forty. Until that time his powers were ripening, not so much slowly as secretly. His friends knew that he was unique, but neither he nor they foresaw what direction his studies would take. He was born in 1872 in Groningen, the most northerly of the chief towns of the Netherlands, and there he went to school and to the University. He studied Dutch history and literature and also Oriental languages and mythology and sociology; he was a good linguist and he steadily accumulated great learning, but he was neither an infant prodigy nor a universal scholar. Science and current affairs scarcely interested him, and until his maturity imagination seemed to satisfy him more than research. Until he was over thirty he was a schoolmaster at Haarlem, a teacher of history; but it was still uncertain whether European or Oriental studies would claim him in the end. For two or three years before giving up school-teaching he lectured in the University of Amsterdam on Sanskrit, and it was almost an accident that he became professor of history in the University of his native town. All through his life it was characteristic of him that after a spell of creative work, when he had finished a book, he would turn aside from the subject that had absorbed him and plunge into some other subject or period, so that the books and articles in the eight volumes of his collected works (with one more volume still to come) cover a very wide range. As time went on he examined aspects of history which at first he had passed over, and he acquired a clear insight into the political and economic life of the past. It has been well said of him that he never became either a pedant or a doctrinaire. During the ten years that he spent as professor at Groningen, he found himself. He was happily married, with a growing family, and the many elements of his mind drew together into a unity. His sensitiveness to style and beauty came to terms with his conscientious scholarship. He was rooted in the traditional freedoms of his national and academic environment, but his curiosity, like the historical adventures of his people and his profession, was not limited by time or space or prejudice. He came more and more definitely to find his central theme in civilization as a realized ideal, something that men have created in an endless variety of forms, but always in order to raise the level of their lives.

While this interior fulfilment was bringing Huizinga to his best, the world about him changed completely. In 1914, Holland became a neutral country surrounded by nations at war. In 1914, also, his wife died, and it was as a lonely widower that he was appointed in the next year to the chair of general history at Leyden, which he was to hold for the rest of his academic life. Yet the year after the end of the war saw the publication of his masterpiece, the book which gave him his high place among historical writers and was translated as *The Waning of the Middle Ages*. This is a study of the forms of life and thought in France and the Netherlands in the fourteenth and fifteenth centuries, the last phase of one of the great European eras of civilization. In England, where the Middle Ages had been idealized for generations, some of its leading thoughts did not seem so novel as they did in Holland, where many people regarded the Renaissance and more still regarded the Reformation as a new beginning of a better world; but in England and America, which had been drawn, unlike Holland, into the vortex of war, it had the poignancy of a recall to the standards of reasonableness. It will long maintain its place as a historical book and as a work of literature.

The shorter book on Erasmus is a companion to this great work. It was first published in 1924 and so belongs to the same best period of the author. Its subject is the central intellectual figure of the next generation after the period which Huizinga called the waning, or rather the autumn, of the Middle Ages; but Erasmus was also, as will appear from many of its pages, a man for whom he had a very special sympathy. Something of what he wrote about Erasmus might also have been written about himself, or at least about his own response to the transformation of the world that he had known.

This is not the place for an analysis of that questioning and illuminating response, nor for a considered estimate of Huizinga's work as a whole; but there is room for a word about his last years. He was recognized as one of the intellectual leaders of his country, and a second marriage in 1937 brought back his private happiness; but the shadows were darkening over the western world. From the time when national socialism began to reveal itself in Germany, he took his stand against it with perfect simplicity and calm. After the invasion of Holland he addressed these memorable words to some of his colleagues: 'When it comes, as it soon will, to defending our University and the freedom of science and learning in the Netherlands, we must be ready to give everything for that: our possessions, our freedom, and even our lives.' The Germans closed the University. For a time they held Johan Huizinga, now an old man and in failing health, as a hostage; then they banished him to open arrest in a remote parish in the eastern part of the country. Even in these conditions he still wrote, and wrote well. In the last winter of the war the liberating armies approached and he suffered the hardships of the civilian population in a theatre of war; but his spirit was unbroken. He died on 1 February 1945, a few weeks before his country was set free.

Oriel College, Oxford

G. N. CLARK

April 1952

ERASMUS

and the Age of Reformation

CHAPTER I

CHILDHOOD AND EARLY YOUTH
1466–88

*The Low Countries in the fifteenth century—The Burgundian power—
Connections with the German Empire and with France—The northern
Netherlands outskirts in every sense—Movement of Devotio moderna:
brethren of the Common Life and Windesheim monasteries—Erasmus's
birth: 1466—His relations and name—At school at Gouda, Deventer and
Bois-le-Duc—He takes the vows: probably in 1488*

WHEN Erasmus was born Holland had for about twenty years
formed part of the territory which the dukes of Burgundy had
succeeded in uniting under their dominion—that complexity
of lands, half French in population, like Burgundy, Artois,
Hainault, Namur; half Dutch like Flanders, Brabant, Zealand,
Holland. The appellation 'Holland' was, as yet, strictly limited
to the county of that name (the present provinces of North and
South Holland), with which Zealand, too, had long since been
united. The remaining territories which, together with those
last mentioned, make up the present kingdom of the Netherlands, had not yet been brought under Burgundian dominion,
although the dukes had cast their eyes on them. In the bishopric
of Utrecht, whose power extended to the regions on the far
side of the river Ysel, Burgundian influence had already begun
to make itself manifest. The projected conquest of Friesland
was a political inheritance of the counts of Holland, who preceded the Burgundians. The duchy of Guelders, alone, still
preserved its independence inviolate, being more closely
connected with the neighbouring German territories, and
consequently with the Empire itself.

All these lands—about this time they began to be regarded
collectively under the name of 'Low Countries by the Sea'—
had in most respects the character of outskirts. The authority
of the German emperors had for some centuries been little

more than imaginary. Holland and Zealand hardly shared the dawning sense of a national German union. They had too long looked to France in matters political. Since 1299 a French-speaking dynasty, that of Hainault, had ruled Holland. Even the house of Bavaria that succeeded it about the middle of the fourteenth century had not restored closer contact with the Empire, but had itself, on the contrary, early become Gallicized, attracted as it was by Paris and soon twined about by the tentacles of Burgundy to which it became linked by means of a double marriage.

The northern half of the Low Countries were 'outskirts' also in ecclesiastical and cultural matters. Brought over rather late to the cause of Christianity (the end of the eighth century), they had, as borderlands, remained united under a single bishop: the bishop of Utrecht. The meshes of ecclesiastical organization were wider here than elsewhere. They had no university. Paris remained, even after the designing policy of the Burgundian dukes had founded the university of Louvain in 1425, the centre of doctrine and science for the northern Netherlands. From the point of view of the wealthy towns of Flanders and Brabant, now the heart of the Burgundian possessions, Holland and Zealand formed a wretched little country of boatmen and peasants. Chivalry, which the dukes of Burgundy attempted to invest with new splendour, had but moderately thrived among the nobles of Holland. The Dutch had not enriched courtly literature, in which Flanders and Brabant zealously strove to follow the French example, by any contribution worth mentioning.

Whatever was coming up in Holland flowered unseen; it was not of a sort to attract the attention of Christendom. It was a brisk navigation and trade, mostly transit trade, by which the Hollanders already began to emulate the German Hansa, and which brought them into continual contact with France and Spain, England and Scotland, Scandinavia, North Germany and the Rhine from Cologne upward. It was herring fishery, a humble trade, but the source of great prosperity—a rising industry, shared by a number of small towns.

Not one of those towns in Holland and Zealand, neither Dordrecht nor Leyden, Haarlem, Middelburg, Amsterdam, could compare with Ghent, Bruges, Lille, Antwerp or Brussels in the south. It is true that in the towns of Holland also the highest products of the human mind germinated, but those towns themselves were still too small and too poor to be centres of art and science. The most eminent men were irresistibly drawn to one of the great foci of secular and ecclesiastical culture. Sluter, the great sculptor, went to Burgundy, took service with the dukes, and bequeathed no specimen of his art to the land of his birth. Dirk Bouts, the artist of Haarlem, removed to Louvain, where his best work is preserved; what was left at Haarlem has perished. At Haarlem, too, and earlier, perhaps, than anywhere else, obscure experiments were being made in that great art, craving to be brought forth, which was to change the world: the art of printing.

There was yet another characteristic spiritual phenomenon, which originated here and gave its peculiar stamp to life in these countries. It was a movement designed to give depth and fervour to religious life; started by a burgher of Deventer, Geert Groote, toward the end of the fourteenth century. It had embodied itself in two closely connected forms—the fraterhouses, where the brethren of the Common Life lived together without altogether separating from the world, and the congregation of the monastery of Windesheim, of the order of the regular Augustinian canons. Originating in the regions on the banks of the Ysel, between the two small towns of Deventer and Zwolle, and so on the outskirts of the diocese of Utrecht, this movement soon spread, eastward to Westphalia, northward to Groningen and the Frisian country, westward to Holland proper. Fraterhouses were erected everywhere and monasteries of the Windesheim congregation were established or affiliated. The movement was spoken of as 'modern devotion', *devotio moderna*. It was rather a matter of sentiment and practice than of definite doctrine. The truly Catholic character of the movement had early been acknowledged by the church authorities. Sincerity and modesty, simplicity and industry, and, above all, constant ardour of religious emotion and thought, were its objects. Its energies were devoted to tending the sick and other works of charity, but especially to instruction and the art of writing. It is in this that it especially differed from the revival of the Franciscan and Dominican orders of about the same time, which turned to preaching. The Windesheimians and the Hieronymians (as the brethren of the Common Life were also called) exerted their crowning activities in the seclusion of the schoolroom and the silence of the writing cell. The schools of the brethren soon drew pupils from a wide area. In this way the foundations were laid, both here in the northern Netherlands and in lower Germany, for a generally diffused culture among the middle classes; a culture of a very narrow, strictly ecclesiastical nature, indeed, but which for that very reason was fit to permeate broad layers of the people.

What the Windesheimians themselves produced in the way of devotional literature is chiefly limited to edifying booklets and biographies of their own members; writings which were distinguished rather by their pious tenor and sincerity than by daring or novel thoughts.

But of them all, the greatest was that immortal work of Thomas à Kempis, Canon of Saint Agnietenberg, near Zwolle, the *Imitatio Christi*.

Foreigners visiting these regions north of the Scheldt and the Meuse laughed at the rude manners and the deep drinking of the inhabitants, but they also mentioned their sincere piety. These countries were already, what they have ever remained, somewhat contemplative and self-contained, better adapted for speculating on the world and for reproving it than for astonishing it with dazzling wit.

Rotterdam and Gouda, situated upward of twelve miles apart in the lowest region of Holland, an extremely watery region, were not among the first towns of the county. They were small country towns, ranking after Dordrecht, Haarlem, Leyden, and rapidly rising Amsterdam. They were not centres of culture. Erasmus was born at Rotterdam on 27 October, most probably in the year 1466. The illegitimacy of his birth has thrown a veil of mystery over his descent and kinship. It is possible that Erasmus himself learned the circumstances of his coming into the world only in his later years. Acutely sensitive to the taint in his origin, he did more to veil the secret than to reveal it. The picture which he painted of it in his ripe age was romantic and pathetic. He imagined that his father when a young man made love to a girl, a physician's daughter, in the hope of marrying her. The parents and brothers of the young fellow, indignant, tried to persuade him to take holy orders. The young man fled before the child was born. He went to Rome and made a living by copying. His relations sent him false tidings that his beloved had died; out of grief he became a priest and devoted himself to religion altogether. Returned to his native country he discovered the deceit. He abstained from all contact with her whom he now could no longer marry, but took great pains to give his son a liberal education. The mother continued to care for the child, till an early death took her from him. The father soon followed her to the grave. To Erasmus's recollection he was only twelve or thirteen years old when his mother died. It seems to be practically certain that her death did not occur before 1483, when, therefore, he was already seventeen years old. His sense of chronology was always remarkably ill developed.

Unfortunately it is beyond doubt that Erasmus himself knew, or had known, that not all particulars of this version were correct. In all probability his father was already a priest at the time of the relationship to which he owed his life; in any case it was not the impatience of a betrothed couple, but an irregular alliance of long standing, of which a brother, Peter, had been born three years before.

We can only vaguely discern the outlines of a numerous and commonplace middle-class family. The father had nine brothers, who were all married. The grandparents on his father's side and the uncles on his mother's side attained to a very great age. It is strange that a host of cousins—their progeny—has not boasted of a family connection with the great

Erasmus. Their descendants have not even been traced. What were their names? The fact that in burgher circles family names had, as yet, become anything but fixed, makes it difficult to trace Erasmus's kinsmen. Usually people were called by their own and their father's name; but it also happened that the father's name became fixed and adhered to the following generation. Erasmus calls his father Gerard, his brother Peter Gerard, while a papal letter styles Erasmus himself Erasmus Rogerii. Possibly the father was called Roger Gerard or Gerards.

Although Erasmus and his brother were born at Rotterdam, there is much that points to the fact that his father's kin did not belong there, but at Gouda. At any rate they had near relatives at Gouda.

Erasmus was his Christian name. There is nothing strange in the choice, although it was rather unusual. St. Erasmus was one of the fourteen Holy Martyrs, whose worship so much engrossed the attention of the multitude in the fifteenth century. Perhaps the popular belief that the intercession of St. Erasmus conferred wealth, had some weight in choosing the name. Up to the time when he became better acquainted with Greek, he used the form Herasmus. Later on he regretted that he had not also given that name the more correct and melodious form Erasmius. On a few occasions he half jocularly called himself so, and his godchild, Johannes Froben's son, always used this form.

It was probably for similar aesthetic considerations that he soon altered the barbaric Rotterdammensis to Roterdamus, later Roterodamus, which he perhaps accentuated as a proparoxytone. Desiderius was an addition selected by himself, which he first used in 1496; it is possible that the study of his favourite author Jerome, among whose correspondents there is a Desiderius, suggested the name to him. When, therefore, the full form, Desiderius Erasmus Roterodamus, first appears, in the second edition of the *Adagia*, published by Josse Badius at Paris in 1506, it is an indication that Erasmus, then forty years of age, had found himself.

Circumstances had not made it easy for him to find his way. Almost in his infancy, when hardly four years old, he thinks, he had been put to school at Gouda, together with his brother. He was nine years old when his father sent him to Deventer to continue his studies in the famous school of the chapter of St. Lebuin. His mother accompanied him. His stay at Deventer must have lasted, with an interval during which he was a choir boy in the minster at Utrecht, from 1475 to 1484. Erasmus's explicit declaration that he was fourteen years old when he left Deventer may be explained by assuming that in later years he confused his temporary absence from Deventer (when at Utrecht) with the definite end of his stay at Deventer. Reminiscences of his life there repeatedly crop up in Erasmus's writings. Those concerning the teaching he got inspired him with little gratitude; the school was still barbaric, then, he said; ancient medieval text-books were used there of whose silliness and cumbrousness we can hardly conceive. Some of the masters were of the brotherhood of the Common Life. One of them, Johannes Synthen, brought to his task a certain degree of understanding of classic antiquity in its purer form. Toward the end of Erasmus's residence Alexander Hegius was placed at the head of the school, a friend of the Frisian humanist, Rudolf Agricola, who on his return from Italy was gaped at by his compatriots as a prodigy. On festal days, when the rector made his oration before all the pupils, Erasmus heard Hegius; on one single occasion he listened to the celebrated Agricola himself, which left a deep impression on his mind.

His mother's death of the plague that ravaged the town brought Erasmus's school-time at Deventer to a sudden close. His father called him and his brother back to Gouda, only to die himself soon afterwards. He must have been a man of culture. For he knew Greek, had heard the famous humanists in Italy, had copied classic authors and left a library of some value.

Erasmus and his brother were now under the protection of three guardians whose care and intentions he afterwards placed in an unfavourable light. How far he exaggerated their treatment of him it is difficult to decide. That the guardians, among whom one Peter Winckel, schoolmaster at Gouda, occupied the principal place, had little sympathy with the new classicism, about which their ward already felt enthusiastic, need not be doubted. 'If you should write again so elegantly, please to add a commentary', the schoolmaster replied grumblingly to an epistle on which Erasmus, then fourteen years old, had expended much care. That the guardians sincerely considered it a work pleasing to God to persuade the youths to enter a monastery can no more be doubted than that this was for them the easiest way to get rid of their task. For Erasmus this pitiful business assumes the colour of a grossly selfish attempt to cloak dishonest administration; an altogether reprehensible abuse of power and authority. More than this: in later years it obscured for him the image of his own brother, with whom he had been on terms of cordial intimacy.

Winckel sent the two young fellows, twenty-one and eighteen years old, to school again, this time at Bois-le-Duc. There they lived in the Fraterhouse itself, to which the school was attached. There was nothing here of the glory that had shone about Deventer. The brethren, says Erasmus, knew of no other purpose than that of destroying all natural gifts, with blows, reprimands and severity, in order to fit the soul for the monastery. This, he thought, was just what his guardians were aiming at; although ripe for the university they were deliberately kept away from it. In this way more than two years were wasted.

One of his two masters, one Rombout, who liked young Erasmus, tried hard to prevail on him to join the brethren of the Common Life. In later years Erasmus occasionally regretted that he had not yielded; for the brethren took no such irrevocable vows as were now in store for him.

An epidemic of the plague became the occasion for the brothers to leave Bois-le-Duc and return to Gouda. Erasmus was attacked by a fever that sapped his power of resistance, of which he now stood in such need. The guardians (one of the three had died in the meantime) now did their utmost to make the two young men enter a monastery. They had good cause for it, as they had ill administered the slender fortune of their wards, and, says Erasmus, refused to render an account. Later he saw everything connected with this dark period of his life in the most gloomy colours—except himself. Himself he sees as a boy of not yet sixteen years (it is nearly certain that he must have been twenty already) weakened by fever, but nevertheless resolute and sensible in refusing. He has persuaded his brother to fly with him and to go to a university. The one guardian is a narrow-minded tyrant, the other, Winckel's brother, a merchant, a frivolous coaxer. Peter, the elder of the youths, yields first and enters the monastery of Sion, near Delft (of the order of the regular Augustinian canons), where the guardian had found a place for him. Erasmus resisted longer. Only after a visit to the monastery of Steyn or Emmaus, near Gouda, belonging to the same order, where he found a schoolfellow from Deventer, who pointed out the bright side of monastic life, did Erasmus yield and enter Steyn, where soon after, probably in 1488, he took the vows.

CHAPTER II

IN THE MONASTERY

1488–95

Erasmus as an Augustinian canon at Steyn—His friends—Letters to Servatius—Humanism in the monasteries: Latin poetry—Aversion to cloister-life—He leaves Steyn to enter the service of the Bishop of Cambray: 1493—James Batt—Antibarbari—He gets leave to study at Paris: 1495

In his later life—under the influence of the gnawing regret which his monkhood and all the trouble he took to escape from it caused him—the picture of all the events leading up to his entering the convent became distorted in his mind. Brother Peter, to whom he still wrote in a cordial vein from Steyn, became a worthless fellow, even his evil spirit, a Judas. The schoolfellow whose advice had been decisive now appeared a traitor, prompted by self-interest, who himself had chosen convent-life merely out of laziness and the love of good cheer.

The letters that Erasmus wrote from Steyn betray no vestige of his deep-seated aversion to monastic life, which afterwards he asks us to believe he had felt from the outset. We may, of course, assume that the supervision of his superiors prevented him from writing all that was in his heart, and that in the depths of his being there had always existed the craving for freedom and for more civilized intercourse than Steyn could offer. Still he must have found in the monastery some of the good things that his schoolfellow had led him to expect. That at this period he should have written a 'Praise of Monastic Life', 'to please a friend who wanted to decoy a cousin', as he himself says, is one of those naïve assertions, invented afterwards, of which Erasmus never saw the unreasonable quality.

He found at Steyn a fair degree of freedom, some food for an intellect craving for classic antiquity, and friendships with men of the same turn of mind. There were three who especially attracted him. Of the schoolfellow who had induced

him to become a monk, we hear no more. His friends are
Servatius Roger of Rotterdam and William Hermans of
Gouda, both his companions at Steyn, and the older Cornelius
Gerard of Gouda, usually called Aurelius (a quasi-latinization
of Goudanus), who spent most of his time in the monastery of
Lopsen, near Leyden. With them he read and conversed
sociably and jestingly; with them he exchanged letters when
they were not together.

Out of the letters to Servatius there rises the picture of an
Erasmus whom we shall never find again—a young man of
more than feminine sensitiveness; of a languishing need for
sentimental friendship. In writing to Servatius, Erasmus runs
the whole gamut of an ardent lover. As often as the image of
his friend presents itself to his mind tears break from his eyes.
Weeping he re-reads his friend's letter every hour. But he is
mortally dejected and anxious, for the friend proves averse to
this excessive attachment. 'What do you want from me?' he
asks. 'What is wrong with you?' the other replies. Erasmus
cannot bear to find that this friendship is not fully returned.
'Do not be so reserved; do tell me what is wrong! I repose my
hope in you alone; I have become yours so completely that you
have left me naught of myself. You know my pusillanimity,
which when it has no one on whom to lean and rest, makes
me so desperate that life becomes a burden.'

Let us remember this. Erasmus never again expresses himself so passionately. He has given us here the clue by which we
may understand much of what he becomes in his later years.

These letters have sometimes been taken as mere literary
exercises; the weakness they betray and the complete absence
of all reticence, seem to tally ill with his habit of cloaking his
most intimate feelings which, afterwards, Erasmus never quite
relinquishes. Dr. Allen, who leaves this question undecided,
nevertheless inclines to regard the letters as sincere effusions,
and to me they seem so, incontestably. This exuberant friendship accords quite well with the times and the person.

Sentimental friendships were as much in vogue in secular
circles during the fifteenth century as towards the end of the

eighteenth century. Each court had its pairs of friends, who dressed alike, and shared room, bed, and heart. Nor was this cult of fervent friendship restricted to the sphere of aristocratic life. It was among the specific characteristics of the *devotio moderna*, as, for the rest, it seems from its very nature to be inseparably bound up with pietism. To observe one another with sympathy, to watch and note each other's inner life, was a customary and approved occupation among the brethren of the Common Life and the Windesheim monks. And though Steyn and Sion were not of the Windesheim congregation, the spirit of the *devotio moderna* was prevalent there.

As for Erasmus himself, he has rarely revealed the foundation of his character more completely than when he declared to Servatius: 'My mind is such that I think nothing can rank higher than friendship in this life, nothing should be desired more ardently, nothing should be treasured more jealously'. A violent affection of a similar nature troubled him even at a later date when the purity of his motives was questioned. Afterwards he speaks of youth as being used to conceive a fervent affection for certain comrades. Moreover, the classic examples of friends, Orestes and Pylades, Damon and Pythias, Theseus and Pirithous, as also David and Jonathan, were ever present before his mind's eye. A young and very tender heart, marked by many feminine traits, replete with all the sentiment and with all the imaginings of classic literature, who was debarred from love and found himself placed against his wish in a coarse and frigid environment, was likely to become somewhat excessive in his affections.

He was obliged to moderate them. Servatius would have none of so jealous and exacting a friendship and, probably at the cost of more humiliation and shame than appears in his letters, young Erasmus resigns himself, to be more guarded in expressing his feelings in the future. The sentimental Erasmus disappears for good and presently makes room for the witty latinist, who surpasses his older friends, and chats with them about poetry and literature, advises them about their Latin style, and lectures them if necessary.

The opportunities for acquiring the new taste for classic antiquity cannot have been so scanty at Deventer, and in the monastery itself, as Erasmus afterwards would have us believe, considering the authors he already knew at this time. We may conjecture, also, that the books left by his father, possibly brought by him from Italy, contributed to Erasmus's culture, though it would be strange that, prone as he was to disparage his schools and his monastery, he should not have mentioned the fact. Moreover, we know that the humanistic knowledge of his youth was not exclusively his own, in spite of all he afterwards said about Dutch ignorance and obscurantism. Cornelius Aurelius and William Hermans likewise possessed it.

In a letter to Cornelius he mentions the following authors as his poetic models—Virgil, Horace, Ovid, Juvenal, Statius, Martial, Claudian, Persius, Lucan, Tibullus, Propertius. In prose he imitates Cicero, Quintilian, Sallust, and Terence, whose metrical character had not yet been recognized. Among Italian humanists he was especially acquainted with Lorenzo Valla, who on account of his *Elegantiae* passed with him for the pioneer of *bonae literae*; but Filelfo, Aeneas Sylvius, Guarino, Poggio, and others, were also not unknown to him. In ecclesiastical literature he was particularly well read in Jerome. It remains remarkable that the education which Erasmus received in the schools of the *devotio moderna* with their ultra-puritanical object, their rigid discipline intent on breaking the personality, could produce such a mind as he manifests in his monastic period—the mind of an accomplished humanist. He is only interested in writing Latin verses and in the purity of his Latin style. We look almost in vain for piety in the correspondence with Cornelius of Gouda and William Hermans. They manipulate with ease the most difficult Latin metres and the rarest terms of mythology. Their subject-matter is bucolic or amatory, and, if devotional, their classicism deprives it of the accent of piety. The prior of the neighbouring monastery of Hem, at whose request Erasmus sang the Archangel Michael, did not dare to paste up his Sapphic ode:

it was so 'poetic', he thought, as to seem almost Greek. In those days poetic meant classic. Erasmus himself thought he had made it so bald that it was nearly prose—'the times were so barren, then', he afterwards sighed.

These young poets felt themselves the guardians of a new light amidst the dullness and barbarism which oppressed them. They readily believed each other's productions to be immortal, as every band of youthful poets does, and dreamt of a future of poetic glory for Steyn by which it would vie with Mantua. Their environment of clownish, narrow-minded conventional divines—for as such they saw them—neither acknowledged nor encouraged them. Erasmus's strong propensity to fancy himself menaced and injured tinged this position with the martyrdom of oppressed talent. To Cornelius he complains in fine Horatian measure of the contempt in which poetry was held; his fellow-monk orders him to let his pen, accustomed to writing poetry, rest. Consuming envy forces him to give up making verses. A horrid barbarism prevails, the country laughs at the laurel-bringing art of high-seated Apollo; the coarse peasant orders the learned poet to write verses. 'Though I had mouths as many as the stars that twinkle in the silent firmament on quiet nights, or as many as the roses that the mild gale of spring strews on the ground, I could not complain of all the evils by which the sacred art of poetry is oppressed in these days. I am tired of writing poetry.' Of this effusion Cornelius made a dialogue which highly pleased Erasmus.

Though in this art nine-tenths may be rhetorical fiction and sedulous imitation, we ought not, on that account, to undervalue the enthusiasm inspiring the young poets. Let us, who have mostly grown blunt to the charms of Latin, not think too lightly of the elation felt by one who, after learning this language out of the most absurd primers and according to the most ridiculous methods, nevertheless discovered it in its purity, and afterwards came to handle it in the charming rhythm of some artful metre, in the glorious precision of its structure and in all the melodiousness of its sound.

I. ERASMUS AT THE AGE OF 51

II. VIEW OF ROTTERDAM, EARLY SIXTEENTH CENTURY

Nec si quot placidis ignea noctibus
Scintillant tacito sydera culmine,
Nec si quot tepidum flante Favonio
 Ver suffundit humo rosas,
Tot sint ora mihi . . .

Was it strange that the youth who could say this felt himself
a poet?—or who, together with his friend, could sing of spring
in a Meliboean song of fifty distichs? Pedantic work, if you
like, laboured literary exercises, and yet full of the freshness
and the vigour which spring from the Latin itself.

Out of these moods was to come the first comprehensive
work that Erasmus was to undertake, the manuscript of which
he was afterwards to lose, to recover in part, and to publish
only after many years—the *Antibarbari*, which he commenced
at Steyn, according to Dr. Allen. In the version in which eventually the first book of the *Antibarbari* appeared, it reflects, it is
true, a somewhat later phase of Erasmus's life, that which
began after he had left the monastery; neither is the comfortable tone of his witty defence of profane literature any longer
that of the poet at Steyn. But the ideal of a free and noble life
of friendly intercourse and the uninterrupted study of the
Ancients had already occurred to him within the convent
walls.

In the course of years those walls probably hemmed him in
more and more closely. Neither learned and poetic correspondence nor the art of painting with which he occupied himself,[1]
together with one Sasboud, could sweeten the oppression of
monastic life and a narrow-minded, unfriendly environment.
Of the later period of his life in the monastery, no letters at all
have been preserved, according to Dr. Allen's carefully considered dating. Had he dropped his correspondence out of
spleen, or had his superiors forbidden him to keep it up, or are
we merely left in the dark because of accidental loss? We

[1] Allen No. 16.12 cf. IV p. xx, and *vide* LB. IV 756, where surveying
the years of his youth he also writes 'Pingere dum meditor tenueis sine
corpore formas'.

know nothing about the circumstances and the frame of mind in which Erasmus was ordained on 25 April 1492, by the Bishop of Utrecht, David of Burgundy. Perhaps his taking holy orders was connected with his design to leave the monastery. He himself afterwards declared that he had but rarely read mass. He got his chance to leave the monastery when offered the post of secretary to the Bishop of Cambray, Henry of Bergen. Erasmus owed this preferment to his fame as a Latinist and a man of letters; for it was with a view to a journey to Rome, where the bishop hoped to obtain a cardinal's hat, that Erasmus entered his service. The authorization of the Bishop of Utrecht had been obtained, and also that of the prior and the general of the order. Of course, there was no question yet of taking leave for good, since, as the bishop's servant, Erasmus continued to wear his canon's dress. He had prepared for his departure in the deepest secrecy. There is something touching in the glimpse we get of his friend and fellow-poet, William Hermans, waiting in vain outside of Gouda to see his friend just for a moment, when on his way south he would pass the town. It seems there had been consultations between them as to leaving Steyn together, and Erasmus, on his part, had left him ignorant of his plans. William had to console himself with the literature that might be had at Steyn.

Erasmus, then twenty-five years old—for in all probability the year when he left the monastery was 1493—now set foot on the path of a career that was very common and much coveted at that time: that of an intellectual in the shadow of the great. His patron belonged to one of the numerous Belgian noble families, which had risen in the service of the Burgundians and were interestedly devoted to the prosperity of that house. The Glimes were lords of the important town of Bergen-op-Zoom, which, situated between the River Scheldt and the Meuse delta, was one of the links between the northern and the southern Netherlands. Henry, the Bishop of Cambray, had just been appointed chancellor of the Order of the Golden Fleece, the most distinguished spiritual dignity at court, which although now Habsburg in fact, was still named after Burgundy. The service of such an important personage promised almost unbounded honour and profit. Many a man would under the circumstances, at the cost of some patience, some humiliation, and a certain laxity of principle, have risen even to be a bishop. But Erasmus was never a man to make the most of his situation.

Serving the bishop proved to be rather a disappointment. Erasmus had to accompany him on his frequent migrations from one residence to another in Bergen, Brussels, or Mechlin. He was very busy, but the exact nature of his duties is unknown. The journey to Rome, the acme of things desirable to every divine or student, did not come off. The bishop, although taking a cordial interest in him for some months, was less accommodating than he had expected. And so we shortly find Erasmus once more in anything but a cheerful frame of mind. 'The hardest fate,' he calls his own, which robs him of all his old sprightliness. Opportunities to study he has none. He now envies his friend William, who at Steyn in the little cell can write beautiful poetry, favoured by his 'lucky stars'. It befits him, Erasmus, only to weep and sigh; it has already so dulled his mind and withered his heart that his former studies no longer appeal to him. There is rhetorical exaggeration in this and we shall not take his pining for the monastery too seriously, but still it is clear that deep dejection had mastered him. Contact with the world of politics and ambition had probably unsettled Erasmus. He never had any aptitude for it. The hard realities of life frightened and distressed him. When forced to occupy himself with them he saw nothing but bitterness and confusion about him. 'Where is gladness or repose? Wherever I turn my eyes I only see disaster and harshness. And in such a bustle and clamour about me you wish me to find leisure for the work of the Muses?'

Real leisure Erasmus was never to find during his life. All his reading, all his writing, he did hastily, *tumultuarie*, as he calls it repeatedly. Yet he must nevertheless have worked with intensest concentration and an incredible power of assimilation.

Whilst staying with the bishop he visited the monastery of Groenendael near Brussels, where in former times Ruysbroeck wrote. Possibly Erasmus did not hear the inmates speak of Ruysbroeck and he would certainly have taken little pleasure in the writings of the great mystic. But in the library he found the works of St. Augustine and these he devoured. The monks of Groenendael were surprised at his diligence. He took the volumes with him even to his bedroom.

He occasionally found time to compose at this period. At Halsteren, near Bergen-op-Zoom, where the bishop had a country house, he revised the *Antibarbari*, begun at Steyn, and elaborated it in the form of a dialogue. It would seem as if he sought compensation for the agitation of his existence in an atmosphere of idyllic repose and cultured conversation. He conveys us to the scene (he will afterwards use it repeatedly) which ever remained the ideal pleasure of life to him: a garden or a garden house outside the town, where in the gladness of a fine day a small number of friends meet to talk during a simple meal or a quiet walk, in Platonic serenity, about things of the mind. The personages whom he introduces, besides himself, are his best friends. They are the valued and faithful friend whom he got to know at Bergen, James Batt, schoolmaster and afterwards also clerk of that town, and his old friend William Hermans of Steyn, whose literary future he continued somewhat to promote. William, arriving unexpectedly from Holland, meets the others, who are later joined by the Burgomaster of Bergen and the town physician. In a lightly jesting, placid tone they engage in a discussion about the appreciation of poetry and literature—Latin literature. These are not incompatible with true devotion, as barbarous dullness wants us to believe. A cloud of witnesses is there to prove it, among them and above all St. Augustine, whom Erasmus had studied recently, and St. Jerome, with whom Erasmus had been longer acquainted and whose mind was, indeed, more congenial to him. Solemnly, in ancient Roman guise, war is declared on the enemies of classic culture. O ye Goths, by what right do you occupy, not only the Latin provinces (the *disciplinae liberales* are meant) but the capital, that is Latinity itself?

It was Batt who, when his prospects with the Bishop of Cambray ended in disappointment, helped to find a way out for Erasmus. He himself had studied at Paris, and thither Erasmus also hoped to go, now that Rome was denied him. The bishop's consent and the promise of a stipend were obtained and Erasmus departed for the most famous of all universities, that of Paris, probably in the late summer of 1495. Batt's influence and efforts had procured him this lucky chance.

CHAPTER III

THE UNIVERSITY OF PARIS

1495-9

The University of Paris — Traditions and schools of Philosophy and Theology — The College of Montaigu — Erasmus's dislike of scholasticism — Relations with the humanist, Robert Gaguin, 1495 — How to earn a living — First drafts of several of his educational works — Travelling to Holland and back — Batt and the Lady of Veere — To England with Lord Mountjoy: 1499

THE University of Paris was, more than any other place in Christendom, the scene of the collision and struggle of opinions and parties. University life in the Middle Ages was in general tumultuous and agitated. The forms of scientific intercourse themselves entailed an element of irritability: never-ending disputations, frequent elections and rowdyism of the students. To those were added old and new quarrels of all sorts of orders, schools and groups. The different colleges contended among themselves, the secular clergy were at variance with the regular. The Thomists and the Scotists, together called the Ancients, had been disputing at Paris for half a century with the Terminists, or Moderns, the followers of Ockam and Buridan. In 1482 some sort of peace was concluded between those two groups. Both schools were on their last legs, stuck fast in sterile technical disputes, in systematizing and sub-dividing, a method of terms and words by which science and philosophy benefited no longer. The theological colleges of the Dominicans and Franciscans at Paris were declining; theo-logical teaching was taken over by the secular colleges of Navarre and Sorbonne, but in the old style.

The general traditionalism had not prevented humanism from penetrating Paris also during the last quarter of the fifteenth century. Refinement of Latin style and the taste for classic poetry here, too, had their fervent champions, just as revived Platonism, which had sprung up in Italy. The Parisian humanists were partly Italians as Girolamo Balbi and

Fausto Andrelini, but at that time a Frenchman was considered to be their leader, Robert Gaguin, general of the order of the Mathurins or Trinitarians, diplomatist, French poet and humanist. Side by side with the new Platonism a clearer understanding of Aristotle penetrated, which had also come from Italy. Shortly before Erasmus's arrival Jacques Lefèvre d'Étaples had returned from Italy, where he had visited the Platonists, such as Marsilio Ficino, Pico della Mirandola, and Ermolao Barbaro, the reviver of Aristotle. Though theoretical theology and philosophy generally were conservative at Paris, yet here as well as elsewhere movements to reform the Church were not wanting. The authority of Jean Gerson, the University's great chancellor (about 1400), had not yet been forgotten. But reform by no means meant inclination to depart from the doctrine of the Church; it aimed, in the first place, at restoration and purification of the monastic orders and afterwards at the extermination of abuses which the Church acknowledged and lamented as existing within its fold. In that spirit of reformation of spiritual life the Dutch movement of the *devotio moderna* had recently begun to make itself felt, also, at Paris. The chief of its promoters was John Standonck of Mechlin, educated by the brethren of the Common Life at Gouda and imbued with their spirit in its most rigorous form. He was an ascetic more austere than the spirit of the Windesheimians, strict indeed but yet moderate, required; far beyond ecclesiastical circles his name was proverbial on account of his abstinence—he had definitely denied himself the use of meat. As provisor of the college of Montaigu he had instituted the most stringent rules there, enforced by chastisement for the slightest faults. To the college he had annexed a home for poor scholars, where they lived in a semi-monastic community.

To this man Erasmus had been recommended by the Bishop of Cambray. Though he did not join the community of poor students—he was nearly thirty years old—he came to know all the privations of the system. They embittered the earlier part of his stay at Paris and instilled in him a deep, permanent aversion to abstinence and austerity. Had he come to Paris for this—to experience the dismal and depressing influences of his youth anew in a more stringent form?

The purpose for which Erasmus went to Paris was chiefly to obtain the degree of doctor of theology. This was not too difficult for him: as a regular he was exempt from previous study in the faculty of arts, and his learning and astonishing intelligence and energy enabled him to prepare in a short time for the examinations and disputations required. Yet he did not attain this object at Paris. His stay, which with interruptions lasted, first till 1499, to be continued later, became to him a period of difficulties and exasperations, of struggle to make his way by all the humiliating means which at the time were indispensable to that end; of dawning success, too, which, however, failed to gratify him.

The first cause of his reverses was a physical one; he could not endure the hard life in the college of Montaigu. The addled eggs and squalid bedrooms stuck in his memory all his life; there he thinks he contracted the beginnings of his later infirmity. In the *Colloquia* he has commemorated with abhorrence Standonck's system of abstinence, privation and chastisement. For the rest his stay there lasted only until the spring of 1496.

Meanwhile he had begun his theological studies. He attended lectures on the Bible and on the Book of the Sentences, the medieval handbook of theology and still the one most frequently used. He was even allowed to give some lessons in the college on Holy Scripture. He preached a few sermons in honour of the Saints, probably in the neighbouring abbey of St. Geneviève. But his heart was not in all this. The subtleties of the schools could not please him. That aversion to all scholasticism, which he rejected in one sweeping condemnation, struck root in his mind, which, however broad, always judged unjustly that for which it had no room. 'Those studies can make a man opinionated and contentious; can they make him wise? They exhaust the mind by a certain jejune and barren subtlety, without fertilizing or inspiring it. By their stammering and by the stains of their impure style they disfigure theology which had been enriched and adorned by the eloquence of the ancients. They involve everything whilst trying to resolve everything.' 'Scotist', with Erasmus, became a handy epithet for all schoolmen, nay, for everything super-annuated and antiquated. He would rather lose the whole of Scotus than Cicero's or Plutarch's works. These he feels the better for reading, whereas he rises from the study of scholas-ticism frigidly disposed towards true virtue, but irritated into a disputatious mood.

It would, no doubt, have been difficult for Erasmus to find in the arid traditionalism which prevailed in the University of Paris the heyday of scholastic philosophy and theology. From the disputations which he heard in the Sorbonne he brought back nothing but the habit of scoffing at doctors of theology, or as he always ironically calls them by their title of honour: *Magistri nostri*. Yawning, he sat among 'those holy Scotists' with their wrinkled brows, staring eyes, and puzzled faces, and on his return home he writes a disrespectful fantasy to his young friend Thomas Grey, telling him how he sleeps the sleep of Epimenides with the divines of the Sorbonne. Epi-menides awoke after his forty-seven years of slumber, but the majority of our present theologians will never wake up. What may Epimenides have dreamt? What but subtleties of the Scotists: quiddities, formalities, etc.! Epimenides himself was reborn in Scotus, or rather, Epimenides was Scotus's prototype. For did not he, too, write theological books, in which he tied such syllogistic knots as he would never have been able to loosen? The Sorbonne preserves Epimenides's skin written over with mysterious letters, as an oracle which men may only see after having borne the title of *Magister noster* for fifteen years.

It is not a far cry from caricatures like these to the *Sorbonistres* and the *Barbouillamenta Scoti* of Rabelais. 'It is said', thus Erasmus concludes his *boutade*, 'that no one can understand the mysteries of this science who has had the least intercourse with the Muses or the Graces. All that you have learned in the way of *bonae literae* has to be unlearned first; if you have drunk of Helicon you must first vomit the draught. I do my utmost to say nothing according to the Latin taste, and nothing graceful or witty; and I am already making progress, and there is hope that one day they will acknowledge Erasmus.'

It was not only the dryness of the method and the barrenness of the system which revolted Erasmus. It was also the qualities of his own mind, which, in spite of all its breadth and acuteness, did not tend to penetrate deeply into philosophical or dogmatic speculations. For it was not only scholasticism that repelled him; the youthful Platonism and the rejuvenated Aristotelianism taught by Lefèvre d'Étaples also failed to attract him. For the present he remained a humanist of aesthetic bias, with the substratum of a biblical and moral disposition, resting mainly on the study of his favourite Jerome. For a long time to come Erasmus considered himself, and also introduced himself, as a poet and an orator, by which latter term he meant what we call a man of letters.

Immediately on arriving at Paris he must have sought contact with the headquarters of literary humanism. The obscure Dutch regular introduced himself in a long letter (not preserved) full of eulogy, accompanied by a much-laboured poem, to the general, not only of the Trinitarians but, at the same time, of Parisian humanists, Robert Gaguin. The great man answered very obligingly: 'From your lyrical specimen I conclude that you are a scholar; my friendship is at your disposal; do not be so profuse in your praise, that looks like flattery'. The correspondence had hardly begun when Erasmus found a splendid opportunity to render this illustrious personage a service and, at the same time, in the shadow of his name, make himself known to the reading public. The matter is also of importance because it affords us an opportunity, for the first time, to notice the connection that is always found between Erasmus's career as a man of letters and a scholar and the technical conditions of the youthful art of printing.

Gaguin was an all-round man and his Latin text-book of the history of France, *De origine et gestis Francorum Compendium*, was just being printed. It was the first specimen of humanistic historiography in France. The printer had finished his work on 30 September 1495, but of the 136 leaves, two remained blank. This was not permissible according to the notions of that time. Gaguin was ill and could not help matters. By judicious spacing the compositor managed to fill up folio 135 with a poem by Gaguin, the colophon and two panegyrics by Faustus Andrelinus and another humanist. Even then there was need of matter, and Erasmus dashed into the breach and furnished a long commendatory letter, completely filling the superfluous blank space of folio 136.[1] In this way his name and style suddenly became known to the numerous public which was interested in Gaguin's historical work, and at the same time he acquired another title to Gaguin's protection, on whom the exceptional qualities of Erasmus's diction had evidently not been lost. That his history would remain known chiefly because it had been a stepping stone to Erasmus, Gaguin could hardly have anticipated.

Although Erasmus had now, as a follower of Gaguin, been introduced into the world of Parisian humanists, the road to fame, which had latterly begun to lead through the printing press, was not yet easy for him. He showed the *Antibarbari* to Gaguin, who praised them, but no suggestion of publication resulted. A slender volume of Latin poems by Erasmus was published in Paris in 1496, dedicated to Hector Boys, a Scotchman, with whom he had become acquainted at Montaigu. But the more important writings at which he worked during his stay in Paris all appeared in print much later.

While intercourse with men like Robert Gaguin and Faustus Andrelinus might be honourable, it was not directly profitable. The support of the Bishop of Cambray was scantier than he wished. In the spring of 1496 he fell ill and left Paris. Going first to Bergen, he had a kind welcome from his patron, the bishop; and then, having recovered his health, he went on to Holland to his friends. It was his intention to stay there, he says.

---

[1] Allen No. 43, p. 145, where the particulars of the case are expounded with peculiar acuteness and conclusions drawn with regard to the chronology of Erasmus's stay at Paris.

The friends themselves, however, urged him to return to Paris, which he did in the autumn of 1496. He carried poetry by William Hermans and a letter from this poet to Gaguin. A printer was found for the poems and Erasmus also brought his friend and fellow-poet into contact with Faustus Andrelinus.

The position of a man who wished to live by intellectual labour was far from easy at that time and not always dignified. He had either to live on church prebends or on distinguished patrons, or on both. But such a prebend was difficult to get and patrons were uncertain and often disappointing. The publishers paid considerable copy-fees only to famous authors. As a rule the writer received a number of copies of his work and that was all. His chief advantage came from a dedication to some distinguished personage, who could compliment him for it with a handsome gift. There were authors who made it a practice to dedicate the same work repeatedly to different persons. Erasmus has afterwards defended himself explicitly from that suspicion and carefully noted how many of those whom he honoured with a dedication gave nothing or very little.

The first need, therefore, to a man in Erasmus's circumstances was to find a Maecenas. Maecenas with the humanists was almost synonymous with paymaster. Under the adage *Ne bos quidem pereat* Erasmus has given a description of the decent way of obtaining a Maecenas. Consequently, when his conduct in these years appears to us to be actuated, more than once, by an undignified pushing spirit, we should not gauge it by our present standards. These were his years of weakness.

On his return to Paris he did not again lodge in Montaigu. He tried to make a living by giving lessons to young men of fortune. A merchant's sons of Lübeck, Christian and Henry Northoff, who lodged with one Augustine Vincent, were his pupils. He composed beautiful letters for them, witty, fluent and a trifle scented. At the same time he taught two young Englishmen, Thomas Grey and Robert Fisher, and conceived such a doting affection for Grey as to lead to trouble with the youth's guardian, a Scotchman, by whom Erasmus was excessively vexed.

Paris did not fail to exercise its refining influence on Erasmus. It made his style affectedly refined and sparkling—he pretends to disdain the rustic products of his youth in Holland. In the meantime, the works through which afterwards his influence was to spread over the whole world began to grow, but only to the benefit of a few readers. They remained unprinted as yet. For the Northoffs was composed the little compendium of polite conversation (in Latin), *Familiarium colloquiorum formulae*, the nucleus of the world-famous *Colloquia*. For Robert Fisher he wrote the first draft of *De conscribendis epistolis*, the great dissertation on the art of letter-writing (Latin letters), probably also the paraphrase of Valla's *Elegantiae*, a treatise on pure Latin, which had been a beacon-light of culture to Erasmus in his youth. *De copia verborum ac rerum* was also such a help for beginners, to provide them with a vocabulary and abundance of turns and expressions; and also the germs of a larger work: *De ratione studii*, a manual for arranging courses of study, lay in the same line.

It was a life of uncertainty and unrest. The bishop gave but little support. Erasmus was not in good health and felt continually depressed. He made plans for a journey to Italy, but did not see much chance of effecting them. In the summer of 1498 he again travelled to Holland and to the bishop. In Holland his friends were little pleased with his studies. It was feared that he was contracting debts at Paris. Current reports about him were not favourable. He found the bishop, in the commotion of his departure for England on a mission, irritable and full of complaints. It became more and more evident that he would have to look out for another patron. Perhaps he might turn to the Lady of Veere, Anna of Borselen, with whom his faithful and helpful friend Batt had now taken service, as a tutor to her son, in the castle of Tournehem, between Calais and Saint Omer.

Upon his return to Paris, Erasmus resumed his old life, but it was hateful slavery to him. Batt had an invitation for him to come to Tournehem, but he could not yet bear to leave Paris. Here he had now as a pupil the young Lord Mountjoy,

William Blount. That meant two strings to his bow. Batt is incited to prepare the ground for him with Anna of Veere; William Hermans is charged with writing letters to Mountjoy, in which he is to praise the latter's love of literature. 'You should display an erudite integrity, commend me, and proffer your services kindly. Believe me, William, your reputation, too, will benefit by it. He is a young man of great authority with his own folk; you will have some one to distribute your writings in England. I pray you again and again, if you love me, take this to heart.'

The visit to Tournehem took place at the beginning of 1499, followed by another journey to Holland. Henceforward Anna of Veere passed for his patroness. In Holland he saw his friend William Hermans and told him that he thought of leaving for Bologna after Easter. The Dutch journey was one of unrest and bustle; he was in a hurry to return to Paris, not to miss any opportunity which Mountjoy's affection might offer him. He worked hard at the various writings on which he was engaged, as hard as his health permitted after the difficult journey in winter. He was busily occupied in collecting the money for travelling to Italy, now postponed until August. But evidently Batt could not obtain as much for him as he had hoped, and, in May, Erasmus suddenly gave up the Italian plan, and left for England with Mountjoy at the latter's request.

CHAPTER IV

FIRST STAY IN ENGLAND
1499–1500

First stay in England: 1499–1500 — Oxford: John Colet — Erasmus's aspirations directed towards divinity — He is as yet mainly a literate — Fisher and More — Mishap at Dover when leaving England: 1500 — Back in France he composes the Adagia *— Years of trouble and penury*

ERASMUS'S first stay in England, which lasted from the early summer of 1499 till the beginning of 1500, was to become for him a period of inward ripening. He came there as an erudite poet, the protégé of a nobleman of rank, on the road to closer contact with the great world which knew how to appreciate and reward literary merit. He left the country with the fervent desire in future to employ his gifts, in so far as circumstances would permit, in more serious tasks. This change was brought about by two new friends whom he found in England, whose personalities were far above those who had hitherto crossed his path: John Colet and Thomas More.

During all the time of his sojourn in England Erasmus is in high spirits, for him. At first it is still the man of the world who speaks, the refined man of letters, who must needs show his brilliant genius. Aristocratic life, of which he evidently had seen but little at the Bishop of Cambray's and the Lady of Veere's at Tournehem, pleased him fairly well, it seems. 'Here in England', he writes in a light vein to Faustus Andrelinus, 'we have, indeed, progressed somewhat. The Erasmus whom you know is almost a good hunter already, not too bad a horseman, a not unpractised courtier. He salutes a little more courteously, he smiles more kindly. If you are wise, you also will alight here.' And he teases the volatile poet by telling him about the charming girls and the laudable custom, which he found in England, of accompanying all compliments by kisses.[1]

---

[1] Allen No. 103.17. Cf. *Chr. Matrim. inst.* LB. V. 678 and *Cent nouvelles nouvelles* 2.63, 'ung baiser, dont les dames et demoiselles du dit pays d'Angleterre sont assez libérales de l'accorder'.

It even fell to his lot to make the acquaintance of royalty. From Mountjoy's estate at Greenwich, More, in the course of a walk, took him to Eltham Palace, where the royal children were educated. There he saw, surrounded by the whole royal household, the youthful Henry, who was to be Henry VIII, a boy of nine years, together with two little sisters and a young prince, who was still an infant in arms. Erasmus was ashamed that he had nothing to offer and, on returning home, he composed (not without exertion, for he had not written poetry at all for some time) a panegyric on England, which he presented to the prince with a graceful dedication.

In October Erasmus was at Oxford which, at first, did not please him, but whither Mountjoy was to follow him. He had been recommended to John Colet, who declared that he required no recommendations: he already knew Erasmus from the letter to Gaguin in the latter's historical work and thought very highly of his learning. There followed during the remainder of Erasmus's stay at Oxford a lively intercourse, in conversation and in correspondence, which definitely decided the bent of Erasmus's many-sided mind.

John Colet, who did not differ much from Erasmus in point of age, had found his intellectual path earlier and more easily. Born of well-to-do parents (his father was a London magistrate and twice lord mayor), he had been able leisurely to prosecute his studies. Not seduced by quite such a brilliant genius as Erasmus possessed into literary digressions, he had from the beginning fixed his attention on theology. He knew Plato and Plotinus, though not in Greek, was very well read in the older Fathers and also respectably acquainted with scholasticism, not to mention his knowledge of mathematics, law, history and the English poets. In 1496 he had established himself at Oxford. Without possessing a degree in divinity, he expounded St. Paul's epistles. Although, owing to his ignorance of Greek, he was restricted to the Vulgate, he tried to penetrate to the original meaning of the sacred texts, discarding the later commentaries.

Colet had a deeply serious nature, always warring against

III. JOHN COLET, DEAN OF ST. PAUL'S

IV. SIR THOMAS MORE, 1527

the tendencies of his vigorous being, and he kept within bounds his pride and the love of pleasure. He had a keen sense of humour, which, without doubt, endeared him to Erasmus. He was an enthusiast. When defending a point in theology his ardour changed the sound of his voice, the look in his eyes, and a lofty spirit permeated his whole person.

Out of his intercourse with Colet came the first of Erasmus's theological writings. At the end of a discussion regarding Christ's agony in the garden of Gethsemane, in which Erasmus had defended the usual view that Christ's fear of suffering proceeded from his human nature, Colet had exhorted him to think further about the matter. They exchanged letters about it and finally Erasmus committed both their opinions to paper in the form of a 'Little disputation concerning the anguish, fear and sadness of Jesus', *Disputatiuncula de tedio, pavore, tristicia Jesu*, etc., being an elaboration of these letters.

While the tone of this pamphlet is earnest and pious, it is not truly fervent. The man of letters is not at once and completely superseded. 'See, Colet,' thus Erasmus ends his first letter, referring half ironically to himself, 'how I can observe the rules of propriety in concluding such a theologic disputation with poetic fables (he had made use of a few mythologic metaphors). But as Horace says, *Naturam expellas furca, tamen usque recurret.*'

This ambiguous position which Erasmus still occupied, also in things of the mind, appears still more clearly from the report which he sent to his new friend, the Frisian John Sixtin, a Latin poet like himself, of another disputation with Colet, at a repast, probably in the hall of Magdalen College, where Wolsey, too, was perhaps present. To his fellow-poet, Erasmus writes as a poet, loosely and with some affectation. It was a meal such as he liked, and afterwards frequently pictured in his *Colloquies*: cultured company, good food, moderate drinking, noble conversation. Colet presided. On his right hand sat the prior Charnock of St. Mary's College, where Erasmus resided (he had also been present at the disputation about Christ's agony). On his left was a divine whose name is not mentioned, an advocate of scholasticism; next to him came Erasmus, 'that the poet should not be wanting at the banquet'. The discussion was about Cain's guilt by which he displeased the Lord. Colet defended the opinion that Cain had injured God by doubting the Creator's goodness, and, in reliance on his own industry, tilling the earth, whereas Abel tended the sheep and was content with what grew of itself. The divine contended with syllogisms, Erasmus with arguments of 'rhetoric'. But Colet kindled, and got the better of both. After a while, when the dispute had lasted long enough and had become more serious than was suitable for table-talk —'then I said, in order to play my part, the part of the poet that is—to abate the contention and at the same time cheer the meal with a pleasant tale: "it is a very old story, it has to be unearthed from the very oldest authors. I will tell you what I found about it in literature, if you will promise me first that you will not look upon it as a fable." '

And now he relates a witty story of some very ancient codex in which he had read how Cain, who had often heard his parents speak of the glorious vegetation of Paradise, where the ears of corn were as high as the alders with us, had prevailed upon the angel who guarded it, to give him some Paradisal grains. God would not mind it, if only he left the apples alone. The speech by which the angel is incited to disobey the Almighty is a masterpiece of Erasmian wit. 'Do you find it pleasant to stand there by the gate with a big sword? We have just begun to use dogs for that sort of work. It is not so bad on earth and it will be better still; we shall learn, no doubt, to cure diseases. What that forbidden knowledge matters I do not see very clearly. Though, in that matter, too, unwearied industry surmounts all obstacles.' In this way the guardian is seduced. But when God beholds the miraculous effect of Cain's agricultural management, punishment does not fail to ensue. A more delicate way of combining Genesis and the Prometheus myth no humanist had yet invented.

But still, though Erasmus went on conducting himself as a

man of letters among his fellow-poets, his heart was no longer in those literary exercises. It is one of the peculiarities of Erasmus's mental growth that it records no violent crises. We never find him engaged in those bitter inward struggles which are in the experience of so many great minds. His transition from interest in literary matters to interest in religious matters is not in the nature of a process of conversion. There is no Tarsus in Erasmus's life. The transition takes place gradually and is never complete. For many years to come Erasmus can, without suspicion of hypocrisy, at pleasure, as his interests or his moods require, play the man of letters or the theologian. He is a man with whom the deeper currents of the soul gradually rise to the surface; who raises himself to the height of his ethical consciousness under the stress of circumstances, rather than at the spur of some irresistible impulse.

The desire to turn only to matters of faith he shows early. 'I have resolved', he writes in his monastic period to Cornelius of Gouda, 'to write no more poems in the future, except such as savour of praise of the saints, or of sanctity itself.' But that was the youthful pious resolve of a moment. During all the years previous to the first voyage to England, Erasmus's writings, and especially his letters, betray a worldly disposition. It only leaves him in moments of illness and weariness. Then the world displeases him and he despises his own ambition; he desires to live in holy quiet, musing on Scripture and shedding tears over his old errors. But these are utterances inspired by the occasion, which one should not take too seriously.

It was Colet's word and example which first changed Erasmus's desultory occupation with theological studies into a firm and lasting resolve to make their pursuit the object of his life. Colet urged him to expound the Pentateuch or the prophet Isaiah at Oxford, just as he himself treated of Paul's epistles. Erasmus declined; he could not do it. This bespoke insight and self-knowledge, by which he surpassed Colet. The latter's intuitive Scripture interpretation without knowledge of the original language failed to satisfy Erasmus. 'You are acting imprudently, my dear Colet, in trying to obtain water

from a pumice-stone (in the words of Plautus). How shall I
be so impudent as to teach that which I have not learned myself? How shall I warm others while shivering and trembling
with cold? . . . You complain that you find yourself deceived
in your expectations regarding me. But I have never promised
you such a thing; you have deceived yourself by refusing to
believe me when I was telling you the truth regarding myself.
Neither did I come here to teach poetics or rhetoric (Colet had
hinted at that); these have ceased to be sweet to me, since they
ceased to be necessary to me. I decline the one task because it
does not come up to my aim in life; the other because it is
beyond my strength . . . But when, one day, I shall be con-
scious that the necessary power is in me, I, too, shall choose
your part and devote to the assertion of divinity, if no excellent, yet sincere labour.'

The inference which Erasmus drew first of all was that he
should know Greek better than he had thus far been able to
learn it.

Meanwhile his stay in England was rapidly drawing to a
close; he had to return to Paris. Towards the end of his sojourn
he wrote to his former pupil, Robert Fisher, who was in Italy,
in a high-pitched tone about the satisfaction which he experienced in England. A most pleasant and wholesome climate
(he was most sensitive to it); so much humanity and erudition
—not of the worn-out and trivial sort, but of the recondite,
genuine, ancient, Latin and Greek stamp—that he need hardly
any more long to go to Italy. In Colet he thought he heard
Plato himself. Grocyn, the Grecian scholar; Linacre, the
learned physician, who would not admire them! And whose
spirit was ever softer, sweeter or happier than that of Thomas
More!

A disagreeable incident occurred as Erasmus was leaving
English soil in January 1500. Unfortunately it not only obscured his pleasant memories of the happy island, but also
placed another obstacle in the path of his career, and left in
his supersensitive soul a sting which vexed him for years
afterwards.

The livelihood which he had been gaining at Paris of late years was precarious. The support from the bishop had probably been withdrawn; that of Anna of Veere had trickled but languidly; he could not too firmly rely on Mountjoy. Under these circumstances a modest fund, some provision against a rainy day, was of the highest consequence. Such savings he brought from England, twenty pounds. An act of Edward III, re-enacted by Henry VII not long before, prohibited the export of gold and silver, but More and Mountjoy had assured Erasmus that he could safely take his money with him, if only it was not in English coin. At Dover he learned that the custom-house officers were of a different opinion. He might only keep six 'angels'—the rest was left behind in the hands of the officials and was evidently confiscated.

The shock which this incident gave him perhaps contributed to his fancying himself threatened by robbers and murderers on the road from Calais to Paris. The loss of his money plunged him afresh into perplexity as to his support from day to day. It forced him to resume the profession of a *bel esprit*, which he already began to loathe, and to take all the humiliating steps to get what was due to it from patrons. And, above all, it affected his mental balance and his dignity. Yet this mishap had its great advantage for the world, and for Erasmus, too, after all. To it the world owes the *Adagia*; and he the fame, which began with this work.

The feelings with which his misfortune at Dover inspired Erasmus were bitter anger and thirst for revenge. A few months later he writes to Batt: 'Things with me are as they are wont to be in such cases: the wound received in England begins to smart only now that it has become inveterate, and that the more as I cannot have my revenge in any way'. And six months later, 'I shall swallow it. An occasion may offer itself, no doubt, to be even with them.' Yet meanwhile true insight told this man, whose strength did not always attain to his ideals, that the English, whom he had just seen in such a favourable light, let alone his special friends among them, were not accessaries to the misfortune. He never reproached

More and Mountjoy, whose inaccurate information, he tells us, had done the harm. At the same time his interest, which he always saw in the garb of virtue, told him that now especially it would be essential not to break off his relations with England, and that this gave him a splendid chance of strengthening them. Afterwards he explained this with a naïveté which often causes his writings, especially where he tries to suppress or cloak matters, to read like confessions.

'Returning to Paris a poor man, I understood that many would expect I should take revenge with my pen for this mishap, after the fashion of men of letters, by writing something venomous against the king or against England. At the same time I was afraid that William Mountjoy, having indirectly caused my loss of money, would be apprehensive of losing my affection. In order, therefore, both to put the expectations of those people to shame, and to make known that I was not so unfair as to blame the country for a private wrong, or so inconsiderate as, because of a small loss, to risk making the king displeased with myself or with my friends in England, and at the same time to give my friend Mountjoy a proof that I was no less kindly disposed towards him than before, I resolved to publish something as quickly as possible. As I had nothing ready, I hastily brought together, by a few days' reading, a collection of Adagia, in the supposition that such a booklet, however it might turn out, by its mere usefulness would get into the hands of students. In this way I demonstrated that my friendship had not cooled off at all. Next, in a poem I subjoined, I protested that I was not angry with the king or with the country at being deprived of my money. And my scheme was not ill received. That moderation and candour procured me a good many friends in England at the time—erudite, upright and influential men.'

This is a characteristic specimen of semi-ethical conduct. In this way Erasmus succeeded in dealing with his indignation, so that later on he could declare, when the recollection came up occasionally, 'At one blow I had lost all my fortune, but I was so unconcerned that I returned to my books all the more cheerfully and ardently'. But his friends knew how deep the wound had been. 'Now (on hearing that Henry VIII had ascended the throne) surely all bitterness must have suddenly left your soul,' Mountjoy writes to him in 1509, possibly through the pen of Ammonius.

The years after his return to France were difficult ones. He was in great need of money and was forced to do what he could, as a man of letters, with his talents and knowledge. He had again to be the *homo poeticus* or *rhetoricus*. He writes polished letters full of mythology and modest mendicity. As a poet he had a reputation; as a poet he could expect support. Meanwhile the elevating picture of his theological activities remained present before his mind's eye. It nerves him to energy and perseverance. 'It is incredible', he writes to Batt, 'how my soul yearns to finish all my works, at the same time becoming somewhat proficient in Greek, and afterwards to devote myself entirely to the sacred learning after which my soul has been hankering for a long time. I am in fairly good health, so I shall have to strain every nerve this year (1501) to get the work we gave the printer published, and by dealing with theological problems, to expose our cavillers, who are very numerous, as they deserve. If three more years of life are granted me, I shall be beyond the reach of envy.'

Here we see him in a frame of mind to accomplish great things, though not merely under the impulse of true devotion. Already he sees the restoration of genuine divinity as his task; unfortunately the effusion is contained in a letter in which he instructs the faithful Batt as to how he should handle the Lady of Veere in order to wheedle money out of her.

For years to come the efforts to make a living were to cause him almost constant tribulations and petty cares. He had had more than enough of France and desired nothing better than to leave it. Part of the year 1500 he spent at Orléans. Adversity made him narrow. There is the story of his relations with Augustine Vincent Caminade, a humanist of lesser rank (he ended as syndic of Middelburg), who took young men as lodgers. It is too long to detail here, but remarkable enough as revealing Erasmus's psychology, for it shows how deeply he mistrusted his friends. There are also his relations with Jacobus Voecht, in whose house he evidently lived gratuitously and for whom he managed to procure a rich lodger in the person of an illegitimate brother of the Bishop of Cambray. At this time, Erasmus asserts, the bishop (Antimaecenas he now calls him) set Standonck to dog him in Paris.

Much bitterness there is in the letters of this period. Erasmus is suspicious, irritable, exacting, sometimes rude in writing to his friends. He cannot bear William Hermans any longer because of his epicureanism and his lack of energy, to which he, Erasmus, certainly was a stranger. But what grieves us most is the way he speaks to honest Batt. He is highly praised, certainly. Erasmus promises to make him immortal, too. But how offended he is, when Batt cannot at once comply with his imperious demands. How almost shameless are his instructions as to what Batt is to tell the Lady of Veere, in order to solicit her favour for Erasmus. And how meagre the expressions of his sorrow, when the faithful Batt is taken from him by death in the first half of 1502.

It is as if Erasmus had revenged himself on Batt for having been obliged to reveal himself to his true friend in need more completely than he cared to appear to anyone; or for having disavowed to Anna of Borselen his fundamental convictions, his most refined taste, for the sake of a meagre gratuity. He has paid homage to her in that ponderous Burgundian style with which dynasties in the Netherlands were familiar, and which must have been hateful to him. He has flattered her formal piety. 'I send you a few prayers, by means of which you could, as by incantations, call down, even against her will, from Heaven, so to say, not the moon, but her who gave birth to the sun of justice.'

Did you smile your delicate smile, O author of the *Colloquies*, while writing this? So much the worse for you.

CHAPTER V

ERASMUS AS A HUMANIST

Significance of the Adagia and similar works of later years — Erasmus as a divulger of classical culture — Latin — Estrangement from Holland — Erasmus as a Netherlander

MEANWHILE renown came to Erasmus as the fruit of those literary studies which, as he said, had ceased to be dear to him. In 1500 that work appeared which Erasmus had written after his misfortune at Dover, and had dedicated to Mountjoy, the *Adagiorum Collectanea*. It was a collection of about eight hundred proverbial sayings drawn from the Latin authors of antiquity and elucidated for the use of those who aspired to write an elegant Latin style. In the dedication Erasmus pointed out the profit an author may derive, both in ornamenting his style and in strengthening his argumentation, from having at his disposal a good supply of sentences hallowed by their antiquity. He proposes to offer such a help to his readers. What he actually gave was much more. He familiarized a much wider circle than the earlier humanists had reached with the spirit of antiquity.

Until this time the humanists had, to some extent, monopolized the treasures of classic culture, in order to parade their knowledge of which the multitude remained destitute, and so to become strange prodigies of learning and elegance. With his irresistible need of teaching and his sincere love for humanity and its general culture, Erasmus introduced the classic spirit, in so far as it could be reflected in the soul of a sixteenth-century Christian, among the people. Not he alone; but none more extensively and more effectively. Not among all the people, it is true, for by writing in Latin he limited his direct influence to the educated classes, which in those days were the upper classes.

Erasmus made current the classic spirit. Humanism ceased to be the exclusive privilege of a few. According to Beatus Rhenanus he had been reproached by some humanists, when about to publish the *Adagia*, for divulging the mysteries of their craft. But he desired that the book of antiquity should be open to all.

The literary and educational works of Erasmus, the chief of which were begun in his Parisian period, though most of them appeared much later, have, in truth, brought about a transmutation of the general modes of expression and of argumentation. It should be repeated over and over again that this was not achieved by him single-handed; countless others at that time were similarly engaged. But we have only to cast an eye on the broad current of editions of the *Adagia*, of the *Colloquia*, etc., to realize of how much greater consequence he was in this respect than all the others. 'Erasmus' is the only name in all the host of humanists which has remained a household word all over the globe.

Here we will anticipate the course of Erasmus's life for a moment, to enumerate the principal works of this sort. Some years later the *Adagia* increased from hundreds to thousands, through which not only Latin, but also Greek, wisdom spoke. In 1514 he published in the same manner a collection of similitudes, *Parabolae*. It was a partial realization of what he had conceived to supplement the *Adagia*—metaphors, saws, allusions, poetical and scriptural allegories, all to be dealt with in a similar way. Towards the end of his life he published a similar thesaurus of the witty anecdotes and the striking words or deeds of wisdom of antiquity, the *Apophthegmata*. In addition to these collections, we find manuals of a more grammatical nature, also piled up treasury-like: 'On the stock of expressions', *De copia verborum et rerum*, 'On letter-writing', *De conscribendis epistolis*, not to mention works of less importance. By a number of Latin translations of Greek authors Erasmus had rendered a point of prospect accessible to those who did not wish to climb the whole mountain. And, finally, as inimitable models of the manner in which to apply all that knowledge, there were the *Colloquia* and that almost countless multitude of letters which have flowed from Erasmus's pen.

All this collectively made up antiquity (in such quantity and quality as it was obtainable in the sixteenth century) exhibited in an emporium where it might be had at retail. Each student could get what was to his taste; everything was to be had there in a great variety of designs. 'You may read my *Adagia* in such a manner', says Erasmus (of the later augmented edition), 'that as soon as you have finished one, you may imagine you have finished the whole book.' He himself made indices to facilitate its use.

In the world of scholasticism he alone had up to now been considered an authority who had mastered the technicalities of its system of thought and its mode of expression in all its details and was versed in biblical knowledge, logic and philosophy. Between scholastic parlance and the spontaneously written popular languages, there yawned a wide gulf. Humanism since Petrarch had substituted for the rigidly syllogistic structure of an argument the loose style of the antique, free, suggestive phrase. In this way the language of the learned approached the natural manner of expression of daily life and raised the popular languages, even where it continued to use Latin, to its own level.

The wealth of subject-matter was found with no one in greater abundance than with Erasmus. What knowledge of life, what ethics, all supported by the indisputable authority of the Ancients, all expressed in that fine, airy form for which he was admired. And such knowledge of antiquities in addition to all this! Illimitable was the craving for and illimitable the power to absorb what is extraordinary in real life. This was one of the principal characteristics of the spirit of the Renaissance. These minds never had their desired share of striking incidents, curious details, rarities and anomalies. There was, as yet, no symptom of that mental dyspepsia of later periods, which can no longer digest reality and relishes it no more. Men revelled in plenty.

And yet, were not Erasmus and his fellow-workers as leaders of civilization on a wrong track? Was it true reality they were aiming at? Was their proud Latinity not a fatal error? There is one of the crucial points of history.

A present-day reader who should take up the *Adagia* or the *Apophthegmata* with a view to enriching his own life (for they were meant for this purpose and it is what gave them value), would soon ask himself: 'What matter to us, apart from strictly philological or historical considerations, those endless details concerning obscure personages of antique society, of Phrygians, of Thessalians? They are nothing to me.' And—he will continue—they really mattered nothing to Erasmus's contemporaries either. The stupendous history of the sixteenth century was not enacted in classic phrases or turns; it was not based on classic interests or views of life. There were no Phrygians and Thessalians, no Agesilauses or Dionysiuses. The humanists created out of all this a mental realm, emancipated from the limitations of time.

And did their own times pass without being influenced by them? That is the question, and we shall not attempt to answer it: to what extent did humanism influence the course of events?

In any case Erasmus and his coadjutors greatly heightened the international character of civilization which had existed throughout the Middle Ages because of Latin and of the Church. If they thought they were really making Latin a vehicle for daily international use, they overrated their power. It was, no doubt, an amusing fancy and a witty exercise to plan, in such an international *milieu* as the Parisian student world, such models of sports and games in Latin as the *Colloquiorum formulae* offered. But can Erasmus have seriously thought that the next generation would play at marbles in Latin?

Still, intellectual intercourse undoubtedly became very easy in so wide a circle as had not been within reach in Europe since the fall of the Roman Empire. Henceforth it was no longer the clergy alone, and an occasional literate, but a numerous multitude of sons of burghers and nobles, qualifying for some magisterial office, who passed through a grammar-school and found Erasmus in their path.

Erasmus could not have attained to his world-wide celebrity if it had not been for Latin. To make his native tongue a universal language was beyond him. It may well puzzle a fellow-countryman of Erasmus to guess what a talent like his, with his power of observation, his delicacy of expression, his gusto and wealth, might have meant to Dutch literature. Just imagine the *Colloquia* written in the racy Dutch of the sixteenth century! What could he not have produced if, instead of gleaning and commenting upon classic Adagia, he had, for his themes, availed himself of the proverbs of the vernacular? To us such a proverb is perhaps even more sapid than the sometimes slightly finical turns praised by Erasmus.

This, however, is to reason unhistorically; this was not what the times required and what Erasmus could give. It is quite clear why Erasmus could only write in Latin. Moreover, in the vernacular everything would have appeared too direct, too personal, too real, for his taste. He could not do without that thin veil of vagueness, of remoteness, in which everything is wrapped when expressed in Latin. His fastidious mind would have shrunk from the pithy coarseness of a Rabelais, or the rustic violence of Luther's German.

Estrangement from his native tongue had begun for Erasmus as early as the days when he learned reading and writing. Estrangement from the land of his birth set in when he left the monastery of Steyn. It was furthered not a little by the ease with which he handled Latin. Erasmus, who could express himself as well in Latin as in his mother tongue, and even better, consequently lacked the experience of, after all, feeling thoroughly at home and of being able to express himself fully, only among his compatriots. There was, however, another psychological influence which acted to alienate him from Holland. After he had seen at Paris the perspectives of his own capacities, he became confirmed in the conviction that Holland failed to appreciate him, that it distrusted and slandered him. Perhaps there was indeed some ground for this conviction. But, partly, it was also a reaction of injured self-love. In Holland people knew too much about him. They had seen him in his smallnesses and feebleness. There he had been obliged to obey others—he who, above all things, wanted to be free. Distaste of the narrow-mindedness, the coarseness and intemperance which he knew to prevail there, were summed up, within him, in a general condemnatory judgement of the Dutch character.

Henceforth he spoke as a rule about Holland with a sort of apologetic contempt. 'I see that you are content with Dutch fame,' he writes to his old friend William Hermans, who like Cornelius Aurelius had begun to devote his best forces to the history of his native country. 'In Holland the air is good for me,' he writes elsewhere, 'but the extravagant carousals annoy me; add to this the vulgar uncultured character of the people, the violent contempt of study, no fruit of learning, the most egregious envy.' And excusing the imperfection of his juvenilia, he says: 'At that time I wrote not for Italians, but for Hollanders, that is to say, for the dullest ears'. And, in another place, 'eloquence is demanded from a Dutchman, that is, from a more hopeless person than a Bœotian'. And again, 'If the story is not very witty, remember it is a Dutch story'. No doubt, false modesty had its share in such sayings.

After 1496 he visited Holland only on hasty journeys. There is no evidence that after 1501 he ever set foot on Dutch soil. He dissuaded his own compatriots abroad from returning to Holland.

Still, now and again, a cordial feeling of sympathy for his native country stirred within him. Just where he would have had an opportunity, in explaining Martial's *Auris Batava* in the *Adagia*, for venting his spleen, he availed himself of the chance of writing an eloquent panegyric on what was dearest to him in Holland, 'a country that I am always bound to honour and revere, as that which gave me birth. Would I might be a credit to it, just as, on the other hand, I need not be ashamed of it.' Their reputed boorishness rather redounds to their honour. 'If a "Batavian ear" means a horror of Martial's obscene jokes, I could wish that all Christians might have Dutch ears. When we consider their morals, no nation is more inclined to humanity and benevolence, less savage or cruel. Their mind is upright and void of cunning and all humbug. If they are somewhat sensual and excessive at meals, it results partly from their plentiful supply: nowhere is import so easy and fertility so great. What an extent of lush meadows, how many navigable rivers! Nowhere are so many towns crowded together within so small an area; not large towns, indeed, but excellently governed. Their cleanliness is praised by everybody. Nowhere are such large numbers of moderately learned persons found, though extraordinary and exquisite erudition is rather rare.'

They were Erasmus's own most cherished ideals which he here ascribes to his compatriots—gentleness, sincerity, simplicity, purity. He sounds that note of love for Holland on other occasions. When speaking of lazy women, he adds: 'In France there are large numbers of them, but in Holland we find countless wives who by their industry support their idling and revelling husbands'. And in the colloquy entitled 'The Shipwreck', the people who charitably take in the castaways are Hollanders. 'There is no more humane people than this, though surrounded by violent nations.'

In addressing English readers it is perhaps not superfluous to point out once again that Erasmus when speaking of Holland, or using the epithet 'Batavian', refers to the county of Holland, which at present forms the provinces of North and South Holland of the kingdom of the Netherlands, and stretches from the Wadden islands to the estuaries of the Meuse. Even the nearest neighbours, such as Zealanders and Frisians, are not included in this appellation.

But it is a different matter when Erasmus speaks of *patria*, the fatherland, or of *nostras*, a compatriot. In those days a national consciousness was just budding all over the Netherlands. A man still felt himself a Hollander, a Frisian, a Fleming, a Brabantine in the first place; but the community of language and customs, and still more the strong political influence which for nearly a century had been exercised by the Burgundian dynasty, which had united most of these low countries under its sway, had cemented a feeling of solidarity which did not even halt at the linguistic frontier in Belgium. It was still rather a strong Burgundian patriotism (even after Habsburg had *de facto* occupied the place of Burgundy) than a strictly Netherlandish feeling of nationality. People liked, by using a heraldic symbol, to designate the Netherlanders as 'the Lions'. Erasmus, too, employs the term. In his works we gradually see the narrower Hollandish patriotism gliding into the Burgundian Netherlandish. In the beginning, *patria* with him still means Holland proper, but soon it meant the Netherlands. It is curious to trace how by degrees his feelings regarding Holland, made up of disgust and attachment, are transferred to the Low Countries in general. 'In my youth', he says in 1535, repeating himself, 'I did not write for Italians but for Hollanders, the people of Brabant and Flemings.' So they now all share the reputation of bluntness. To Louvain is applied what formerly was said of Holland: there are too many compotations; nothing can be done without a drinking bout. Nowhere, he repeatedly complains, is there so little sense of the *bonae literae*, nowhere is study so despised as in the Netherlands, and nowhere are there more cavillers and slanderers. But also his affection has expanded. When Longolius of Brabant plays the Frenchman, Erasmus is vexed: 'I devoted nearly three days to Longolius; he was uncommonly pleasing, except only that he is too French, whereas it is well known that he is one of us'.[1] When Charles V has obtained the crown of Spain, Erasmus notes: 'a singular stroke of luck, but I pray that it may also prove a blessing to the fatherland, and not only to the prince'. When his strength was beginning to fail he began to think more and more of returning to his native country. 'King Ferdinand invites me, with large promises, to come to Vienna,' he writes from Basle, 1 October 1528, 'but nowhere would it please me better to rest than in Brabant.'

[1] Allen No. 1026.4, cf. 914, intr. p. 473. Later Erasmus was made to believe that Longolius was a Hollander, cf. LBE. 1507 A.

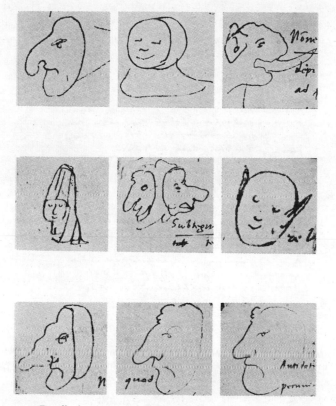

v. Doodles by Erasmus in the margin of one of his manuscripts

VI. A manuscript page of Erasmus

CHAPTER VI

THEOLOGICAL ASPIRATIONS

1501

At Tournehem: 1501 — The restoration of theology now the aim of his life — He learns Greek — John Vitrier — Enchiridion Militis Christiani

THE lean years continued with Erasmus. His livelihood remained uncertain, and he had no fixed abode. It is remarkable that, in spite of his precarious means of support, his movements were ever guided rather by the care for his health than for his sustenance, and his studies rather by his burning desire to penetrate to the purest sources of knowledge than by his advantage. Repeatedly the fear of the plague drives him on: in 1500 from Paris to Orléans, where he first lodges with Augustine Caminade; but when one of the latter's boarders falls ill, Erasmus moves. Perhaps it was the impressions dating from his youth at Deventer that made him so excessively afraid of the plague, which in those days raged practically without intermission. Faustus Andrelinus sent a servant to upbraid him in his name with cowardice: 'That would be an intolerable insult', Erasmus answers, 'if I were a Swiss soldier, but a poet's soul, loving peace and shady places, is proof against it'. In the spring of 1501 he leaves Paris once more for fear of the plague: 'the frequent burials frighten me', he writes to Augustine.

He travelled first to Holland, where, at Steyn, he obtained leave to spend another year outside the monastery, for the sake of study; his friends would be ashamed if he returned, after so many years of study, without having acquired some authority. At Haarlem he visited his friend William Hermans, then turned to the south, once again to pay his respects to the Bishop of Cambray, probably at Brussels. Thence he went to Veere, but found no opportunity to talk to his patroness. In July 1501, he subsided into quietness at the castle of Tournehem with his faithful friend Batt.

In all his comings and goings he does not for a moment lose sight of his ideals of study. Since his return from England he is mastered by two desires: to edit Jerome, the great Father of the Church, and, especially, to learn Greek thoroughly. 'You understand how much all this matters to my fame, nay, to my preservation,' he writes (from Orléans towards the end of 1500) to Batt. But, indeed, had Erasmus been an ordinary fame and success hunter he might have had recourse to plenty of other expedients. It was the ardent desire to penetrate to the source and to make others understand that impelled him, even when he availed himself of these projects of study to raise a little money. 'Listen,' he writes to Batt, 'to what more I desire from you. You must wrest a gift from the abbot (of Saint Bertin). You know the man's disposition; invent some modest and plausible reason for begging. Tell him that I purpose something grand, viz., to restore the whole of Jerome, however comprehensive he may be, and spoiled, mutilated, entangled by the ignorance of divines; and to re-insert the Greek passages. I venture to say, I shall be able to lay open the antiquities and the style of Jerome, understood by no one as yet. Tell him that I shall want not a few books for the purpose, and moreover the help of Greeks, and that therefore I require support. In saying this, Battus, you will be telling no lies. For I really mean to do all this.'

He was, indeed, in a serious mood on this point, as he was soon to prove to the world. His conquest of Greek was a veritable feat of heroism. He had learned the simplest rudiments at Deventer, but these evidently amounted to very little. In March, 1500, he writes to Batt: 'Greek is nearly killing me, but I have no time and I have no money to buy books or to take a master'. When Augustine Caminade wants his Homer back which he had lent to him, Erasmus complains: 'You deprive me of my sole consolation in my tedium. For I so burn with love for this author, though I cannot understand him, that I feast my eyes and re-create my mind by looking at him.' Was Erasmus aware that in saying this he almost literally reproduced feelings which Petrarch had expressed a hundred and fifty years before? But he had already begun to study. Whether he had a master is not quite clear, but it is probable. He finds the language difficult at first. Then gradually he ventures to call himself 'a candidate in this language', and he begins with more confidence to scatter Greek quotations through his letters. It occupies him night and day and he urges all his friends to procure Greek books for him. In the autumn of 1502 he declares that he can properly write all he wants in Greek, and that extempore. He was not deceived in his expectation that Greek would open his eyes to the right understanding of Holy Scripture. Three years of nearly uninterrupted study amply rewarded him for his trouble. Hebrew, which he had also taken up, he abandoned. At that time (1504) he made translations from the Greek, he employed it critically in his theological studies, he taught it, amongst others, to William Cop, the French physician-humanist. A few years later he was to find little in Italy to improve his proficiency in Greek; he was afterwards inclined to believe that he carried more of the two ancient languages to that country than he brought back.

Nothing testifies more to the enthusiasm with which Erasmus applied himself to Greek than his zeal to make his best friends share in its blessings. Batt, he decided, should learn Greek. But Batt had no time, and Latin appealed more to him. When Erasmus goes to Haarlem to visit William Hermans, it is to make him a Greek scholar too; he has brought a handbag full of books. But he had only his trouble for his pains. William did not take at all kindly to this study and Erasmus was so disappointed that he not only considered his money and trouble thrown away, but also thought he had lost a friend.

Meanwhile he was still undecided where he should go in the near future. To England, to Italy, or back to Paris? In the end he made a fairly long stay as a guest, from the autumn of 1501 till the following summer, first at Saint Omer, with the prior of Saint Bertin, and afterwards at the castle of Courtebourne, not far off.

At Saint Omer, Erasmus became acquainted with a man whose image he was afterwards to place beside that of Colet as that of a true divine, and of a good monk at the same time: Jean Vitrier, the warden of the Franciscan monastery at Saint Omer. Erasmus must have felt attracted to a man who was burdened with a condemnation pronounced by the Sorbonne on account of his too frank expressions regarding the abuses of monastic life. Vitrier had not given up the life on that account, but he devoted himself to reforming monasteries and convents. Having progressed from scholasticism to Saint Paul, he had formed a very liberal conception of Christian life, strongly opposed to practices and ceremonies. This man, without doubt, considerably influenced the origin of one of Erasmus's most celebrated and influential works, the *Enchiridion militis Christiani*.

Erasmus himself afterwards confessed that the *Enchiridion* was born by chance. He did not reflect that some outward circumstance is often made to serve an inward impulse. The outward circumstance was that the castle of Tournehem was frequented by a soldier, a friend of Batt, a man of very dissolute conduct, who behaved very badly towards his pious wife, and who was, moreover, an uncultured and violent hater of priests.[1] For the rest he was of a kindly disposition and excepted Erasmus from his hatred of divines. The wife used her influence with Batt to get Erasmus to write something which might bring her husband to take an interest in religion. Erasmus complied with the request and Jean Vitrier concurred so cordially with the views expressed in these notes that Erasmus afterwards elaborated them at Louvain; in 1504 they were published at Antwerp by Dirck Maertensz.

This is the outward genesis of the *Enchiridion*. But the inward cause was that sooner or later Erasmus was bound to formulate his attitude towards the religious conduct of the life of his day and towards ceremonial and soulless conceptions of Christian duty, which were an eyesore to him.

In point of form the *Enchiridion* is a manual for an illiterate

[1] That this man should have been John of Trazegnies as Allen thinks possible and Renaudet accepts, is still all too uncertain; A. 164 t. I. p. 373; Renaudet, Préréforme 428.

soldier to attain to an attitude of mind worthy of Christ; as with a finger he will point out to him the shortest path to Christ. He assumes the friend to be weary of life at court—a common theme of contemporary literature. Only for a few days does Erasmus interrupt the work of his life, the purification of theology, to comply with his friend's request for instruction. To keep up a soldierly style he chooses the title, *Enchiridion*, the Greek word that even in antiquity meant both a poniard and a manual:[1] 'The poniard of the militant Christian'.[2] He reminds him of the duty of watchfulness and enumerates the weapons of Christ's militia. Self-knowledge is the beginning of wisdom. The general rules of the Christian conduct of life are followed by a number of remedies for particular sins and faults.

Such is the outward frame. But within this scope Erasmus finds an opportunity, for the first time, to develop his theological programme. This programme calls upon us to return to Scripture. It should be the endeavour of every Christian to understand Scripture in its purity and original meaning. To that end he should prepare himself by the study of the Ancients, orators, poets, philosophers; Plato especially. Also the great Fathers of the Church, Jerome, Ambrose, Augustine will be found useful, but not the large crowd of subsequent exegetists. The argument chiefly aims at subverting the conception of religion as a continual observance of ceremonies. This is Judaic ritualism and of no value. It is better to understand a single verse of the psalms well, by this means to deepen one's understanding of God and of oneself, and to draw a moral and line of conduct from it, than to read the whole psalter without attention. If the ceremonies do not renew the soul they are valueless and hurtful. 'Many are wont to count

---

[1] In 1500 (A. 123.21) Erasmus speaks of the *Enchiridion* of the Father Augustine, cf. 135, 138; in 1501, A. 152.33, he calls the *Officia* of Cicero a 'pugiunculus'—a dagger. So the appellation had been in his mind for some time.

[2] *Miles* with Erasmus has no longer the meaning of 'knight' which it had in medieval Latin.

how many masses they have heard every day, and referring to them as to something very important, as though they owed Christ nothing else, they return to their former habits after leaving church.' 'Perhaps you sacrifice every day and yet you live for yourself. You worship the saints, you like to touch their relics; do you want to earn Peter and Paul? Then copy the faith of the one and the charity of the other and you will have done more than if you had walked to Rome ten times.' He does not reject formulae and practices; he does not want to shake the faith of the humble but he cannot suffer that Christ is offered a cult made up of practices only. And why is it the monks, above all, who contribute to the deterioration of faith? 'I am ashamed to tell how superstitiously most of them observe certain petty ceremonies, invented by puny human minds (and not even for this purpose), how hatefully they want to force others to conform to them, how implicitly they trust them, how boldly they condemn others.'

Let Paul teach them true Christianity. 'Stand fast therefore in the liberty wherewith Christ hath made us free, and be not entangled again with the yoke of bondage.' This word to the Galatians contains the doctrine of Christian liberty, which soon at the Reformation was to resound so loudly. Erasmus did not apply it here in a sense derogatory to the dogmatics of the Catholic Church; but still it is a fact that the *Enchiridion* prepared many minds to give up much that he still wanted to keep.

The note of the *Enchiridion* is already what was to remain the note of Erasmus's life-work: how revolting it is that in this world the substance and the shadow differ so and that the world reverences those whom it should not reverence; that a hedge of infatuation, routine and thoughtlessness prevents mankind from seeing things in their true proportions. He expresses it later in the *Praise of Folly* and in the *Colloquies*. It is not merely religious feeling, it is equally social feeling that inspired him. Under the heading: Opinions worthy of a Christian, he laments the extremes of pride of class, national hostility, professional envy, and rivalry between religious

orders, which keep men apart. Let everybody sincerely concern himself about his brother. 'Throwing dice cost you a
thousand gold pieces in one night, and meanwhile some
wretched girl, compelled by poverty, sold her modesty; and a
soul is lost for which Christ gave his own. You say, what is
that to me? I mind my own business, according to my lights.
And yet you, holding such opinions, consider yourself a Christian, who are not even a man!'

In the *Enchiridion* of the militant Christian, Erasmus had for
the first time said the things which he had most at heart, with
fervour and indignation, with sincerity and courage. And yet
one would hardly say that this booklet was born of an irresistible impulse of ardent piety. Erasmus treats it, as we have
seen, as a trifle, composed at the request of a friend in a couple
of days stolen from his studies (though, strictly speaking, this
only holds good of the first draft, which he elaborated afterwards). The chief object of his studies he had already conceived to be the restoration of theology. One day he will
expound Paul, 'that the slanderers who consider it the height
of piety to know nothing of *bonae literae*, may understand that
we in our youth embraced the cultured literature of the
Ancients, and that we acquired a correct knowledge of the
two languages, Greek and Latin—not without many vigils—
not for the purpose of vainglory or childish satisfaction, but
because, long before, we premeditated adorning the temple of
the Lord (which some have too much desecrated by their
ignorance and barbarism) according to our strength, with
help from foreign parts, so that also in noble minds the love of
Holy Scripture may be kindled'. Is it not still the Humanist
who speaks?

We hear, moreover, the note of personal justification. It is
sounded also in a letter to Colet written towards the close of
1504, accompanying the edition of the *Lucubrationes* in which
the *Enchiridion* was first published. 'I did not write the
Enchiridion to parade my invention or eloquence, but only
that I might correct the error of those whose religion is usually
composed of more than Judaic ceremonies and observances of

a material sort, and who neglect the things that conduce to piety.' He adds, and this is typically humanistic, 'I have tried to give the reader a sort of art of piety, as others have written the theory of certain sciences'.

The art of piety! Erasmus might have been surprised had he known that another treatise, written more than sixty years before, by another canon of the Low Countries would continue to appeal much longer and much more urgently to the world than his manual: the *Imitatio Christi* by Thomas à Kempis.

The *Enchiridion*, collected with some other pieces into a volume of *Lucubrationes*, did not meet with such a great and speedy success as had been bestowed upon the *Adagia*. That Erasmus's speculations on true piety were considered too bold was certainly not the cause. They contained nothing antagonistic to the teachings of the Church, so that even at the time of the Counter-Reformation, when the Church had become highly suspicious of everything that Erasmus had written, the divines who drew up the *index expurgatorius* of his work found only a few passages in the *Enchiridion* to expunge. Moreover, Erasmus had inserted in the volume some writings of unsuspected Catholic tenor. For a long time it was in great repute, especially with theologians and monks. A famous preacher at Antwerp used to say that a sermon might be found in every page of the *Enchiridion*. But the book only obtained its great influence in wide cultured circles when, upheld by Erasmus's world-wide reputation, it was available in a number of translations, English, Czech, German, Dutch, Spanish, and French. But then it began to fall under suspicion, for that was the time when Luther had unchained the great struggle. 'Now they have begun to nibble at the *Enchiridion* also, that used to be so popular with divines,' Erasmus writes in 1526. For the rest it was only two passages to which the orthodox critics objected.

CHAPTER VII

YEARS OF TROUBLE—LOUVAIN, PARIS, ENGLAND

1502–6

Death of Batt: 1502—First stay at Louvain: 1502–4—Translations from the Greek—At Paris again—Valla's Annotationes on the New Testament—Second stay in England: 1505–6—More patrons and friends—Departure for Italy: 1506—Carmen Alpestre

CIRCUMSTANCES continued to remain unfavourable for Erasmus. 'This year fortune has truly been raging violently against me,' he writes in the autumn of 1502. In the spring his good friend Batt had died. It is a pity that no letters written by Erasmus directly after his bereavement have come down to us. We should be glad to have for that faithful helper a monument in addition to that which Erasmus erected to his memory in the *Antibarbari*. Anna of Veere had remarried and, as a patroness, might henceforth be left out of account. In October 1502, Henry of Bergen passed away. 'I have commemorated the Bishop of Cambray in three Latin epitaphs and a Greek one; they sent me but six guilders, that also in death he should remain true to himself.' In Francis of Busleiden, Archbishop of Besançon, he lost at about the same time a prospective new patron. He still felt shut out from Paris, Cologne and England by the danger of the plague.

In the late summer of 1502 he went to Louvain, 'flung thither by the plague,' he says. The university of Louvain, established in 1425 to wean the Netherlands in spiritual matters from Paris, was, at the beginning of the sixteenth century, one of the strongholds of theological tradition, which, however, did not prevent the progress of classical studies. How else should Adrian of Utrecht, later pope but at that time Dean of Saint Peter's and professor of theology, have forthwith undertaken to get him a professorship? Erasmus declined the offer, however, 'for certain reasons,' he says. Considering his great distress, the reasons must have been cogent indeed. One of them which he mentioned is not very clear to us: 'I am here so near to Dutch tongues which know how to hurt much, it is true, but have not learned to profit any one'. His spirit of liberty and his ardent love of the studies to which he wanted to devote himself entirely, were, no doubt, his chief reasons for declining.

But he had to make a living. Life at Louvain was expensive and he had no regular earnings. He wrote some prefaces and dedicated to the Bishop of Arras, Chancellor of the University, the first translation from the Greek: some *Declamationes* by Libanius. When in the autumn of 1503 Philip le Beau was expected back in the Netherlands from his journey to Spain Erasmus wrote, with sighs of distaste, a panegyric to celebrate the safe return of the prince. It cost him much trouble. 'It occupies me day and night,' says the man who composed with such incredible facility, when his heart was in the work. 'What is harder than to write with aversion; what is more use-less than to write something by which we unlearn good writing?' It must be acknowledged that he really flattered as sparingly as possible; the practice was so repulsive to him that in his preface he roundly owned that, to tell the truth, this whole class of composition was not to his taste.

At the end of 1504 Erasmus was back at Paris, at last. Probably he had always meant to return and looked upon his stay at Louvain as a temporary exile. The circumstances under which he left Louvain are unknown to us, because of the almost total lack of letters of the year 1504. In any case, he hoped that at Paris he would sooner be able to attain his great end of devoting himself entirely to the study of theology. 'I cannot tell you, dear Colet,' he writes towards the end of 1504, 'how I hurry on, with all sails set, to holy literature; how I dislike everything that keeps me back, or retards me. But the disfavour of Fortune, who always looks at me with the same face, has been the reason why I have not been able to get clear of those vexations. So I returned to France with the purpose, if I cannot solve them, at any rate of ridding myself of them in one way or another. After that I shall devote myself, with all my heart, to the *divinae literae*, to give up the remainder of my life to them.' If only he can find the means to work for some months entirely for himself and disentangle himself from profane literature. Can Colet not find out for him how matters stand with regard to the proceeds of the hundred copies of the *Adagia* which, at one time, he sent to England at his own expense? The liberty of a few months may be bought for little money.

There is something heroic in Erasmus scorning to make money out of his facile talents and enviable knowledge of the humanities, daring indigence so as to be able to realize his shining ideal of restoring theology.

It is remarkable that the same Italian humanist who in his youth had been his guide and example on the road to pure Latinity and classic antiquity, Lorenzo Valla, by chance became his leader and an outpost in the field of critical theology. In the summer of 1504, hunting in the old library of the Premonstratensian monastery of Parc, near Louvain ('in no preserves is hunting a greater delight'), he found a manuscript of Valla's *Annotationes* on the New Testament. It was a collection of critical notes on the text of the Gospels, the Epistles and Revelation. That the text of the Vulgate was not stainless had been acknowledged by Rome itself as early as the thirteenth century. Monastic orders and individual divines had set themselves to correct it, but that purification had not amounted to much, in spite of Nicholas of Lyra's work in the fourteenth century.

It was probably the falling in with Valla's *Annotationes* which led Erasmus, who was formerly more inspired with the resolution to edit Jerome and to comment upon Paul (he was to do both at a later date), to turn to the task of taking up the New Testament as a whole, in order to restore it in its purity. In March 1505 already Josse Badius at Paris printed Valla's *Annotationes* for Erasmus, as a sort of advertisement of what he himself one day hoped to achieve. It was a feat of courage.

Erasmus did not conceal from himself that Valla, the humanist, had an ill name with divines, and that there would be an outcry about 'the intolerable temerity of the *homo grammaticus*, who after having harassed all the *disciplinae*, did not scruple to assail holy literature with his petulant pen'. It was another programme much more explicit and defiant than the *Enchiridion* had been.

Once more it is not clear why and how Erasmus left Paris again for England in the autumn of 1505. He speaks of serious reasons and the advice of sensible people. He mentions one reason: lack of money. The reprint of the *Adagia*, published by John Philippi at Paris in 1505, had probably helped him through, for the time being; the edition cannot have been to his taste, for he had been dissatisfied with his work and wanted to extend it by weaving his new Greek knowledge into it. From Holland a warning voice had sounded, the voice of his superior and friend Servatius, demanding an account of his departure from Paris. Evidently his Dutch friends had still no confidence in Erasmus, his work, and his future.

In many respects that future appeared more favourable to him in England than it had seemed anywhere, thus far. There he found the old friends, men of consideration and importance: Mountjoy, with whom, on his arrival, he stayed some months, Colet, and More. There he found some excellent Greek scholars, whose conversation promised to be profitable and amusing; not Colet, who knew little Greek, but More, Linacre, Grocyn, Latimer, and Tunstall. He soon came in contact with some high ecclesiastics who were to be his friends and patrons: Richard Foxe, Bishop of Winchester, John Fisher, Bishop of Rochester and William Warham, Archbishop of Canterbury. Soon he would also find a friend whose congenial spirit and interests, to some extent, made up for the loss of Batt: the Italian Andrew Ammonius, of Lucca. And lastly, the king promised him an ecclesiastical benefice. It was not long before Erasmus was armed with a dispensation from Pope Julius II, dated 4 January 1506, cancelling the obstacles in the way of accepting an English benefice.

Translations from Greek into Latin were for him an easy

and speedy means to obtain favour and support: a dialogue by Lucian, followed by others, for Foxe; the *Hecuba* and the *Iphigenia* of Euripides for Warham. He now also thought of publishing his letters.

Clearly his relations with Holland were not yet satisfactory. Servatius did not reply to his letters. Erasmus ever felt hanging over him a menace to his career and his liberty embodied in the figure of that friend, to whom he was linked by so many silken ties, yonder in the monastery of Steyn, where his return was looked forward to, sooner or later, as a beacon-light of Christendom. Did the prior know of the papal dispensation exempting Erasmus from the 'statutes and customs of the monastery of Steyn in Holland, of the order of Saint Augustine?' Probably he did. On 1 April 1506, Erasmus writes to him: 'Here in London I am, it seems, greatly esteemed by the most eminent and erudite men of all England. The king has promised me a curacy: the visit of the prince necessitated a postponement of this business.'[1]

He immediately adds: 'I am deliberating again how best to devote the remainder of my life (how much that will be, I do not know) entirely to piety, to Christ. I see life, even when it is long, as evanescent and dwindling; I know that I am of a delicate constitution and that my strength has been encroached upon, not a little, by study and also, somewhat, by misfortune. I see that no deliverance can be hoped from study, and that it seems as if we had to begin over again, day after day. Therefore I have resolved, content with my mediocrity (especially now that I have learned as much Greek as suffices me), to apply myself to meditation about death and the training of my soul. I should have done so before and have husbanded the precious years when they were at their best. But though it is a tardy husbandry that people practise when only little remains at the bottom, we should be the more economical accordingly as the quantity and quality of what is left diminishes.'

[1] A. 189, Philip le Beau, who had unexpectedly come to England because of a storm, which obliged Mountjoy to do court-service.

Was it a fit of melancholy which made Erasmus write those words of repentance and renunciation? Was he surprised in the middle of the pursuit of his life's aim by the consciousness of the vanity of his endeavours, the consciousness, too, of a great fatigue? Is this the deepest foundation of Erasmus's being, which he reveals for a moment to his old and intimate friend? It may be doubted. The passage tallies very ill with the first sentences of the letter, which are altogether concerned with success and prospects. In a letter he wrote the next day, also to Gouda and to a trusted friend, there is no trace of the mood: he is again thinking of his future. We do not notice that the tremendous zeal with which he continues his studies is relaxed for a moment. And there are other indications that towards Servatius, who knew him better than he could wish, and who, moreover, as prior of Steyn, had a threatening power over him, he purposely demeaned himself as though he despised the world.

Meanwhile nothing came of the English prebend. But suddenly the occasion offered to which Erasmus had so often looked forward: the journey to Italy. The court-physician of Henry VII, Giovanni Battista Boerio, of Genoa, was looking for a master to accompany his sons in their journey to the universities of Italy. Erasmus accepted the post, which charged him neither with the duties of tuition nor with attending to the young fellows, but only with supervising and guiding their studies. In the beginning of June 1506, he found himself on French soil once more. For two summer months the party of travellers stayed at Paris and Erasmus availed himself of the opportunity to have several of his works, which he had brought from England, printed at Paris. He was by now a well-known and favourite author, gladly welcomed by the old friends (he had been reputed dead) and made much of. Josse Badius printed all Erasmus offered him: the translations of Euripides and Lucian, a collection of *Epigrammata*, a new but still unaltered edition of the *Adagia*.

In August the journey was continued. As he rode on horse-back along the Alpine roads the most important poem Erasmus has written, the echo of an abandoned pursuit, originated. He had been vexed about his travelling company, had abstained from conversing with them, and sought consolation in composing poetry. The result was the ode which he called *Carmen equestre vel potius alpestre*, about the inconveniences of old age, dedicated to his friend William Cop.

Erasmus was one of those who early feel old. He was not forty and yet fancied himself across the threshold of old age. How quickly it had come! He looks back on the course of his life: he sees himself playing with nuts as a child, as a boy eager for study, as a youth engrossed in poetry and scholasticism, also in painting. He surveys his enormous erudition, his study of Greek, his aspiration to scholarly fame. In the midst of all this, old age has suddenly come. What remains to him? And again we hear the note of renunciation of the world and of devotion to Christ. Farewell jests and trifles, farewell philosophy and poetry, a pure heart full of Christ is all he desires henceforward.

Here, in the stillness of the Alpine landscape, there arose something more of Erasmus's deepest aspirations than in the lament to Servatius. But in this case, too, it is a stray element of his soul, not the strong impulse that gave direction and fullness to his life and with irresistible pressure urged him on to ever new studies.

CHAPTER VIII

IN ITALY

1506–9

Erasmus in Italy: 1506–9 — He takes his degree at Turin — Bologna and Pope Julius II — Erasmus in Venice with Aldus: 1507–8 — The art of printing — Alexander Stewart — To Rome: 1509 — News of Henry VIII's accession — Erasmus leaves Italy

At Turin Erasmus received, directly upon his arrival, on 4 September 1506, the degree of doctor of theology. That he did not attach much value to the degree is easy to understand. He regarded it, however, as an official warrant of his competence as a writer on theological subjects, which would strengthen his position when assailed by the suspicion of his critics. He writes disdainfully about the title, even to his Dutch friends who in former days had helped him on in his studies for the express purpose of obtaining the doctor's degree. As early as 1501, to Anna of Borselen he writes, 'Go to Italy and obtain the doctor's degree? Foolish projects, both of them. But one should conform to the customs of the times.' Again to Servatius and Johannes Obrecht, half apologetically, he says: 'I have obtained the doctor's degree in theology, and that quite contrary to my intention, only because I was overcome by the prayers of friends.'

Bologna was now the destination of his journey. But when Erasmus arrived there, a war was in progress which forced him to retire to Florence for a time. Pope Julius II, allied with the French, at the head of an army, marched on Bologna to conquer it from the Bentivogli. This purpose was soon attained, and Bologna was a safe place to return to. On 11 November 1506, Erasmus witnessed the triumphal entry of the martial pope.

Of these days nothing but short, hasty letters of his have come down to us. They speak of unrest and rumours of war. There is nothing to show that he was impressed by the beauty of the Italy of the Renaissance. The scanty correspondence

VII. Title-page of the *Adagia*, printed by Aldus Manutius in 1508

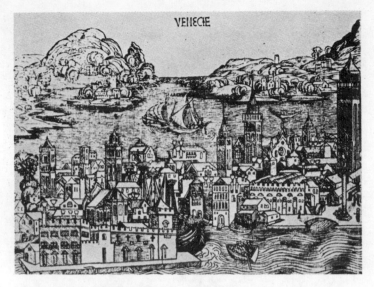

VIII. VIEW OF VENICE, 1493

IX. PORTRAIT MEDAL OF ALDUS MANUTIUS
On the reverse the Aldine emblem

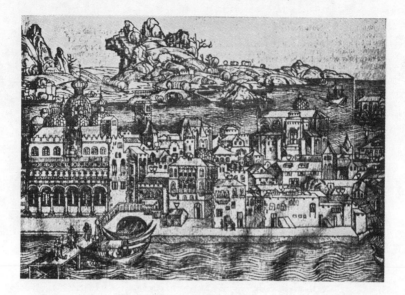

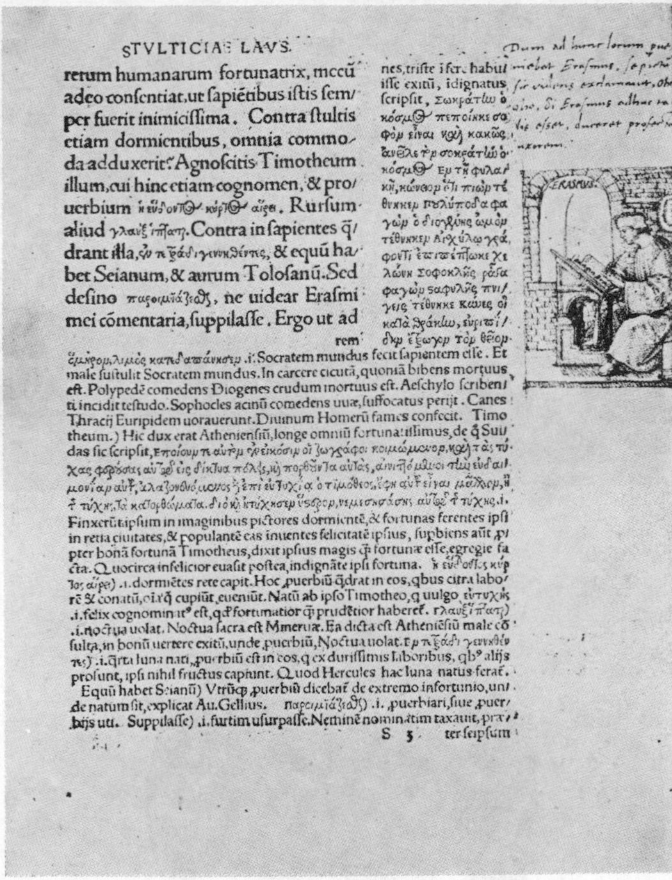

STVLTICIAE LAVS.

retum humanarum fortunatrix, mecū adeo consentiat, ut sapiētibus istis semper fuerit inimicissima. Contra stultis etiam dormientibus, omnia commoda adduxerit. Agnoscitis Timotheum illum, cui hinc etiam cognomen, & prouerbium ἡ εὕδοντος κύρτος αἱρεῖ. Rursum aliud γλαὺξ ἵπταται. Contra in sapientes quadrant illa, ἐν τετράδι γεννηθέντες, & equū habet Seianum, & aurum Tolosanū. Sed desino παροιμιάζεσθαι, ne uidear Erasmi mei cōmentaria, suppilasse. Ergo ut ad rem

nes, triste ferè habuisse exitū, idignatus scripsit, Σωκράτην ὁ κόσμος πεποίηκε σοφὸν εἶναι καὶ κακῶς ἀνεῖλε τὸν Σωκράτην ὁ κόσμος ἐν τῇ φυλακῇ, κώνειον ὅτι πιὼν τέθνηκεν πολύποδα φαγὼν ὁ Διογένης ὠμὸν τέθνηκεν Αἰσχύλῳ γράφοντι ἐπιπέπτωκε χελώνη Σοφοκλῆς ῥᾶγα φαγὼν σταφυλῆς πνιγεὶς τέθνηκε κύνες οἱ κατὰ Θρᾴκην, Εὐριπίδην ἔξωγον τὸν θεῖον Ὅμηρον λιμὸς κατεδαπάνησεν .i. Socratem mundus fecit sapientem esse. Et male sustulit Socratem mundus. In carcere cicutā, quoniā bibens mortuus est. Polypedē comedens Diogenes crudum mortuus est. Aeschylo scribenti incidit testudo. Sophocles acinū comedens uuae, suffocatus perijt. Canes Thracij Euripidem uorauerunt. Diuinum Homerū fames confecit. Timotheum.) Hic dux erat Atheniensiū, longe omniū fortunatissimus, de quo Suidas sic scripsit, ἐποίουν τε αὐτὸν ἐν εἰκόσιν οἱ ζωγράφοι κοιμώμενον, καὶ τὰς τύχας φερούσας αὐτῷ εἰς δίκτυα πόλεις, καὶ πορθοῦντα αὐτάς, ἀντιπαρόμενοι τὴν εὐδαιμονίαν αὐτοῦ, ἀλαζονευόμενος δὲ ἐπὶ εὐτυχίᾳ ὁ Τιμόθεος, ἔφη αὐτοῦ εἶναι μᾶλλον, ἢ τῆς τύχης, τὰ κατορθώματα. διὸ καὶ ἠτύχησεν ὕστερον, νεμεσησάσης αὐτῷ τῆς τύχης. .i. Finxerūt ipsum in imaginibus pictores dormientē, & fortunas ferentes ipsi in retia ciuitates, & populantē eas inuentes felicitatē ipsius, supbiens aūt propter bonā fortunā Timotheus, dixit ipsius magis quam fortunae esse, egregie facta. Quocirca infelicior euasit postea, indignāte ipsi fortuna. ἡ εὕδοντος κύρτος αἱρεῖ) .i. dormiētes rete capit. Hoc puerbiū quadrat in eos, qbus citra laborē & conatū, omnia quae cupiūt, eueniūt. Natū ab ipso Timotheo, q uulgo εὐτυχὴς .i. felix cognominatus est, quod fortunatior quam prudētior haberet. γλαὺξ ἵπταται) .i. noctua uolat. Noctua sacra est Mineruae. Ea dicta est Atheniēsiū male cōsulta, in bonū uertere exitū, unde puerbiū, Noctua uolat. ἐν τετράδι γεννηθέντες) .i. quarta luna nati, puerbiū est in eos, q ex durissimis laboribus, qbus alijs prosunt, ipsi nihil fructus capiunt. Quod Hercules hac luna natus ferat. Equū habet Seianū) Vtrūque puerbiū dicebat de extremo infortunio, unde natum sit, explicat Au. Gellius. παροιμιάζεσθαι) .i. puerbiari, siue puerbijs uti. Suppilasse) .i. furtim usurpasse. Neminē nominatim taxauit, praeter seipsum

S 5

Dum ad hunc locum perueniebat Erasmus, sapientis [illegible] ... Si Erasmus adhuc [illegible] ... esset, duceret [illegible]

ERASMUS

x. A page from the *Praise of Folly* with a drawing by Holbein of Erasmus at his desk dating from his stay in Italy mentions neither architecture, nor sculpture, nor pictures. When much later he happened to remember his visit to the Chartreuse of Pavia, it is only to give an instance of useless waste and magnificence. Books alone seemed to occupy and attract Erasmus in Italy.

At Bologna, Erasmus served as a mentor to the young Boerios to the end of the year for which he had bound himself. It seemed a very long time to him. He could not stand any encroachment upon his liberty. He felt caught in the contract as in a net. The boys, it seems, were intelligent enough, if not so brilliant as Erasmus had seen them in his first joy; but with their private tutor Clyfton, whom he at first extolled to the sky, he was soon at loggerheads. At Bologna he experienced many vexations for which his new relations with Paul Bombasius could only in part indemnify him. He worked there at an enlarged edition of his *Adagia*, which now, by the addition of the Greek ones, increased from eight hundred to some thousands of items.

From Bologna, in October 1507, Erasmus addressed a letter to the famous Venetian printer, Aldus Manutius, in which he requested him to publish, anew, the two translated dramas of Euripides, as the edition of Badius was out of print and too defective for his taste. What made Aldus attractive in his eyes was, no doubt, besides the fame of the business, though it was languishing at the time, the printer's beautiful type—'those most magnificent letters, especially those very small ones'. Erasmus was one of those true book-lovers who pledge their heart to a type or a size of a book, not because of any artistic preference, but because of readableness and handiness, which to them are of the very greatest importance. What he asked of Aldus was a small book at a low price. Towards the end of the year their relations had gone so far that Erasmus gave up his projected journey to Rome, for the time, to remove to Venice, there personally to superintend the publication of his works. Now there was no longer merely the question of a little book of translations, but Aldus had declared himself willing to print the enormously increased collection of the *Adagia*.

Beatus Rhenanus tells a story which, no doubt, he had heard from Erasmus himself: how Erasmus on his arrival at Venice had gone straight to the printing-office and was kept waiting there for a long time. Aldus was correcting proofs and thought his visitor was one of those inquisitive people by whom he used to be pestered. When he turned out to be Erasmus, he welcomed him cordially and procured him board and lodging in the house of his father-in-law, Andrea Asolani. Fully eight months did Erasmus live there, in the environment which, in future, was to be his true element: the printing-office. He was in a fever of hurried work, about which he would often sigh, but which, after all, was congenial to him. The augmented collection of the *Adagia* had not yet been made ready for the press at Bologna. 'With great temerity on my part,' Erasmus himself testifies, 'we began to work at the same time, I to write, Aldus to print.' Meanwhile the literary friends of the New Academy whom he got to know at Venice, Johannes Lascaris, Baptista Egnatius, Marcus Musurus and the young Jerome Aleander, with whom, at Asolani's, he shared room and bed, brought him new Greek authors, unprinted as yet, furnishing fresh material for augmenting the *Adagia*. These were no inconsiderable additions: Plato in the original, Plutarch's *Lives* and *Moralia*, Pindar, Pausanias, and others. Even people whom he did not know and who took an interest in his work, brought new material to him. Amid the noise of the press-room, Erasmus, to the surprise of his publisher, sat and wrote, usually from memory, so busily occupied that, as he picturesquely expressed it, he had no time to scratch his ears. He was lord and master of the printing-office. A special corrector had been assigned to him; he made his textual changes in the last impression. Aldus also read the proofs. 'Why?' asked Erasmus. 'Because I am studying at the same time,' was the reply. Meanwhile Erasmus suffered from the first attack of his tormenting nephrolithic malady; he ascribed it to the food he got at Asolani's and later took revenge by painting that boarding-house and its landlord in very spiteful colours in the *Colloquies*.

When in September 1508, the edition of the *Adagia* was ready, Aldus wanted Erasmus to remain in order to write more for him. Till December he continued to work at Venice on editions of Plautus, Terence, and Seneca's tragedies. Visions of joint labour to publish all that classic antiquity still held in the way of hidden treasures, together with Hebrew and Chaldean stores, floated before his mind.

Erasmus belonged to the generation which had grown up together with the youthful art of printing. To the world of those days it was still like a newly acquired organ; people felt rich, powerful, happy in the possession of this 'almost divine implement'. The figure of Erasmus and his *œuvre* were only rendered possible by the art of printing. He was its glorious triumph and, equally, in a sense, its victim. What would Erasmus have been without the printing-press? To broadcast the ancient documents, to purify and restore them was his life's passion. The certainty that the printed book places exactly the same text in the hands of thousands of readers, was to him a consolation that former generations had lacked.

Erasmus is one of the first who, after his name as an author was established, worked directly and continually for the press. It was his strength, but also his weakness. It enabled him to exercise an immediate influence on the reading public of Europe such as had emanated from none before him; to become a focus of culture in the full sense of the word, an intellectual central station, a touchstone of the spirit of the time. Imagine for a moment what it would have meant if a still greater mind than his, say Cardinal Nicholas of Cusa, that universal spirit who had helped in nursing the art of printing in its earliest infancy, could have availed himself of the art as it was placed at the disposal of Erasmus!

The dangerous aspect of this situation was that printing enabled Erasmus, having once become a centre and an authority, to address the world at large immediately about all that occurred to him. Much of his later mental labour is, after all, really but repetition, ruminating digression, unnecessary vindication from assaults to which his greatness alone would have been a sufficient answer, futilities which he might have better left alone. Much of this work written directly for the press is journalism at bottom, and we do Erasmus an injustice by applying to it the tests of lasting excellence. The consciousness that we can reach the whole world at once with our writings is a stimulant which unwittingly influences our mode of expression, a luxury that only the highest spirits can bear with impunity.

The link between Erasmus and book-printing was Latin. Without his incomparable Latinity his position as an author would have been impossible. The art of printing undoubtedly furthered the use of Latin. It was the Latin publications which in those days promised success and a large sale for a publisher, and established his reputation, for they were broadcast all over the world. The leading publishers were themselves scholars filled with enthusiasm for humanism. Cultured and well-to-do people acted as proof-readers to printers; such as Peter Gilles, the friend of Erasmus and More, the town clerk of Antwerp, who corrected proof-sheets for Dirck Maertensz. The great printing-offices were, in a local sense, too, the foci of intellectual intercourse. The fact that England had lagged behind, thus far, in the evolution of the art of printing, contributed not a little, no doubt, to prevent Erasmus from settling there, where so many ties held and so many advantages allured him.

To find a permanent place of residence was, indeed, and apart from this fact, very hard for him. Towards the end of 1508 he accepted the post of tutor in rhetorics to the young Alexander Stewart, a natural son of James IV of Scotland, and already, in spite of his youth, Archbishop of Saint Andrews, now a student at Padua. The danger of war soon drove them from upper Italy to Siena. Here Erasmus obtained leave to visit Rome. He arrived there early in 1509, no longer an unknown canon from the northern regions but a celebrated and honoured author. All the charms of the Eternal City lay open to him and he must have felt keenly gratified by the consideration and courtesy with which cardinals and prelates, such as Giovanni de' Medici, afterwards Leo X, Domenico Grimani,

Riario and others, treated him. It seems that he was even offered some post in the curia. But he had to return to his youthful archbishop with whom he thereupon visited Rome again, incognito, and afterwards travelled in the neighbourhood of Naples. He inspected the cave of the Sibylla of Cumae, but what it meant to him we do not know. This entire period following his departure from Padua and all that follows till the spring of 1511—in certain respects the most important part of his life—remains unrecorded in a single letter that has come down to us. Here and there he has occasionally, and at a much later date, touched upon some impressions of Rome,[1] but the whole remains vague and dim. It is the incubation period of the *Praise of Folly* that is thus obscured from view.

On 21 April 1509, King Henry VII of England died. His successor was the young prince whom Erasmus had saluted at Eltham in 1499, to whom he had dedicated his poem in praise of Great Britain, and who, during his stay at Bologna, had distinguished him by a Latin letter as creditable to Erasmus as to the fifteen-year-old royal latinist.[2] If ever the chance of obtaining a patron seemed favourable, it was now, when this promising lover of letters ascended the throne as Henry VIII. Lord Mountjoy, Erasmus's most faithful Maecenas, thought so, too, and pointed out the fact to him in a letter of 27 May 1509. It was a pleasure to see, he wrote, how vigorous, how upright and just, how zealous in the cause of literature and men of letters was the conduct of the youthful prince. Mountjoy—or Ammonius, who probably drew up the flowery document for him—was exultant. A laughing sky and tears of joy are the themes of the letter. Evidently, however, Erasmus himself had, on his side, already sounded Mountjoy as to his chances, as soon as the tidings of Henry VII's death became known at Rome; not without lamentations about cares and weakened

[1] LBE. No. 1175 c. 1375, visit to Grimani.

[2] A. 206, where from Allen's introduction one can form an opinion about the prince's share in the composition.

health. 'The Archbishop of Canterbury', Mountjoy was able to apprise Erasmus, 'is not only continually engrossed in your *Adagia* and praises you to the skies, but he also promises you a benefice on your return and sends you five pounds for travelling expenses,' which sum was doubled by Mountjoy.

We do not know whether Erasmus really hesitated before he reached his decision. Cardinal Grimani, he asserts, tried to hold him back, but in vain, for in July, 1509, he left Rome and Italy, never to return.

As he crossed the Alps for the second time, not on the French side now, but across the Splügen, through Switzerland, his genius touched him again, as had happened in those high regions three years before on the road to Italy. But this time it was not in the guise of the Latin Muse, who then drew from him such artful and pathetic poetical meditations about his past life and pious vows for the future;—it was something much more subtle and grand: the *Praise of Folly*.

CHAPTER IX

THE PRAISE OF FOLLY

*Moriae Encomium, The Praise of Folly: 1509, as a work of art—Folly,
the motor of all life: Indispensable, salutary, cause and support of states and
of heroism—Folly keeps the world going—Vital energy incorporated with
folly—Lack of folly makes unfit for life—Need of self-complacency—
Humbug beats truth—Knowledge a plague—Satire of all secular and
ecclesiastical vocations—Two themes throughout the work—The highest
folly: Ecstasy—The Moria to be taken as a gay jest—Confusion of fools
and lunatics—Erasmus treats his Moria slightingly—Its value*

WHILE he rode over the mountain passes,[1] Erasmus's restless
spirit, now unfettered for some days by set tasks, occupied
itself with everything he had studied and read in the last few
years, and with everything he had seen. What ambition, what
self-deception, what pride and conceit filled the world! He
thought of Thomas More, whom he was now to see again—
that most witty and wise of all his friends, with that curious
name *Moros*, the Greek word for a fool, which so ill became his
personality. Anticipating the gay jests which More's conversation promised, there grew in his mind that masterpiece of
humour and wise irony, *Moriae Encomium*, the *Praise of Folly*.
The world as the scene of universal folly; folly as the indispensable element making life and society possible and all this
put into the mouth of Stultitia—Folly—itself (true antitype of
Minerva), who in a panegyric on her own power and usefulness, praises herself. As to form it is a *Declamatio*, such as he
had translated from the Greek of Libanius. As to the spirit,
a revival of Lucian, whose *Gallus*, translated by him three
years before, may have suggested the theme. It must have been
in the incomparably lucid moments of that brilliant intellect.
All the particulars of classic reading which the year before he
worked up in the new edition of the *Adagia* were still at his

[1] That he conceived the work in the Alps follows from the fact that
he tells us explicitly that it happened while riding, whereas, after passing
through Switzerland, he travelled by boat. A. 1, IV 216.62.

immediate disposal in that retentive and capacious memory. Reflecting at his ease on all that wisdom of the ancients, he secreted the juices required for his expostulation.

He arrived in London, took up his abode in More's house in Bucklersbury, and there, tortured by nephritic pains, he wrote down in a few days, without having his books with him, the perfect work of art that must have been ready in his mind. Stultitia was truly born in the manner of her serious sister Pallas.

As to form and imagery the *Moria* is faultless, the product of the inspired moments of creative impulse. The figure of an orator confronting her public is sustained to the last in a masterly way. We see the faces of the auditors light up with glee when Folly appears in the pulpit; we hear the applause interrupting her words. There is a wealth of fancy, coupled with so much soberness of line and colour, such reserve, that the whole presents a perfect instance of that harmony which is the essence of Renaissance expression. There is no exuberance, in spite of the multiplicity of matter and thought, but a temperateness, a smoothness, an airiness and clearness which are as gladdening as they are relaxing. In order perfectly to realize the artistic perfection of Erasmus's book we should compare it with Rabelais.

'Without me', says Folly, 'the world cannot exist for a moment. For is not all that is done at all among mortals, full of folly; is it not performed by fools and for fools?' 'No society, no cohabitation can be pleasant or lasting without folly; so much so, that a people could not stand its prince, nor the master his man, nor the maid her mistress, nor the tutor his pupil, nor the friend his friend, nor the wife her husband for a moment longer, if they did not now and then err together, now flatter each other; now sensibly conniving at things, now smearing themselves with some honey of folly.' In that sentence the summary of the *Laus* is contained. Folly here is worldly wisdom, resignation and lenient judgement.

He who pulls off the masks in the comedy of life is ejected. What is the whole life of mortals but a sort of play in which each actor appears on the boards in his specific mask and acts his part till the stage-manager calls him off? He acts wrongly who does not adapt himself to existing conditions, and demands that the game shall be a game no longer. It is the part of the truly sensible to mix with all people, either conniving readily at their folly, or affably erring like themselves.

And the necessary driving power of all human action is 'Philautia', Folly's own sister: self-love. He who does not please himself effects little. Take away that condiment of life and the word of the orator cools, the poet is laughed at, the artist perishes with his art.

Folly in the garb of pride, of vanity, of vainglory, is the hidden spring of all that is considered high and great in this world. The state with its posts of honour, patriotism and national pride; the stateliness of ceremonies, the delusion of caste and nobility—what is it but folly? War, the most foolish thing of all, is the origin of all heroism. What prompted the Deciuses, what Curtius, to sacrifice themselves? Vainglory. It is this folly which produces states; through her, empires, religion, law-courts, exist.

This is bolder and more chilling than Machiavelli, more detached than Montaigne. But Erasmus will not have it credited to him: it is Folly who speaks. He purposely makes us tread the round of the *circulus vitiosus*, as in the old saw: A Cretan said, all Cretans are liars.

Wisdom is to folly as reason is to passion. And there is much more passion than reason in the world. That which keeps the world going, the fount of life, is folly. For what else is love? Why do people marry, if not out of folly, which sees no objections? All enjoyment and amusement is only a condiment of folly. When a wise man wishes to become a father, he has first to play the fool. For what is more foolish than the game of procreation?

Unperceived the orator has incorporated here with folly all that is vitality and the courage of life. Folly is spontaneous energy that no one can do without. He who is perfectly sensible and serious cannot live. The more people get away from me, Stultitia, the less they live. Why do we kiss and cuddle little children, if not because they are still so delightfully foolish. And what else makes youth so elegant?

Now look at the truly serious and sensible. They are awkward at everything, at meal-time, at a dance, in playing, in social intercourse. If they have to buy, or to contract, things are sure to go wrong. Quintilian says that stage fright bespeaks the intelligent orator, who knows his faults. Right! But does not, then, Quintilian confess openly that wisdom is an impediment to good execution? And has not Stultitia the right to claim prudence for herself, if the wise, out of shame, out of bashfulness, undertake nothing in circumstances where fools pluckily set to work?

Here Erasmus goes to the root of the matter in a psychological sense. Indeed the consciousness of falling short in achievement is the brake clogging action, is the great inertia retarding the progress of the world. Did he know himself for one who is awkward when not bending over his books, but confronting men and affairs?

Folly is gaiety and lightheartedness, indispensable to happiness. The man of mere reason without passion is a stone image, blunt and without any human feeling, a spectre or monster, from whom all fly, deaf to all natural emotions, susceptible neither to love nor compassion. Nothing escapes him, in nothing he errs; he sees through everything, he weighs everything accurately, he forgives nothing, he is only satisfied with himself; he alone is healthy; he alone is king, he alone is free. It is the hideous figure of the doctrinaire which Erasmus is thinking of. Which state, he exclaims, would desire such an absolutely wise man for a magistrate?

He who devotes himself to tasting all the bitterness of life with wise insight would forthwith deprive himself of life. Only folly is a remedy: to err, to be mistaken, to be ignorant is to be human. How much better it is in marriage to be blind to a wife's shortcomings than to make away with oneself out of jealousy and to fill the world with tragedy! Adulation is virtue. There is no cordial devotion without a little adulation.

It is the soul of eloquence, of medicine and poetry; it is the honey and the sweetness of all human customs.

Again a series of valuable social qualities is slyly incorporated with folly: benevolence, kindness, inclination to approve and to admire.

But especially to approve of oneself. There is no pleasing others without beginning by flattering ourselves a little and approving of ourselves. What would the world be if everyone was not proud of his standing, his calling, so that no person would change places with another in point of good appearance, of fancy, of good family, of landed property?

Humbug is the right thing. Why should any one desire true erudition? The more incompetent a man, the pleasanter his life is and the more he is admired. Look at professors, poets, orators. Man's mind is so made that he is more impressed by lies than by the truth. Go to church: if the priest deals with serious subjects the whole congregation is dozing, yawning, feeling bored. But when he begins to tell some cock-and-bull story, they awake, sit up, and hang on his lips.

To be deceived, philosophers say, is a misfortune, but not to be deceived is a superlative misfortune. If it is human to err, why should a man be called unhappy because he errs, since he was so born and made, and it is the fate of all? Do we pity a man because he cannot fly or does not walk on four legs? We might as well call the horse unhappy because it does not learn grammar or eat cakes. No creature is unhappy, if it lives according to its nature. The sciences were invented to our utmost destruction; far from conducing to our happiness, they are even in its way, though for its sake they are supposed to have been invented. By the agency of evil demons they have stolen into human life with the other pests. For did not the simple-minded people of the Golden Age live happily, unprovided with any science, only led by nature and instinct? What did they want grammar for, when all spoke the same language? Why have dialectics, when there were no quarrels and no differences of opinion? Why jurisprudence, when there were no bad morals from which good laws sprang? They were too religious to investigate with impious curiosity the secrets of nature, the size, motions, influence of the stars, the hidden cause of things.

It is the old idea, which germinated in antiquity, here lightly touched upon by Erasmus, afterwards proclaimed by Rousseau in bitter earnest: civilization is a plague.

Wisdom is misfortune, but self-conceit is happiness. Grammarians, who wield the sceptre of wisdom—schoolmasters, that is—would be the most wretched of all people if I, Folly, did not mitigate the discomforts of their miserable calling by a sort of sweet frenzy. But what holds good of schoolmasters, also holds good of poets, orators, authors. For them, too, all happiness merely consists in vanity and delusion. The lawyers are no better off and after them come the philosophers. Next there is a numerous procession of clergy: divines, monks, bishops, cardinals, popes, only interrupted by princes and courtiers.

In the chapters[1] which review these offices and callings, satire has shifted its ground a little. Throughout the work two themes are intertwined: that of salutary folly, which is true wisdom, and that of deluded wisdom, which is pure folly. As they are both put into the mouth of Folly, we should have to invert them both to get truth, if Folly . . . were not wisdom. Now it is clear that the first is the principal theme. Erasmus starts from it; and he returns to it. Only in the middle, as he reviews human accomplishments and dignities in their universal foolishness, the second theme predominates and the book becomes an ordinary satire on human folly, of which there are many though few are so delicate. But in the other parts it is something far deeper.

Occasionally the satire runs somewhat off the line, when Stultitia directly censures what Erasmus wishes to censure; for instance, indulgences, silly belief in wonders, selfish worship of the saints; or gamblers whom she, Folly, ought to praise; or the spirit of systematizing and levelling, and the jealousy of the monks.

---

[1] Erasmus did not divide the book into chapters. It was done by an editor as late as 1765.

For contemporary readers the importance of the *Laus Stultitiae* was, to a great extent, in the direct satire. Its lasting value is in those passages where we truly grant that folly is wisdom and the reverse. Erasmus knows the aloofness of the ground of all things: all consistent thinking out of the dogmas of faith leads to absurdity. Only look at the theological quiddities of effete scholasticism. The apostles would not have understood them: in the eyes of latter-day divines they would have been fools. Holy Scripture itself sides with folly. 'The foolishness of God is wiser than men,' says Saint Paul. 'But God hath chosen the foolish things of the world.' 'It pleased God by the foolishness (of preaching) to save them that believe.' Christ loved the simple-minded and the ignorant: children, women, poor fishermen, nay, even such animals as are farthest removed from vulpine cunning: the ass which he wished to ride, the dove, the lamb, the sheep.

Here there is a great deal behind the seemingly light jest: 'Christian religion seems in general to have some affinity with a certain sort of folly'. Was it not thought the apostles were full of new wine? And did not the judge say: 'Paul, thou art beside thyself'? When are we beside ourselves? When the spirit breaks its fetters and tries to escape from its prison and aspires to liberty. That is madness, but it is also other-worldliness and the highest wisdom. True happiness is in selflessness, in the furore of lovers, whom Plato calls happiest of all. The more absolute love is, the greater and more rapturous is the frenzy. Heavenly bliss itself is the greatest insanity; truly pious people enjoy its shadow on earth already in their meditations.

Here Stultitia breaks off her discourse, apologizing in a few words in case she may have been too petulant or talkative, and leaves the pulpit. 'So farewell, applaud, live happily, and drink, Moria's illustrious initiates.'

It was an unrivalled feat of art even in these last chapters neither to lose the light comical touch, nor to lapse into undisguised profanation. It was only feasible by veritable dancing on the tight-rope of sophistry. In the *Moria* Erasmus is all the time hovering on the brink of profound truths. But what a boon it was—still granted to those times—to be able to treat of all this in a vein of pleasantry. For this should be impressed upon our minds: that the *Moriae Encomium* is a true, gay jest. The laugh is more delicate, but no less hearty than Rabelais's. 'Valete, plaudite, vivite, bibite.' 'All common people abound to such a degree, and everywhere, in so many forms of folly that a thousand Democrituses would be insufficient to laugh at them all (and they would require another Democritus to laugh at them).'

How could one take the *Moria* too seriously, when even More's *Utopia*, which is a true companion-piece to it and makes such a grave impression on us, is treated by its author and Erasmus as a mere jest? There is a place where the *Laus* seems to touch both More and Rabelais; the place where Stultitia speaks of her father, Plutus, the god of wealth, at whose beck all things are turned topsy-turvy, according to whose will all human affairs are regulated—war and peace, government and counsel, justice and treaties. He has begotten her on the nymph Youth, not a senile, purblind Plutus, but a fresh god, warm with youth and nectar, like another Gargantua.

The figure of Folly, of gigantic size, looms large in the period of the Renaissance. She wears a fool's cap and bells. People laughed loudly and with unconcern at all that was foolish, without discriminating between species of folly. It is remarkable that even in the *Laus*, delicate as it is, the author does not distinguish between the unwise or the silly, between fools and lunatics. Holbein, illustrating Erasmus, knows but of one representation of a fool: with a staff and ass's ears. Erasmus speaks without clear transition, now of foolish persons and now of real lunatics. They are happiest of all, he makes Stultitia say: they are not frightened by spectres and apparitions; they are not tortured by the fear of impending calamities; everywhere they bring mirth, jests, frolic and laughter. Evidently he here means harmless imbeciles, who, indeed, were often used as jesters. This identification of denseness and insanity is kept up, however, like the confusion of the comic and the simply ridiculous, and all this is well calculated to make us feel how wide the gap has already become that separates us from Erasmus.

In later years he always spoke slightingly of his *Moria*. He considered it so unimportant, he says, as to be unworthy of publication, yet no work of his had been received with such applause. It was a trifle and not at all in keeping with his character. More had made him write it, as if a camel were made to dance. But these disparaging utterances were not without a secondary purpose. The *Moria* had not brought him only success and pleasure. The exceedingly susceptible age in which he lived had taken the satire in very bad part, where it seemed to glance at offices and orders, although in his preface he had tried to safeguard himself from the reproach of irreverence. His airy play with the texts of Holy Scripture had been too venturesome for many. His friend Martin van Dorp upbraided him with having made a mock of eternal life. Erasmus did what he could to convince evil-thinkers that the purpose of the *Moria* was no other than to exhort people to be virtuous. In affirming this he did his work injustice: it was much more than that. But in 1515 he was no longer what he had been in 1509. Repeatedly he had been obliged to defend his most witty work. Had he known that it would offend, he might have kept it back, he writes in 1517 to an acquaintance at Louvain. Even towards the end of his life, he warded off the insinuations of Alberto Pio of Carpi in a lengthy expostulation.

Erasmus made no further ventures in the genre of the *Praise of Folly*. One might consider the treatise *Lingua*, which he published in 1525, as an attempt to make a companion-piece to the *Moria*. The book is called *Of the Use and Abuse of the Tongue*. In the opening pages there is something that reminds us of the style of the *Laus*, but it lacks all the charm both of form and of thought.

Should one pity Erasmus because, of all his publications, collected in ten folio volumes, only the *Praise of Folly* has remained a really popular book? It is, apart from the

Colloquies, perhaps the only one of his works that is still read for its own sake. The rest is now only studied from a historical point of view, for the sake of becoming acquainted with his person or his times. It seems to me that perfect justice has been done in this case. The *Praise of Folly* is his best work. He wrote other books, more erudite, some more pious —some perhaps of equal or greater influence on his time. But each has had its day. *Moriae Encomium* alone was to be immortal. For only when humour illuminated that mind did it become truly profound. In the *Praise of Folly* Erasmus gave something that no one else could have given to the world.

STVLTICIAE LAVS.

æ uelut uïmbra quædã,fit ut præmij quo q̃; illi⁹ aliqñ guſtũ,
aut odoré aliqué ſentiãt.Id tãetſi minutiſſima quædã ſtillu
la eſt ad fonté illũ æternæ felicitatis,tñ longe ſupat uniuer-
ſas corpis uoluptates,etiã ſi oẽs omniũ mortaliũ delitiæ in
unũ côferant.Vſq̃adeo præſtãt ſpiritaliã corpalib⁹,inuiſi/
bilia uiſibilib⁹.Hoc nimirũ eſt,q̃d pollicet̃ ꝓpheta, oculus
nô uidit,nec aũris audiuit,nec in cor hois aſcêdit, quæ præ
parauit deus diligêtibus ſe. Atq̃; hæc eſt Moriæ pars,quæ
nô aufert̃ cômutatióe uitæ,ſed pficit̃.Hoc igit̃qbus ſentire
licuit(côtingit aũt ppaucis) ij patiunt̃ q̃ddã demêtiæ ſimilli
mũ, loquũtur quædã nô ſatis cohærêtia, nec humano more,ſed dant ſine mête ſonũ, deinde ſubinde totã oris ſpecié
uertũt,Nũc alacres,nũc deiecti,nũc lachrymãt, nũc rident,
nũc ſuſpirãt,in ſũma uere toti extra ſe ſunt. Mox ubi ad ſe
ſe redierint,negat ſe ſcire,ubi fuerint,utrũ in corpe,an extra
corp⁹,uigilãtes,an dormiétes,qd audierint, qd uiderint, qd
dixerint,qd ſecerint,nô meminerũt,niſi tãq̃p p nebulam, ac
ſomniũ,tantũ hoc ſciunt,ſe feliciſſimos fuiſſe, dũ ita deſipe
rêt.Itaq̃; plorãt ſeſe reſipuiſſe,nihilq̃; omniũ malint q̃ hoc
inſaniæ genus ꝑpetuo inſanire. Atq̃; hæc eſt futuræ felicita
tis tenuis quædã deguſtatiuncula. Verũ ego iãdudũ oblita
mei ὑπὲρ τὰ ἐσκαμμένα πηδῶ. Quãq̃; ſiqd petulãtius aut loqũa
cius a me dictũ uidebit̃,cogitate & ſtulticiã, & mulierem di
xiſſe.Sed interim tñ memineritis illius Græcanici puerbij,
πολλάκϊοι καὶ μωρὸς ἀνὴρ καταχαίριον ἔιπεμ · Niſi forte putatis hoc
ad mulieres nihil attinere. Video uos epilogũ expectare,
ſed nimiũ deſipitis, ſi qd̃ arbitramini me qd dixerim etiã
dũ meminiſſe.Cũ tantã uerborũ ſarragine effuderim. Ve-
tus illud,μισῶ μνάμονα συμπόταμ.Nouũ hoc,μισῶ μνάμονα ἀκρο-
ατὴν.Quare ualete,plaudite,uiuite,bibite,Moriæ celeberri-
mi Myſtæ.   ΜΩΡΙΑΣ ΕΓΚΩΜΙΩΝ Feliciter abſolutum.

XI. The last page of the *Praise of Folly*, with Holbein's drawing of Folly
descending from the pulpit

Prelum
Ascensianū.

15   20

XII. THE PRINTING PRESS OF JOSSE BADIUS

CHAPTER X

THIRD STAY IN ENGLAND

1509–14

Third stay in England: 1509–14 — No information about two years of Erasmus's life: 1509 summer, till 1511 spring — Poverty — Erasmus at Cambridge — Relations with Badius, the Paris publisher — A mistake profitable to Johannes Froben at Basle — Erasmus leaves England: 1514 — Julius Exclusus — Epistle against war

FROM the moment when Erasmus, back from Italy in the early summer of 1509, is hidden from view in the house of More, to write the *Praise of Folly*, until nearly two years later when he comes to view again on the road to Paris to have the book printed by Gilles Gourmont, every trace of his life has been obliterated. Of the letters which during that period he wrote and received, not a single one has been preserved. Perhaps it was the happiest time of his life, for it was partly spent with his tried patron, Mountjoy, and also in the house of More in that noble and witty circle which to Erasmus appeared ideal. That house was also frequented by the friend whom Erasmus had made during his former sojourn in England, and whose mind was perhaps more congenial to him than any other, Andrew Ammonius. It is not improbable that during these months he was able to work without interruption at the studies to which he was irresistibly attracted, without cares as to the immediate future, and not yet burdened by excessive renown, which afterwards was to cause him as much trouble and loss as joy.

That future was still uncertain. As soon as he no longer enjoys More's hospitality, the difficulties and complaints recommence. Continual poverty, uncertainty and dependence were extraordinarily galling to a mind requiring above all things liberty. At Paris he charged Badius with a new, revised edition of the *Adagia*, though the Aldine might still be had there at a moderate price. The *Laus*, which had just appeared at Gourmont's, was reprinted at Strassburg as early as 1511, with a courteous letter by Jacob Wimpfeling to Erasmus, but evidently without his being consulted in the matter. By that time he was back in England, had been laid up in London with a bad attack of the sweating sickness, and thence had gone to Queens' College, Cambridge, where he had resided before. From Cambridge he writes to Colet, 24 August 1511, in a vein of comical despair. The journey from London had been disastrous: a lame horse, no victuals for the road, rain and thunder. 'But I am almost pleased at this, I see the track of Christian poverty.' A chance to make some money he does not see; he will be obliged to spend everything he can wrest from his Maecenases—he, born under a wrathful Mercury.

This may sound somewhat gloomier than it was meant, but a few weeks later he writes again: 'Oh, this begging; you laugh at me, I know. But I hate myself for it and am fully determined, either to obtain some fortune, which will relieve me from cringing, or to imitate Diogenes altogether.' This refers to a dedication of a translation of Basilius's Commentaries on Isaiah to John Fisher, the Bishop of Rochester.

Colet, who had never known pecuniary cares himself, did not well understand these sallies of Erasmus. He replies to them with delicate irony and covert rebuke, which Erasmus, in his turn, pretends not to understand. He was now 'in want in the midst of plenty', *simul et in media copia et in summa inopia*. That is to say, he was engaged in preparing for Badius's press the *De copia verborum ac rerum*, formerly begun at Paris; it was dedicated to Colet. 'I ask you, who can be more impudent or abject than I, who for such a long time already have been openly begging in England?'

Writing to Ammonius he bitterly regrets having left Rome and Italy; how prosperity had smiled upon him there! In the same way he would afterwards lament that he had not permanently established himself in England. If he had only embraced the opportunity! he thinks. Was not Erasmus rather one of those people whom good fortune cannot help?

He remained in trouble and his tone grows more bitter. 'I am preparing some bait against the 1st of January, though it is pretty sure to be in vain,' he writes to Ammonius, referring to new translations of Lucian and Plutarch.

At Cambridge Erasmus lectured on divinity and Greek, but it brought him little success and still less profit. The long-wished-for prebend, indeed, had at last been given him, in the form of the rectory of Aldington, in Kent, to which Archbishop William Warham, his patron, appointed him in 1512. Instead of residing he was allowed to draw a pension of twenty pounds a year. The archbishop affirms explicitly that, contrary to his custom, he had granted this favour to Erasmus, because he, 'a light of learning in Latin and Greek literature, had, out of love for England, disdained to live in Italy, France, or Germany, in order to pass the rest of his life here, with his friends'. We see how nations already begin to vie with each other for the honour of sheltering Erasmus.

Relief from all cares the post did not bring. Intercourse and correspondence with Colet was a little soured under the light veil of jests and kindness by his constant need of money. Seeking new resources by undertaking new labours, or preparing new editions of his old books, remained a hard necessity for Erasmus. The great works upon which he had set his heart, and to which he had given all his energies at Cambridge, held out no promise of immediate profit. His serious theological labours ranked above all others; and in these hard years, he devoted his best strength to preparation for the great edition of Jerome's works and emendation of the text of the New Testament, a task inspired, encouraged and promoted by Colet.

For his living other books had to serve. He had a sufficient number now, and the printers were eager enough about them, though the profit which the author made by them was not large. After leaving Aldus at Venice, Erasmus had returned to the publisher who had printed for him as early as 1505—Josse Badius, of Brabant, who, at Paris, had established the Ascensian Press (called after his native place, Assche) and who, a scholar himself, rivalled Aldus in point of the accuracy of his editions of the classics. At the time when Erasmus took the *Moria* to Gourmont, at Paris, he had charged Badius with a new edition, still to be revised, of the *Adagia*. Why the *Moria* was published by another, we cannot tell; perhaps Badius did not like it at first. From the *Adagia* he promised himself the more profit, but that was a long work, the alterations and preface of which he was still waiting for Erasmus to send. He felt very sure of his ground, for everyone knew that he, Badius, was preparing the new edition. Yet a rumour reached him that in Germany the Aldine edition was being reprinted. So there was some hurry to finish it, he wrote to Erasmus in May 1512.

Badius, meanwhile, had much more work of Erasmus in hand, or on approval: the *Copia*, which, shortly afterwards, was published by him; the *Moria*, of which, at the same time, a new edition, the fifth, already had appeared; the dialogues by Lucian; the Euripides and Seneca translations, which were to follow. He hoped to add Jerome's letters to these. For the *Adagia* they had agreed upon a copy-fee of fifteen guilders; for Jerome's letters Badius was willing to give the same sum and as much again for the rest of the consignment. 'Ah, you will say, what a very small sum! I own that by no remuneration could your genius, industry, knowledge and labour be requited, but the gods will requite you and your own virtue will be the finest reward. You have already deserved exceedingly well of Greek and Roman literature; you will in this same way deserve well of sacred and divine, and you will help your little Badius, who has a numerous family and no earnings besides his daily trade.'

Erasmus must have smiled ruefully on receiving Badius's letter. But he accepted the proposal readily. He promised to prepare everything for the press and, on 5 January 1513, he finished, in London, the preface to the revised *Adagia*, for which Badius was waiting. But then something happened. An agent who acted as a mediator with authors for several publishers in Germany and France, one Francis Berckman, of Cologne, took the revised copy of the *Adagia* with the preface entrusted to him by Erasmus to hand over to Badius, not to Paris, but to Basle, to Johannes Froben, who had just, without Erasmus's leave, reprinted the Venetian edition! Erasmus pretended to be indignant at this mistake or perfidy, but it is only too clear that he did not regret it. Six months later he betook himself with bag and baggage to Basle, to enter with that same Froben into those most cordial relations by which their names are united. Beatus Rhenanus, afterwards, made no secret of the fact that a connection with the house of Froben, then still called Amerbach and Froben, had seemed attractive to Erasmus ever since he had heard of the *Adagia* being reprinted.

Without conclusive proofs of his complicity, we do not like to accuse Erasmus of perfidy towards Badius, though his attitude is curious, to say the least. But we do want to commemorate the dignified tone in which Badius, who held strict notions, as those times went, about copyright, replied, when Berckman afterwards had come to offer him a sort of explanation of the case. He declares himself satisfied, though Erasmus had, since that time, caused him losses in more ways, amongst others by printing a new edition of the *Copia* at Strassburg. 'If, however, it is agreeable to your interests and honour, I shall suffer it, and that with equanimity.' Their relations were not broken off. In all this we should not lose sight of the fact that publishing at that time was yet a quite new commercial phenomenon and that new commercial forms and relations of trade are wont to be characterized by uncertainty, confusion and lack of established business morals.

The stay at Cambridge gradually became irksome to Erasmus. 'For some months already', he writes to Ammonius in November 1513, 'we have been leading a true snail's life, staying at home and plodding. It is very lonely here; most people have gone for fear of the plague, but even when they are all here, it is lonely.' The cost of sustenance is unbearable and he makes no money at all. If he does not succeed, that winter, in making a nest for himself, he is resolved to fly away, he does not know where. 'If to no other end, to die elsewhere.'

Added to the stress of circumstances, the plague, reappear-
ing again and again, and attacks of his kidney-trouble, there
came the state of war, which depressed and alarmed Erasmus.
In the spring of 1513 the English raid on France, long prepared, took place. In co-operation with Maximilian's army
the English had beaten the French near Guinegate and compelled Therouanne to surrender, and afterwards Tournay.
Meanwhile the Scotch invaded England, to be decisively
beaten near Flodden. Their king, James IV, perished together
with his natural son, Erasmus's pupil and travelling companion
in Italy, Alexander, Archbishop of Saint Andrews.

Crowned with martial fame, Henry VIII returned in
November to meet his parliament. Erasmus did not share the
universal joy and enthusiastic admiration. 'We are circumscribed here by the plague, threatened by robbers; we drink
wine of the worst (because there is no import from France),
but, *io triumphe!* we are the conquerors of the world!'

His deep aversion to the clamour of war, and all it represented, stimulated Erasmus's satirical faculties. It is true that he
flattered the English national pride by an epigram on the rout
of the French near Guinegate, but soon he went deeper. He
remembered how war had impeded his movements in Italy;
how the entry of the pope-conqueror, Julius II, into Bologna
had outraged his feelings. 'The high priest Julius wages
war, conquers, triumphs and truly plays the part of Julius
(Caesar)' he had written then. Pope Julius, he thought,
had been the cause of all the wars spreading more and more
over Europe. Now the Pope had died in the beginning of the
year 1513.

And in the deepest secrecy, between his work on the New
Testament and Jerome, Erasmus took revenge on the martial
Pope, for the misery of the times, by writing the masterly
satire, entitled *Julius exclusus*, in which the Pope appears in all
his glory before the gate of the Heavenly Paradise to plead his
cause and find himself excluded. The theme was not new to
him; for had he not made something similar in the witty Cain
fable, by which, at one time, he had cheered a dinner-party at

Oxford? But that was an innocent jest to which his pious fellow-guests had listened with pleasure. To the satire about the defunct Pope many would, no doubt, also gladly listen, but Erasmus had to be careful about it. The folly of all the world might be ridiculed, but not the worldly propensities of the recently deceased Pope. Therefore, though he helped in circulating copies of the manuscript, Erasmus did his utmost, for the rest of his life, to preserve its anonymity, and when it was universally known and had appeared in print, and he was presumed to be the author, he always cautiously denied the fact; although he was careful to use such terms as to avoid a formal denial. The first edition of the *Julius* was published at Basle, not by Froben, Erasmus's ordinary publisher, but by Cratander, probably in the year 1518.

Erasmus's need of protesting against warfare had not been satisfied by writing the *Julius*. In March 1514, no longer at Cambridge, but in London, he wrote a letter to his former patron, the Abbot of Saint Bertin, Anthony of Bergen, in which he enlarges upon the folly of waging war. Would that a Christian peace were concluded between Christian princes! Perhaps the abbot might contribute to that consummation through his influence with the youthful Charles V and especially with his grandfather Maximilian. Erasmus states quite frankly that the war has suddenly changed the spirit of England. He would like to return to his native country if the prince would procure him the means to live there in peace. It is a remarkable fact and of true Erasmian naïveté that he cannot help mixing up his personal interests with his sincere indignation at the atrocities disgracing a man and a Christian. 'The war has suddenly altered the spirit of this island. The cost of living rises every day and generosity decreases. Through lack of wine I nearly perished by gravel, contracted by taking bad stuff. We are confined in this island, more than ever, so that even letters are not carried abroad.'

This was the first of Erasmus's anti-war writings. He expanded it into the adage *Dulce bellum inexpertis*, which was inserted into the *Adagia* edition of 1515, published by Froben and afterwards also printed separately. Hereafter we shall follow up this line of Erasmus's ideas as a whole.

Though the summer of 1514 was to bring peace between England and France, Erasmus had now definitely made up his mind to leave England. He sent his trunks to Antwerp, to his friend Peter Gilles and prepared to go to the Netherlands, after a short visit to Mountjoy at the castle of Hammes near Calais. Shortly before his departure from London he had a curious interview with a papal diplomat, working in the cause of peace, Count Canossa, at Ammonius's house on the Thames. Ammonius passed him off on Erasmus as a merchant. After the meal the Italian sounded him as to a possible return to Rome, where he might be the first in place instead of living alone among a barbarous nation. Erasmus replied that he lived in a land that contained the greatest number of excellent scholars, among whom he would be content with the humblest place. This compliment was his farewell to England, which had favoured him so. Some days later, in the first half of July 1514, he was on the other side of the Channel. On three more occasions he paid short visits to England, but he lived there no more.

XIII. JOHANNES FROBEN, 1522–3
Reproduced by gracious permission of H.M. The Queen

XIV. THE PRINTER'S EMBLEM OF JOHANNES FROBEN

CHAPTER XI

A LIGHT OF THEOLOGY
1514–16

On the way to success and satisfaction — His Prior calls him back to Steyn —
He refuses to comply — First journey to Basle: 1514–16 — Cordial welcome in
Germany — Johannes Froben — Editions of Jerome and the New Testament —
A Councillor to Prince Charles: Institutio Principis Christiani, 1515 —
Definitive dispensation from Monastic Vows: 1517 — Fame — Erasmus as
a spiritual centre — His correspondence — Letter-writing as an art — Its
dangers — A glorious age at hand

ERASMUS had, as was usual with him, enveloped his departure
from England with mystery. It was given out that he was
going to Rome to redeem a pledge. Probably he had already
determined to try his fortune in the Netherlands; not in
Holland, but in the neighbourhood of the princely court in
Brabant. The chief object of his journey, however, was to visit
Froben's printing-office at Basle, personally to supervise the
publication of the numerous works, old and new, which he
brought with him, among them the material for his chosen
task, the New Testament and Jerome, by which he hoped to
effect the restoration of theology, which he had long felt to be
his life-work. It is easy thus to imagine his anxiety when during
the crossing he discovered that his hand-bag, containing the
manuscripts, was found to have been taken on board another
ship. He felt bereft, having lost the labour of so many years; a
sorrow so great, he writes, as only parents can feel at the loss of
their children.

To his joy, however, he found his manuscripts safe on the
other side. At the castle of Hammes near Calais, he stayed for
some days, the guest of Mountjoy. There, on 7 July, a letter
found him, written on 18 April by his superior, the prior of
Steyn, his old friend Servatius Rogerus, recalling him to the
monastery after so many years of absence. The letter had

already been in the hands of more than one prying person, before it reached him by mere chance.

It was a terrific blow, which struck him in the midst of his course to his highest aspirations. Erasmus took counsel for a day and then sent a refusal. To his old friend, in addressing whom he always found the most serious accents of his being, he wrote a letter which he meant to be a justification and which was self-contemplation, much deeper and more sincere than the one which, at a momentous turning-point of his life, had drawn from him his *Carmen Alpestre*.

He calls upon God to be his witness that he would follow the purest inspiration of his life. But to return to the monastery! He reminds Servatius of the circumstances under which he entered it, as they lived in his memory: the pressure of his relations, his false modesty. He points out to him how ill monastic life had suited his constitution, how it outraged his love of freedom, how detrimental it would be to his delicate health, if now resumed. Had he, then, lived a worse life in the world? Literature had kept him from many vices. His restless life could not redound to his dishonour, though only with diffidence did he dare to appeal to the examples of Solon, Pythagoras, St. Paul and his favourite Jerome. Had he not everywhere won recognition from friends and patrons? He enumerates them: cardinals, archbishops, bishops, Mountjoy, the Universities of Oxford and Cambridge, and, lastly, John Colet. Was there, then, any objection to his works: the *Enchiridion*, the *Adagia*? (He did not mention the *Moria*.) The best was still to follow: Jerome and the New Testament. The fact that, since his stay in Italy, he had laid aside the habit of his order and wore a common clerical dress, he could excuse on a number of grounds.

The conclusion was: I shall not return to Holland. 'I know that I shall not be able to stand the air and the food there; all eyes will be directed to me. I shall return to the country, an old and grey man, who left it as a youth; I shall return a valetudinarian; I shall be exposed to the contempt even of the lowest, I, who am accustomed to be honoured even by the greatest.' 'It is not possible', he concludes, 'to speak out frankly in a letter. I am now going to Basle and thence to Rome, perhaps, but on my return I shall try to visit you . . . I have heard of the deaths of William, Francis and Andrew (his old Dutch friends). Remember me to Master Henry and the others who live with you; I am disposed towards them as befits me. For those old tragedies I ascribe to my errors, or if you like to my fate. Do not omit to commend me to Christ in your prayers. If I knew for sure that it would be pleasing to Him that I should return to live with you, I should prepare for the journey this very day. Farewell, my former sweetest companion, now my venerable father.'

Underlying the immediate motives of his high theological aspirations, this refusal was doubtless actuated by his ancient, inveterate, psychological incentives of disgust and shame.[1]

Through the southern Netherlands, where he visited several friends and patrons and renewed his acquaintance with the University of Louvain, Erasmus turned to the Rhine and reached Basle in the second half of August 1514. There such pleasures of fame awaited him as he had never yet tasted. The German humanists hailed him as the light of the world— in letters, receptions and banquets. They were more solemn and enthusiastic than Erasmus had found the scholars of France, England and Italy, to say nothing of his compatriots; and they applauded him emphatically as being a German himself and an ornament of Germany. At his first meeting with Froben, Erasmus permitted himself the pleasure of a jocular deception: he pretended to be a friend and agent of himself, to enjoy to the full the joy of being recognized. The German environment was rather to his mind: '*My* Germany, which to my regret and shame I got to know so late'.

Soon the work for which he had come was in full swing. He was in his element once more, as he had been at Venice six years before: working hard in a large printing-office, surrounded by scholars, who heaped upon him homage and

[1] For a full translation of this important letter see pp. 212–18.

kindness in those rare moments of leisure which he permitted himself. 'I move in a most agreeable Museon: so many men of learning, and of such exceptional learning!'

Some translations of the lesser works of Plutarch were published by Froben in August. The *Adagia* was passing through the press again with corrections and additions, and the preface which was originally destined for Badius. At the same time Dirck Maertensz, at Louvain, was also at work for Erasmus, who had, on passing through the town, entrusted him with a collection of easy Latin texts; also M. Schürer at Strassburg, who prepared the *Parabolae sive similia* for him. For Froben, too, Erasmus was engaged on a Seneca, which appeared in 1515, together with a work on Latin construction. But Jerome and the New Testament remained his chief occupation.

Jerome's works had been Erasmus's love in early youth, especially his letters. The plan of preparing a correct edition of the great Father of the Church was conceived in 1500, if not earlier, and he had worked at it ever since, at intervals. In 1513 he writes to Ammonius: 'My enthusiasm for emending and annotating Jerome is such that I feel as though inspired by some god. I have almost completely emended him already by collating many old manuscripts. And this I do at incredibly great expense.' In 1512 he negotiated with Badius about an edition of the letters. Froben's partner, Johannes Amerbach, who died before Erasmus's arrival, had been engaged for years on an edition of Jerome. Several scholars, Reuchlin among others, had assisted in the undertaking when Erasmus offered himself and all his material. He became the actual editor. Of the nine volumes, in which Froben published the work in 1516, the first four contained Erasmus's edition of Jerome's letters; the others had been corrected by him and provided with forewords.

His work upon the New Testament was, if possible, still nearer his heart. By its growth it had gradually changed its nature. Since the time when Valla's *Annotationes* had directed his attention to textual criticism of the Vulgate, Erasmus had, probably during his second stay in England from 1505 to 1506, at the instance of Colet, made a new translation of the New Testament from the Greek original, which translation differed greatly from the Vulgate. Besides Colet, few had seen it. Later, Erasmus understood it was necessary to publish also a new edition of the Greek text, with his notes. As to this he had made a provisional arrangement with Froben, shortly after his arrival at Basle. Afterwards he considered that it would be better to have it printed in Italy, and was on the point of going there when, possibly persuaded by new offers from Froben, he suddenly changed his plan of travel and in the spring of 1515 made a short trip to England—probably, among other reasons, for the purpose of securing a copy of his translation of the New Testament, which he had left behind there. In the summer he was back at Basle and resumed the work in Froben's printing-office. In the beginning of 1516 the *Novum Instrumentum* appeared, containing the purified Greek text with notes, together with a Latin translation in which Erasmus had altered too great deviations from the Vulgate.

From the moment of the appearance of two such important and, as regards the second, such daring theological works by Erasmus as Jerome and the New Testament, we may say that he had made himself the centre of the scientific study of divinity, as he was at the same time the centre and touchstone of classic erudition and literary taste. His authority constantly increased in all countries, his correspondence was prodigiously augmented.

But while his mental growth was accomplished, his financial position was not assured. The years 1515 to 1517 are among the most restless of his life; he is still looking out for every chance which presents itself, a canonry at Tournay, a prebend in England, a bishopric in Sicily, always half jocularly regretting the good chances he missed in former times, jesting about his pursuit of fortune, lamenting about his 'spouse, execrable poverty, which even yet I have not succeeded in shaking off my shoulders'. And, after all, ever more the victim of his own restlessness than of the disfavour of fate. He is now fifty years old and still he is, as he says, 'sowing without knowing what I shall reap'. This, however, only refers to his career, not to his life-work.

In the course of 1515 a new and promising patron, John le Sauvage, Chancellor of Brabant, had succeeded in procuring for him the title of councillor of the prince, the youthful Charles V. In the beginning of 1516 he was nominated: it was a mere title of honour, promising a yearly pension of 200 florins, which, however, was paid but irregularly. To habilitate himself as a councillor of the prince, Erasmus wrote the *Institutio Principis Christiani*, a treatise about the education of a prince, which in accordance with Erasmus's naturè and inclination deals rather with moral than with political matters, and is in striking contrast with that other work, written some years earlier, *il Principe* by Machiavelli.

When his work at Basle ceased for the time being, in the spring of 1516, Erasmus journeyed to the Netherlands. At Brussels he met the chancellor, who, in addition to the prince's pension, procured him a prebend at Courtray, which, like the English benefice mentioned above, was compounded for by money payments. At Antwerp lived one of the great friends who helped in his support all his life: Peter Gilles, the young town clerk, in whose house he stayed as often as he came to Antwerp. Peter Gilles is the man who figures in More's *Utopia* as the person in whose garden the sailor tells his experiences; it was in these days that Gilles helped Dirck Maertensz, at Louvain, to pass the first edition of the *Utopia* through the press. Later Quentin Metsys was to paint him and Erasmus, joined in a diptych; a present for Thomas More and for us a vivid memorial of one of the best things Erasmus ever knew: this triple friendship.

In the summer of 1516 Erasmus made another short trip to England. He stayed with More, saw Colet again, also Warham, Fisher, and the other friends. But it was not to visit old friends that he went there. A pressing and delicate matter impelled him. Now that prebends and church dignities began to be presented to him, it was more urgent than ever that the impediments in the way of a free ecclesiastical career should be permanently obviated. He was provided with a dispensation of Pope Julius II, authorizing him to accept English prebends, and another exempting him from the obligation of wearing the habit of his order. But both were of limited scope, and insufficient. The fervent impatience with which he conducted this matter of his definite discharge from the order makes it probable that, as Dr. Allen presumes, the threat of his recall to Steyn had, since his refusal to Servatius in 1514, hung over his head. There was nothing he feared and detested so much.

With his friend Ammonius he drew up, in London, a very elaborate paper, addressed to the apostolic chancery, in which he recounts the story of his own life as that of one Florentius: his half-enforced entrance to the monastery, the troubles which monastic life had brought him, the circumstances which had induced him to lay his monk's dress aside. It is a passionate apology, pathetic and ornate. The letter, as we know it, does not contain a direct request. In an appendix at the end, written in cipher, of which he sent the key in sympathetic ink in another letter, the chancery was requested to obviate the impediments which Erasmus's illegitimate birth placed in the way of his promotion. The addressee, Lambertus Grunnius, apostolic secretary, was most probably an imaginary personage.[1] So much mystery did Erasmus use when his vital interests were at stake.

The Bishop of Worcester, Silvestro Gigli, who was setting out to the Lateran Council, as the envoy of England, took upon himself to deliver the letter and to plead Erasmus's cause. Erasmus, having meanwhile at the end of August returned to the Netherlands, awaited the upshot of his kind offices in the greatest suspense. The matter was finally settled in January 1517. In two letters bearing the signature of Sadolet, Leo X condoned Erasmus's transgressions of ecclesiastical law, relieved him of the obligation to wear the dress of his order, allowed him to live in the world and authorized him to hold

[1] The name Grunnius may have been taken from Jerome's epistles, where it is a nickname for a certain Ruffinus, whom Jerome disliked very much. It appears again in a letter of 5 March 1531, LB. X 1590 A.

church benefices in spite of any disqualifications arising from illegitimacy of birth.

So much his great fame had now achieved. The Pope had moreover accepted the dedication of the edition of the New Testament, and had, through Sadolet, expressed himself in very gracious terms about Erasmus's work in general. Rome itself seemed to further his endeavours in all respects.

Erasmus now thought of establishing himself permanently in the Netherlands, to which everything pointed. Louvain seemed to be the most suitable abode, the centre of studies, where he had already spent two years in former times. But Louvain did not attract him. It was the stronghold of conservative theology. Martin van Dorp, a Dutchman like Erasmus, and professor of divinity at Louvain, had, in 1514, in the name of his faculty, rebuked Erasmus in a letter for the audacity of the *Praise of Folly*, his derision of divines and also his temerity in correcting the text of the New Testament. Erasmus had defended himself elaborately. At present war was being waged in a much wider field: for or against Reuchlin, the great Hebrew scholar, for whom the authors of the *Epistolae obscurorum virorum* had so sensationally taken up the cudgels. At Louvain Erasmus was regarded with the same suspicion with which he distrusted Dorp and the other Louvain divines. He stayed during the remainder of 1516 and the first half of 1517 at Antwerp, Brussels and Ghent, often in the house of Peter Gilles. In February 1517, there came tempting offers from France. Budaeus, Cop, Étienne Poncher, Bishop of Paris, wrote to him that the king, the youthful Francis I, would present him with a generous prebend if he would come to Paris. Erasmus, always shy of being tied down, only wrote polite, evasive answers, and did not go.

In the meantime he received the news of the papal absolution. In connection with this he had, once more, to visit England, little dreaming that it would be the last time he should set foot on British soil. In Ammonius's house of Saint Stephen's Chapel at Westminster on 9 April 1517, the ceremony of absolution took place, ridding Erasmus for good of the night-mare which had oppressed him since his youth. At last he was free!

Invitations and specious promises now came to him from all sides. Mountjoy and Wolsey spoke of high ecclesiastical honours which awaited him in England. Budaeus kept press-ing him to remove to France. Cardinal Ximenes wanted to attach him to the University of Alcalá, in Spain. The Duke of Saxony offered him a chair at Leipzig. Pirckheimer boasted of the perfections of the free imperial city of Nuremberg. Erasmus, meanwhile, overwhelmed again with the labour of writing and editing, according to his wont, did not definitely decline any of these offers; neither did he accept any. He always wanted to keep all his strings on his bow at the same time. In the early summer of 1517 he was asked to accompany the court of the youthful Charles, who was on the point of leaving the Netherlands for Spain. But he declined. His departure to Spain would have meant a long interruption of immediate contact with the great publishing centres, Basle, Louvain, Strassburg, Paris, and that, in turn, would have meant postponement of his life-work. When, in the beginning of July, the prince set out for Middelburg, there to take ship for Spain, Erasmus started for Louvain.

He was thus destined to go to this university environment, although it displeased him in so many respects. There he would have academic duties, young latinists would follow him about to get their poems and letters corrected by him and all those divines, whom he distrusted, would watch him at close quarters. But it was only to be for a few months. 'I have removed to Louvain', he writes to the Archbishop of Canter-bury, 'till I shall decide which residence is best suited to old age, which is already knocking at the gate importunately.'

As it turned out, he was to spend four years (1517–21) at Louvain. His life was now becoming more stationary, but because of outward circumstances rather than of inward quiet. He kept deliberating all those years whether he should go to England, Germany or France, hoping at last to find the brilliant position which he had always coveted and never had been able or willing to grasp.

The years 1516-18 may be called the culmination of Erasmus's career. Applauding crowds surrounded him more and more. The minds of men were seemingly prepared for something great to happen and they looked to Erasmus as the man! At Brussels, he was continually bothered with visits from Spaniards, Italians and Germans who wanted to boast of their interviews with him. The Spaniards, with their verbose solemnity, particularly bored him. Most exuberant of all were the eulogies with which the German humanists greeted him in their letters. This had begun already on his first journey to Basle in 1514. 'Great Rotterdamer', 'ornament of Germany', 'ornament of the world' were some of the simplest effusions. Town councils waited upon him, presents of wine and public banquets were of common occurrence. No one expresses himself so hyperbolically as the jurist Ulrich Zasius of Freiburg. 'I am pointed out in public', he asserts, 'as the man who has received a letter from Erasmus.' 'Thrice greatest hero, you great Jove' is a moderate apostrophe for him. 'The Swiss', Zwingli writes in 1516, 'account it a great glory to have seen Erasmus.' 'I know and I teach nothing but Erasmus now,' writes Wolfgang Capito. Ulrich von Hutten and Henry Glareanus both imagine themselves placed beside Erasmus, as Alcibiades stood beside Socrates. And Beatus Rhenanus devotes to him a life of earnest admiration and helpfulness that was to prove of much more value than these exuberant panegyrics. There is an element of national exaltation in this German enthusiasm for Erasmus: it is the violently stimulated mood into which Luther's word will fall anon.

The other nations also chimed in with praise, though a little later and a little more soberly. Colet and Tunstall promise him immortality, Étienne Poncher exalts him above the celebrated Italian humanists, Germain de Brie declares that French scholars have ceased reading any authors but Erasmus, and Budaeus announces that all Western Christendom resounds with his name.

This increase of glory manifested itself in different ways. Almost every year the rumour of his death was spread abroad, malignantly, as he himself thinks. Again, all sorts of writings were ascribed to him in which he had no share whatever, amongst others the *Epistolae obscurorum virorum*.

But, above all, his correspondence increased immensely. The time was long since past when he asked More to procure him more correspondents. Letters now kept pouring in to him, from all sides, beseeching him to reply. A former pupil laments with tears that he cannot show a single note written by Erasmus. Scholars respectfully sought an introduction from one of his friends, before venturing to address him. In this respect Erasmus was a man of heroic benevolence, and tried to answer what he could, although so overwhelmed by letters every day that he hardly found time to read them. 'If I do not answer, I seem unkind,' says Erasmus, and that thought was intolerable.

We should bear in mind that letter-writing, at that time, occupied more or less the place of the newspaper at present, or rather of the literary monthly, which arose fairly directly out of erudite correspondence. It was, as in antiquity—which in this respect was imitated better and more profitably, perhaps, than in any other sphere—an art. Even before 1500 Erasmus had, at Paris, described that art in the treatise, *De conscribendis epistolis*, which was to appear in print in 1522. People wrote, as a rule, with a view to later publication, for a wider circle, or at any rate, with the certainty that the recipient would show the letter to others. A fine Latin letter was a gem, which a man envied his neighbour. Erasmus writes to Budaeus: 'Tunstall has devoured your letter to me and re-read it as many as three or four times; I had literally to tear it from his hands.'

Unfortunately fate did not always take into consideration the author's intentions as to publicity, semi-publicity or strict secrecy. Often letters passed through many hands before reaching their destination, as did Servatius's letter to Erasmus in 1514. 'Do be careful about letters,' he writes more than once; 'waylayers are on the lookout to intercept them.' Yet, with the curious precipitation that characterizes him, Erasmus was often very careless as to what he wrote. From an early age he preserved and cared for his letters, yet nevertheless, through his itinerant life, many were lost. He could not control their publication. As early as 1509 a friend sent him a manuscript volume of his own (Erasmus's) letters, that he had picked up for sale at Rome. Erasmus had it burnt at once. Since 1515 he himself superintended the publication of his letters; at first only a few important ones; afterwards in 1516 a selection of letters from friends to him, and after that ever larger collections till, at the end of his life, there appeared a new collection almost every year. No article was so much in demand on the book market as letters by Erasmus, and no wonder. They were models of excellent style, tasteful Latin, witty expression and elegant erudition.

The semi-private, semi-public character of the letters often made them compromising. What one could say to a friend in confidence might possibly injure when many read it. Erasmus, who never was aware how injuriously he expressed himself, repeatedly gave rise to misunderstanding and estrangement. Manners, so to say, had not yet adapted themselves to the new art of printing, which increased the publicity of the written word a thousandfold. Only gradually under this new influence was the separation effected between the public word, intended for the press, and the private communication, which remains in writing and is read only by the recipient.

Meanwhile, with the growth of Erasmus's fame, his earlier writings, too, had risen in the public estimation. The great success of the *Enchiridion militis christiani* had begun about 1515, when the times were much riper for it than eleven years before. 'The *Moria* is embraced as the highest wisdom,' writes John Watson to him in 1516. In the same year we find a word used, for the first time, which expresses better than anything else how much Erasmus had become a centre of authority: *Erasmiani*. So his German friends called themselves, according to Johannes Sapidus. More than a year later Dr. Johannes Eck employs the word still in a rather friendly sense, as a generally current term: 'all scholars in Germany are Erasmians,' he says. But Erasmus did not like the word. 'I find nothing in myself', he replies, 'why anyone should wish to be an Erasmicus, and, altogether, I hate those party names. We are all followers of Christ, and to His glory we all drudge, each for his part.' But he knows that now the question is: for or against him! From the brilliant latinist and the man of wit of his prime he had become the international pivot on which the civilization of his age hinged. He could not help beginning to feel himself the brain, the heart and the conscience of his times. It might even appear to him that he was called to speak the great redeeming word or, perhaps, that he had already spoken it. The faith in an easy triumph of pure knowledge and Christian meekness in a near future speaks from the preface of Erasmus's edition of the New Testament.

How clear did the future look in those years! In this period Erasmus repeatedly reverts to the glad motif of a golden age, which is on the point of dawning. Perennial peace is before the door. The highest princes of the world, Francis I of France, Charles, King of Spain, Henry VIII of England, and the emperor Maximilian have ensured peace by the strongest ties. Uprightness and Christian piety will flourish together with the revival of letters and the sciences. As at a given signal the mightiest minds conspire to restore a high standard of culture. We may congratulate the age, it will be a golden one.

But Erasmus does not sound this note long. It is heard for the last time in 1519; after which the dream of universal happiness about to dawn gives place to the usual complaint about the badness of the times everywhere.

CHAPTER XII

ERASMUS'S MIND

Erasmus's mind: Ethical and aesthetic tendencies, aversion to all that is unreasonable, silly and cumbrous—His vision of antiquity pervaded by Christian faith—Renascence of good learning—The ideal life of serene harmony and happy wisdom—Love of the decorous and smooth—His mind neither philosophic nor historical, but strongly philological and moralistic—Freedom, clearness, purity, simplicity—Faith in nature—Educational and social ideas

WHAT made Erasmus the man from whom his contemporaries expected their salvation, on whose lips they hung to catch the word of deliverance? He seemed to them the bearer of a new liberty of the mind, a new clearness, purity and simplicity of knowledge, a new harmony of healthy and right living. He was to them as the possessor of newly discovered, untold wealth which he had only to distribute.

What was there in the mind of the great Rotterdamer which promised so much to the world?

The negative aspect of Erasmus's mind may be defined as a heartfelt aversion to everything unreasonable, insipid, purely formal, with which the undisturbed growth of medieval culture had overburdened and overcrowded the world of thought. As often as he thinks of the ridiculous text-books out of which Latin was taught in his youth, disgust rises in his mind, and he execrates them—Mammetrectus, Brachylogus, Ebrardus and all the rest—as a heap of rubbish which ought to be cleared away. But this aversion to the superannuated, which had become useless and soulless, extended much farther. He found society, and especially religious life, full of practices, ceremonies, traditions and conceptions, from which the spirit seemed to have departed. He does not reject them off-hand and altogether: what revolts him is that they are so often performed without understanding and right feeling. But to his mind, highly susceptible to the foolish and ridiculous things, and with a delicate need of high decorum and inward dignity, all that sphere of ceremony and tradition displays itself as a useless, nay, a hurtful scene of human stupidity and selfishness. And, intellectualist as he is, with his contempt for ignorance, he seems unaware that those religious observances, after all, may contain valuable sentiments of unexpressed and unformulated piety.

Through his treatises, his letters, his *Colloquies* especially, there always passes—as if one was looking at a gallery of Brueghel's pictures—a procession of ignorant and covetous monks who by their sanctimony and humbug impose upon the trustful multitude and fare sumptuously themselves. As a fixed motif (such motifs are numerous with Erasmus) there always recurs his gibe about the superstition that a person was saved by dying in the gown of a Franciscan or a Dominican.

Fasting, prescribed prayers, the observance of holy days, should not be altogether neglected, but they become displeasing to God when we repose our trust in them and forget charity. The same holds good of confession, indulgence, all sorts of blessings. Pilgrimages are worthless. The veneration of the Saints and of their relics is full of superstition and foolishness. The people think they will be preserved from disasters during the day if only they have looked at the painted image of Saint Christopher in the morning. 'We kiss the shoes of the saints and their dirty handkerchiefs and we leave their books, their most holy and efficacious relics, neglected.'

Erasmus's dislike of what seemed antiquated and worn out in his days, went farther still. It comprised the whole intellectual scheme of medieval theology and philosophy. In the syllogistic system he found only subtlety and arid ingenuity. All symbolism and allegory were fundamentally alien to him and indifferent, though he occasionally tried his hand at an allegory; and he never was mystically inclined.

Now here it is just as much the deficiencies of his own mind as the qualities of the system which made him unable to appreciate it. While he struck at the abuse of ceremonies and of Church practices both with noble indignation and well-aimed mockery, a proud irony to which he was not fully entitled preponderates in his condemnation of scholastic theology which he could not quite understand. It was easy always to talk with a sneer of the conservative divines of his time as *magistri nostri*.

His noble indignation hurt only those who deserved castigation and strengthened what was valuable, but his mockery hurt the good as well as the bad in spite of him, assailed both the institution and persons, and injured without elevating them. The individualist Erasmus never understood what it meant to offend the honour of an office, an order, or an establishment, especially when that institution is the most sacred of all, the Church itself.

Erasmus's conception of the Church was no longer purely Catholic. Of that glorious structure of medieval-Christian civilization with its mystic foundation, its strict hierarchic construction, its splendidly fitting symmetry he saw hardly anything but its load of outward details and ornament. Instead of the world which Thomas Aquinas and Dante had described, according to their vision, Erasmus saw another world, full of charm and elevated feeling, and this he held up before his compatriots.

It was the world of Antiquity, but illuminated throughout by Christian faith. It was a world that had never existed as such. For with the historical reality which the times of Constantine and the great fathers of the Church had manifested—that of declining Latinity and deteriorating Hellenism, the oncoming barbarism and the oncoming Byzantinism—it had nothing in common. Erasmus's imagined world was an amalgamation of pure classicism (this meant for him, Cicero, Horace, Plutarch; for to the flourishing period of the Greek mind he remained after all a stranger) and pure, biblical Christianity. Could it be a union? Not really. In Erasmus's mind the light falls, just as we saw in the history of his career, alternately on the pagan antique and on the Christian. But the warp of his mind is Christian; his classicism only serves him as

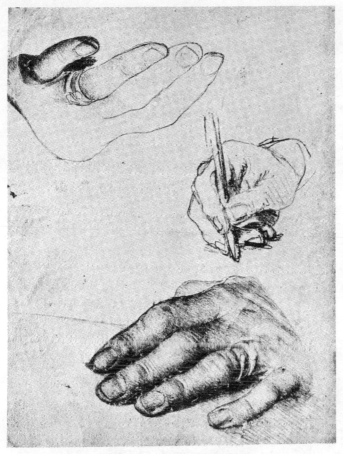

XV. THE HANDS OF ERASMUS

XVI. ERASMUS AT THE AGE OF 57

a form, and from Antiquity he only chooses those elements which in ethical tendency are in conformity with his Christian ideal.

And because of this, Erasmus, although he appeared after a century of earlier Humanism, is yet new to his time. The union of Antiquity and the Christian spirit which had haunted the mind of Petrarch, the father of Humanism, which was lost sight of by his disciples, enchanted as they were by the irresistible brilliance of the antique beauty of form, this union was brought about by Erasmus.

What pure Latinity and the classic spirit meant to Erasmus we cannot feel as he did because its realization does not mean to us, as to him, a difficult conquest and a glorious triumph. To feel it thus one must have acquired, in a hard school, the hatred of barbarism, which already during his first years of authorship had suggested the composition of the *Antibarbari*. The abusive term for all that is old and rude is already Gothic, Goths. The term barbarism as used by Erasmus comprised much of what we value most in the medieval spirit. Erasmus's conception of the great intellectual crisis of his day was distinctly dualistic. He saw it as a struggle between old and new, which, to him, meant evil and good. In the advocates of tradition he saw only obscurantism, conservatism, and ignorant opposition to *bonae literae*, that is, the good cause for which he and his partisans battled. Of the rise of that higher culture Erasmus had already formed the conception which has since dominated the history of the Renaissance. It was a revival, begun two or three hundred years before his time, in which, besides literature, all the plastic arts shared. Side by side with the terms restitution and reflorescence the word renascence crops up repeatedly in his writings. "The world is coming to its senses as if awaking out of a deep sleep. Still there are some left who recalcitrate pertinaciously, clinging convulsively with hands and feet to their old ignorance. They fear that if *bonae literae* are reborn and the world grows wise, it will come to light that they have known nothing.' They do not know how pious the Ancients could be, what sanctity characterizes

Socrates, Virgil, and Horace, or Plutarch's *Moralia*, how rich the history of Antiquity is in examples of forgiveness and true virtue. We should call nothing profane that is pious and conduces to good morals. No more dignified view of life was ever found than that which Cicero propounds in *De Senectute*.

In order to understand Erasmus's mind and the charm which it had for his contemporaries, one must begin with the ideal of life that was present before his inward eye as a splendid dream. It is not his own in particular. The whole Renaissance cherished that wish of reposeful, blithe, and yet serious intercourse of good and wise friends in the cool shade of a house under trees, where serenity and harmony would dwell. The age yearned for the realization of simplicity, sincerity, truth and nature. Their imagination was always steeped in the essence of Antiquity, though, at heart, it is more nearly connected with medieval ideals than they themselves were aware. In the circle of the Medici it is the idyll of Careggi, in Rabelais it embodies itself in the fancy of the abbey of Thélème; it finds voice in More's *Utopia* and in the work of Montaigne. In Erasmus's writings that ideal wish ever recurs in the shape of a friendly walk, followed by a meal in a garden-house. It is found as an opening scene of the *Antibarbari*, in the numerous descriptions of meals with Colet, and the numerous *Convivia* of the *Colloquies*. Especially in the *Convivium religiosum* Erasmus has elaborately pictured his dream, and it would be worth while to compare it, on the one hand with Thélème, and on the other with the fantastic design of a pleasure garden which Bernard Palissy describes. The little Dutch eighteenth-century country-seats and garden-houses in which the national spirit took great delight are the fulfilment of a purely Erasmian ideal. The host of the *Convivium religiosum* says: 'To me a simple country-house, a nest, is pleasanter than any palace, and, if he be king who lives in freedom and according to his wishes, surely I am king here'.

Life's true joy is in virtue and piety. If they are Epicureans who live pleasantly, then none are more truly Epicureans than they who live in holiness and piety.

The ideal joy of life is also perfectly idyllic in so far that it requires an aloofness from earthly concerns and contempt for all that is sordid. It is foolish to be interested in all that happens in the world; to pride oneself on one's knowledge of the market, of the King of England's plans, the news from Rome, conditions in Denmark. The sensible old man of the *Colloquium Senile* has an easy post of honour, a safe mediocrity, he judges no one and nothing and smiles upon all the world. Quiet for oneself, surrounded by books—that is of all things most desirable.

On the outskirts of this ideal of serenity and harmony numerous flowers of aesthetic value blow, such as Erasmus's sense of decorum, his great need of kindly courtesy, his pleasure in gentle and obliging treatment, in cultured and easy manners. Close by are some of his intellectual peculiarities. He hates the violent and extravagant. Therefore the choruses of the Greek drama displease him. The merit of his own poems he sees in the fact that they pass passion by, they abstain from pathos altogether—'there is not a single storm in them, no mountain torrent overflowing its banks, no exaggeration whatever. There is great frugality in words. My poetry would rather keep within bounds than exceed them, rather hug the shore than cleave the high seas.' In another place he says: 'I am always most pleased by a poem that does not differ too much from prose, but prose of the best sort, be it understood. As Philoxenus accounted those the most palatable fishes that are no true fishes and the most savoury meat what is no meat, the most pleasant voyage, that along the shores, and the most agreeable walk, that along the water's edge; so I take especial pleasure in a rhetorical poem and a poetical oration, so that poetry is tasted in prose and the reverse.' That is the man of half-tones, of fine shadings, of the thought that is never completely expressed. But he adds: 'Far-fetched conceits may please others; to me the chief concern seems to be that we draw our speech from the matter itself and apply ourselves less to showing off our invention than to present the thing.' That is the realist.

From this conception results his admirable, simple clarity, the excellent division and presentation of his argument. But it also causes his lack of depth and the prolixity by which he is characterized. His machine runs too smoothly. In the endless *apologiae* of his later years, ever new arguments occur to him; new passages to point, or quotations to support, his idea. He praises laconism, but never practises it. Erasmus never coins a sentence which, rounded off and pithy, becomes a proverb and in this manner lives. There are no current quotations from Erasmus. The collector of the *Adagia* has created no new ones of his own.

The true occupation for a mind like his was paraphrasing, in which, indeed, he amply indulged. Soothing down and unfolding was just the work he liked. It is characteristic that he paraphrased the whole New Testament except the Apocalypse.

Erasmus's mind was neither philosophic nor historic. His was neither the work of exact, logical discrimination, nor of grasping the deep sense of the way of the world in broad historical visions in which the particulars themselves, in their multiplicity and variegation, form the image. His mind is philological in the fullest sense of the word. But by that alone he would not have conquered and captivated the world. His mind was at the same time of a deeply ethical and rather strong aesthetic trend and those three together have made him great.

The foundation of Erasmus's mind is his fervent desire of freedom, clearness, purity, simplicity and rest. It is an old ideal of life to which he gave new substance by the wealth of his mind. Without liberty, life is no life; and there is no liberty without repose. The fact that he never took sides definitely resulted from an urgent need of perfect independence. Each engagement, even a temporary one, was felt as a fetter by Erasmus. An interlocutor in the *Colloquies*, in which he so often, spontaneously, reveals his own ideals of life, declares himself determined neither to marry, nor to take holy orders, nor to enter a monastery, nor into any connection from which he will afterwards be unable to free himself—at least not before he knows himself completely. 'When will that be? Never, perhaps.' 'On no other account do I congratulate myself more than on the fact that I have never attached myself to any party,' Erasmus says towards the end of his life.

Liberty should be spiritual liberty in the first place. 'But he that is spiritual judgeth all things, yet he himself is judged of no man,' is the word of Saint Paul. To what purpose should he require prescriptions who, of his own accord, does better things than human laws require? What arrogance it is to bind by institutions a man who is clearly led by the inspirations of the divine spirit!

In Erasmus we already find the beginning of that optimism which judges upright man good enough to dispense with fixed forms and rules. As More, in *Utopia*, and Rabelais, Erasmus relies already on the dictates of nature, which produces man as inclined to good and which we may follow, provided we are imbued with faith and piety.

In this line of confidence in what is natural and desire of the simple and reasonable, Erasmus's educational and social ideas lie. Here he is far ahead of his times. It would be an attractive undertaking to discuss Erasmus's educational ideals more fully. They foreshadow exactly those of the eighteenth century. The child should learn in playing, by means of things that are agreeable to its mind, from pictures. Its faults should be gently corrected. The flogging and abusive schoolmaster is Erasmus's abomination; the office itself is holy and venerable to him. Education should begin from the moment of birth. Probably Erasmus attached too much value to classicism, here as elsewhere: his friend Peter Gilles should implant the rudiments of the ancient languages in his two-year-old son, that he may greet his father with endearing stammerings in Greek and Latin. But what gentleness and clear good sense shines from all Erasmus says about instruction and education!

The same holds good of his views about marriage and woman. In the problem of sexual relations he distinctly sides with the woman from deep conviction. There is a great deal of tenderness and delicate feeling in his conception of the position of the girl and the woman. Few characters of the

Colloquies have been drawn with so much sympathy as the girl with the lover and the cultured woman in the witty conversation with the abbot. Erasmus's ideal of marriage is truly social and hygienic. Let us beget children for the State and for Christ, says the lover, children endowed by their upright parents with a good disposition, children who see the good example at home which is to guide them. Again and again he reverts to the mother's duty to suckle the child herself. He indicates how the house should be arranged, in a simple and cleanly manner; he occupies himself with the problem of useful children's dress. Who stood up at that time, as he did, for the fallen girl, and for the prostitute compelled by necessity? Who saw so clearly the social danger of marriages of persons infected with the new scourge of Europe, so violently abhorred by Erasmus? He would wish that such a marriage should at once be declared null and void by the Pope. Erasmus does not hold with the easy social theory, still quite current in the literature of his time, which casts upon women all the blame of adultery and lewdness. With the savages who live in a state of nature, he says, the adultery of men is punished, but that of women is forgiven.

Here it appears, at the same time, that Erasmus knew, be it half in jest, the conception of natural virtue and happiness of naked islanders in a savage state. It soon crops up again in Montaigne and the following centuries develop it into a literary dogma.

CHAPTER XIII

ERASMUS'S MIND

(continued)

Erasmus's mind: Intellectual tendencies—The world encumbered by beliefs and forms—Truth must be simple—Back to the pure sources—Holy Scripture in the original languages—Biblical humanism—Critical work on the texts of Scripture—Practice better than dogma—Erasmus's talent and wit—Delight in words and things—Prolixity—Observation of details—A veiled realism—Ambiguousness—The 'Nuance'—Inscrutability of the ultimate ground of all things

SIMPLICITY, naturalness, purity, and reasonableness, those are to Erasmus the dominant requirements, also when we pass from his ethical and aesthetic concepts to his intellectual point of view; indeed, the two can hardly be kept apart.

The world, says Erasmus, is overloaded with human constitutions and opinions and scholastic dogmas, and overburdened with the tyrannical authority of orders, and because of all this the strength of gospel doctrine is flagging. Faith requires simplification, he argued. What would the Turks say of our scholasticism? Colet wrote to him one day: 'There is no end to books and science. Let us, therefore, leave all roundabout roads and go by a short cut to the truth.'

Truth must be simple. 'The language of truth is simple, says Seneca; well then, nothing is simpler nor truer than Christ.' 'I should wish', Erasmus says elsewhere, 'that this simple and pure Christ might be deeply impressed upon the mind of men, and that I deem best attainable in this way, that we, supported by our knowledge of the original languages, should philosophize *at the sources* themselves.'

Here a new watchword comes to the fore: back to the sources! It is not merely an intellectual, philological requirement; it is equally an ethical and aesthetic necessity of life. The original and pure, all that is not yet overgrown or has not passed through many hands, has such a potent charm. Erasmus compared it to an apple which we ourselves pick off the tree. To recall the world to the ancient simplicity of science, to lead it back from the now turbid pools to those living and most pure fountain-heads, those most limpid sources of gospel doctrine—thus he saw the task of divinity. The metaphor of the limpid water is not without meaning here; it reveals the psychological quality of Erasmus's fervent principle.

'How is it', he exclaims, 'that people give themselves so much trouble about the details of all sorts of remote philosophical systems and neglect to go to the sources of Christianity itself?' 'Although this wisdom, which is so excellent that once for all it put the wisdom of all the world to shame, may be drawn from these few books, as from a crystalline source, with far less trouble than is the wisdom of Aristotle from so many thorny books and with much more fruit . . . The equipment for that journey is simple and at everyone's immediate disposal. This philosophy is accessible to everybody. Christ desires that his mysteries shall be spread as widely as possible. I should wish that all good wives read the Gospel and Paul's Epistles; that they were translated into all languages; that out of these the husbandman sang while ploughing, the weaver at his loom; that with such stories the traveller should beguile his wayfaring. . . . This sort of philosophy is rather a matter of disposition than of syllogisms, rather of life than of disputation, rather of inspiration than of erudition, rather of transformation than of logic. . . . What is the philosophy of Christ, which he himself calls *Renascentia*, but the insaturation of Nature created good?—moreover, though no one has taught us this so absolutely and effectively as Christ, yet also in pagan books much may be found that is in accordance with it.'

Such was the view of life of this biblical humanist. As often as Erasmus reverts to these matters, his voice sounds clearest. 'Let no one', he says in the preface to the notes to the New Testament, 'take up this work, as he takes up Gellius's *Noctes atticae* or Poliziano's Miscellanies . . . We are in the presence of holy things; here it is no question of eloquence, these

matters are best recommended to the world by simplicity and
purity; it would be ridiculous to display human erudition here,
impious to pride oneself on human eloquence.' But Erasmus
never was so eloquent himself as just then.

What here raises him above his usual level of force and
fervour is the fact that he fights a battle, the battle for the right
of biblical criticism. It revolts him that people should study
Holy Scripture in the Vulgate when they know that the texts
show differences and are corrupt, although we have the Greek
text by which to go back to the original form and primary
meaning.

He is now reproached because he dares, as a mere gram-
marian, to assail the text of Holy Scripture on the score of
futile mistakes or irregularities. 'Details they are, yes, but
because of these details we sometimes see even great divines
stumble and rave.' Philological trifling is necessary. 'Why are
we so precise as to our food, our clothes, our money-matters
and why does this accuracy displease us in divine literature
alone? He crawls along the ground, they say, he wearies himself out about words and syllables! Why do we slight any
word of Him whom we venerate and worship under the name
of the Word? But, be it so! Let whoever wishes imagine that
I have not been able to achieve anything better, and out of
sluggishness of mind and coldness of heart or lack of erudition
have taken this lowest task upon myself; it is still a Christian
idea to think all work good that is done with pious zeal. We
bring along the bricks, but to build the temple of God.'

He does not want to be intractable. Let the Vulgate be kept
for use in the liturgy, for sermons, in schools, but he who, at
home, reads our edition, will understand his own the better
in consequence. He, Erasmus, is prepared to render account
and acknowledge himself to have been wrong when convicted
of error.

Erasmus perhaps never quite realized how much his philo-
logical-critical method must shake the foundations of the
Church. He was surprised at his adversaries 'who could not
but believe that all their authority would perish at once when

the sacred books might be read in a purified form, and when people tried to understand them in the original'. He did not feel what the unassailable authority of a sacred book meant. He rejoices because Holy Scripture is approached so much more closely, because all sorts of shadings are brought to light by considering not only what is said but also by whom, for whom, at what time, on what occasion, what precedes and what follows, in short, by the method of historical philological criticism. To him it seemed so especially pious when reading Scripture and coming across a place which seemed contrary to the doctrine of Christ or the divinity of his nature, to believe rather that one did not understand the phrase *or that the text might be corrupt*. Unperceived he passed from emendation of the different versions to the correction of the contents. The epistles were not all written by the apostles to whom they are attributed. The apostles themselves made mistakes, at times.

The foundation of his spiritual life was no longer a unity to Erasmus. It was, on the one hand, a strong desire for an upright, simple, pure and homely belief, the earnest wish to be a good Christian. But it was also the irresistible intellectual and aesthetic need of the good taste, the harmony, the clear and exact expression of the Ancients, the dislike of what was cumbrous and involved. Erasmus thought that good learning might render good service for the necessary purification of the faith and its forms. The measure of church hymns should be corrected. That Christian expression and classicism were incompatible, he never believed. The man who in the sphere of sacred studies asked every author for his credentials remained unconscious of the fact that he acknowledged the authority of the Ancients without any evidence. How naïvely he appeals to Antiquity, again and again, to justify some bold feat! He is critical, they say? Were not the Ancients critical? He permits himself to insert digressions? So did the Ancients, etc.

Erasmus is in profound sympathy with that revered Antiquity by his fundamental conviction that it is the practice of life which matters. Not he is the great philosopher who knows the tenets of the Stoics or Peripatetics by rote—but he who expresses the meaning of philosophy by his life and his morals, for that is its purpose. He is truly a divine who teaches, not by artful syllogisms, but by his disposition, by his face and his eyes, by his life itself, that wealth should be despised. To live up to that standard is what Christ himself calls *Renascentia*. Erasmus uses the word in the Christian sense only. But in that sense it is closely allied to the idea of the Renaissance as a historical phenomenon. The worldly and pagan sides of the Renaissance have nearly always been overrated. Erasmus is, much more than Aretino or Castiglione, the representative of the spirit of his age, one over whose Christian sentiment the sweet gale of Antiquity had passed. And that very union of strong Christian endeavour and the spirit of Antiquity is the explanation of Erasmus's wonderful success.

The mere intention and the contents of the mind do not influence the world, if the form of expression does not co-operate. In Erasmus the quality of his talent is a very important factor. His perfect clearness and ease of expression, his liveliness, wit, imagination, gusto and humour have lent a charm to all he wrote which to his contemporaries was irresistible and captivates even us, as soon as we read him. In all that constitutes his talent, Erasmus is perfectly and altogether a representative of the Renaissance. There is, in the first place, his eternal *à propos*. What he writes is never vague, never dark—it is always plausible. Everything seemingly flows of itself like a fountain. It always rings true as to tone, turn of phrase and accent. It has almost the light harmony of Ariosto. And it is, like Ariosto, never tragic, never truly heroic. It carries us away, indeed, but it is never itself truly enraptured.

The more artistic aspects of Erasmus's talent come out most clearly—though they are everywhere in evidence—in those two recreations after more serious labour, the *Moriae Encomium* and the *Colloquia*. But just those two have been of enormous importance for his influence upon his times. For while Jerome reached tens of readers and the New Testament hundreds, the *Moria* and *Colloquies* went out to thousands. And their importance is heightened in that Erasmus has nowhere else expressed himself so spontaneously.

In each of the Colloquies, even in the first purely formulary ones, there is the sketch for a comedy, a novelette or a satire. There is hardly a sentence without its 'point', an expression without a vivid fancy. There are unrivalled niceties. The abbot of the *Abbatis et eruditae colloquium* is a Molière character. It should be noticed how well Erasmus always sustains his characters and his scenes, because he *sees* them. In 'The woman in childbed' he never forgets for a moment that Eutrapelus is an artist. At the end of 'The game of knuckle-bones', when the interlocutors, after having elucidated the whole nomenclature of the Latin game of knuckle-bones, are going to play themselves, Carolus says: 'but shut the door first, lest the cook should see us playing like two boys'.

As Holbein illustrated the *Moria*, we should wish to possess the *Colloquia* with illustrations by Brueghel, so closely allied is Erasmus's witty clear vision of incidents to that of this great master. The procession of drunkards on Palm Sunday, the saving of the shipwrecked crew, the old men waiting for the travelling cart while the drivers are still drinking, all these are Dutch genre pieces of the best sort.

We like to speak of the realism of the Renaissance. Erasmus is certainly a realist in the sense of having an insatiable hunger for knowledge of the tangible world. He wants to know things and their names: the particulars of each thing, be it never so remote, such as those terms of games and rules of games of the Romans. Read carefully the description of the decorative painting on the garden-house of the *Convivium religiosum*: it is nothing but an object lesson, a graphic representation of the forms of reality.

In its joy over the material universe and the supple, pliant word, the Renaissance revels in a profusion of imagery and expressions. The resounding enumerations of names and things, which Rabelais always gives, are not unknown to Erasmus, but he uses them for intellectual and useful purposes.

In *De copia verborum ac rerum* one feat of varied power of expression succeeds another—he gives fifty ways of saying: 'Your letter has given me much pleasure,' or, 'I think that it is going to rain'. The aesthetic impulse is here that of a theme and variations: to display all the wealth and mutations of the logic of language. Elsewhere, too, Erasmus indulges this proclivity for accumulating the treasures of his genius; he and his contemporaries can never restrain themselves from giving all the instances instead of one: in *Ratio verae theologiae*, in *De pronuntiatione*, in *Lingua*, in *Ecclesiastes*. The collections of *Adagia*, *Parabolae*, and *Apophthegmata* are altogether based on this eagerness of the Renaissance (which, by the way, was an inheritance of the Middle Ages themselves) to luxuriate in the wealth of the tangible world, to revel in words and things.

The senses are open for the nice observation of the curious. Though Erasmus does not know that need of proving the secrets of nature, which inspired a Leonardo da Vinci, a Paracelsus, a Vesalius, he is also, by his keen observation, a child of his time. For peculiarities in the habits and customs of nations he has an open eye. He notices the gait of Swiss soldiers, how dandies sit, how Picards pronounce French. He notices that in old pictures the sitters are always represented with half-closed eyes and tightly shut lips, as signs of modesty, and how some Spaniards still honour this expression in life, while German art prefers lips pouting as for a kiss. His lively sense of anecdote, to which he gives the rein in all his writings, belongs here.

And, in spite of all his realism, the world which Erasmus sees and renders, is not altogether that of the sixteenth century. Everything is veiled by Latin. Between the author's mind and reality intervenes his antique diction. At bottom the world of his mind is imaginary. It is a subdued and limited sixteenth-century reality which he reflects. Together with its coarseness he lacks all that is violent and direct in his times. Compared with the artists, with Luther and Calvin, with the statesmen, the navigators, the soldiers and the scientists, Erasmus confronts the world as a recluse. It is only the influence of Latin.

In spite of all his receptiveness and sensitiveness, Erasmus is never fully in contact with life. All through his work not a bird sings, not a wind rustles.

But that reserve or fear of directness is not merely a negative quality. It also results from a consciousness of the indefiniteness of the ground of all things, from the awe of the ambiguity of all that is. If Erasmus so often hovers over the borderline between earnestness and mockery, if he hardly ever gives an incisive conclusion, it is not only due to cautiousness, and fear to commit himself. Everywhere he sees the shadings, the blending of the meaning of words. The terms of things are no longer to him, as to the man of the Middle Ages, as crystals mounted in gold, or as stars in the firmament. 'I like assertions so little that I would easily take sides with the sceptics whereever it is allowed by the inviolable authority of Holy Scripture and the decrees of the Church.' 'What is exempt from error?' All subtle contentions of theological speculation arise from a dangerous curiosity and lead to impious audacity. What have all the great controversies about the Trinity and the Virgin Mary profited? 'We have defined so much that without danger to our salvation might have remained unknown or undecided. . . . The essentials of our religion are peace and unanimity. These can hardly exist unless we make definitions about as few points as possible and leave many questions to individual judgement. Numerous problems are now postponed till the oecumenical Council. It would be much better to put off such questions till the time when the glass shall be removed and the darkness cleared away, and we shall see God face to face.'

'There are sanctuaries in the sacred studies which God has not willed that we should probe, and if we try to penetrate there, we grope in ever deeper darkness the farther we proceed, so that we recognize, in this manner, too, the inscrutable majesty of divine wisdom and the imbecility of human understanding.'

CHAPTER XIV

ERASMUS'S CHARACTER

Erasmus's character: Need of purity and cleanliness—Delicacy—Dislike of contention, need of concord and friendship—Aversion to disturbance of any kind—Too much concerned about other men's opinions—Need of self-justification—Himself never in the wrong—Correlation between inclinations and convictions—Ideal image of himself—Dissatisfaction with himself—Self-centredness—A solitary at heart—Fastidiousness—Suspiciousness—Morbid mistrust—Unhappiness—Restlessness—Unsolved contradictions of his being—Horror of lies—Reserve and insinuation

ERASMUS'S powerful mind met with a great response in the heart of his contemporaries and had a lasting influence on the march of civilization. But one of the heroes of history he cannot be called. Was not his failure to attain to still loftier heights partly due to the fact that his character was not on a level with the elevation of his mind?

And yet that character, a very complicated one, though he took himself to be the simplest man in the world, was determined by the same factors which determined the structure of his mind. Again and again we find in his inclinations the correlates of his convictions.

At the root of his moral being we find—a key to the understanding of his character—that same profound need of purity which drove him to the sources of sacred science. Purity in the material and the moral sense is what he desires for himself and others, always and in all things. Few things revolt him so much as the practices of vintners who doctor wine and dealers who adulterate food. If he continually chastens his language and style, or exculpates himself from mistakes, it is the same impulse which prompts his passionate desire for cleanliness and brightness, of the home and of the body. He has a violent dislike of stuffy air and smelly substances. He regularly takes a roundabout way to avoid a malodorous lane; he loathes shambles and fishmongers' shops. Fetors spread infection, he thinks. Erasmus had, earlier than most people, antiseptic ideas about the danger of infection in the foul air of crowded inns, in the breath of confessants, in baptismal water. Throw aside common cups, he pleaded; let everybody shave himself, let us be cleanly as to bed-sheets, let us not kiss each other by way of greeting. The fear of the horrible venereal disease, imported into Europe during his lifetime, and of which Erasmus watched the unbridled propagation with solicitude, increases his desire for purity. Too little is being done to stop it, he thinks. He cautions against suspected inns; he wants to have measures taken against the marriages of syphilitic persons. In his undignified attitude towards Hutten his physical and moral aversion to the man's evil plays an unmistakable part.

Erasmus is a delicate soul in all his fibres. His body forces him to be that. He is highly sensitive, among other things very susceptible to cold, 'the scholars' disorder', as he calls it. Early in life already the painful malady of the stone begins to torment him, which he resisted so bravely when his work was at stake. He always speaks in a coddling tone about his little body, which cannot stand fasting, which must be kept fit by some exercise, namely riding, and for which he carefully tries to select a suitable climate. He is at times circumstantial in the description of his ailments.[1] He has to be very careful in the matter of his sleep; if once he wakes up, he finds it difficult to go to sleep again, and because of that has often to lose the morning, the best time to work and which is so dear to him. He cannot stand cold, wind and fog, but still less overheated rooms. How he has execrated the German stoves, which are burned nearly all the year through and made Germany almost unbearable to him! Of his fear of illness we have spoken above. It is not only the plague which he flees—for fear of catching cold he gives up a journey from Louvain to Antwerp, where his friend Peter Gilles is in mourning. Although he realizes quite well that 'often a great deal of the disease is in the imagination', yet his own imagination leaves him no peace. Nevertheless, when he is seriously ill he does not fear death.

[1] Cf. the letter to Beatus Rhenanus, pp. 227–8.

His hygienics amount to temperance, cleanliness and fresh air, this last item in moderation: he takes the vicinity of the sea to be unwholesome and is afraid of draughts. His friend Gilles, who is ill, he advises: 'Do not take too much medicine, keep quiet and do not get angry'. Though there is a 'Praise of Medicine' among his works, he does not think highly of physicians and satirizes them more than once in the *Colloquies*.

Also in his outward appearance there were certain features betraying his delicacy. He was of medium height, well-made, of a fair complexion with blond hair and blue eyes, a cheerful face, a very articulate mode of speech, but a thin voice.

In the moral sphere Erasmus's delicacy is represented by his great need of friendship and concord, his dislike of contention. With him peace and harmony rank above all other considerations, and he confesses them to be the guiding principles of his actions. He would, if it might be, have all the world as a friend. 'Wittingly I discharge no one from my friendship,' he says. And though he was sometimes capricious and exacting towards his friends, yet a truly great friend he was: witness the many who never forsook him, or whom he, after a temporary estrangement, always won back—More, Peter Gilles, Fisher, Ammonius, Budaeus, and others too numerous to mention. 'He was most constant in keeping up friendships,' says Beatus Rhenanus, whose own attachment to Erasmus is a proof of the strong affection he could inspire.

At the root of this desire of friendship lies a great and sincere need of affection. Remember the effusions of almost feminine affection towards Servatius during his monastic period. But at the same time it is a sort of moral serenity that makes him so: an aversion to disturbance, to whatever is harsh and inharmonious. He calls it 'a certain occult natural sense' which makes him abhor strife. He cannot abide being at loggerheads with anyone. He always hoped and wanted, he says, to keep his pen unbloody, to attack no one, to provoke no one, even if he were attacked. But his enemies had not willed it, and in later years he became well accustomed to bitter polemics, with Lefèvre d'Étaples, with Lee, with Egmondanus, with Hutten, with Luther, with Beda, with the Spaniards, and the Italians. At first it is still noticeable how he suffers by it, how contention wounds him, so that he cannot bear the pain in silence. 'Do let us be friends again,' he begs Lefèvre, who does not reply. The time which he had to devote to his polemics he regards as lost. 'I feel myself getting more heavy every day,' he writes in 1520, 'not so much on account of my age as because of the restless labour of my studies, nay more even by the weariness of disputes than by the work, which, in itself, is agreeable.' And how much strife was still in store for him then!

If only Erasmus had been less concerned about public opinion! But that seemed impossible: he had a fear of men, or, we may call it, a fervent need of justification. He would always see beforehand, and usually in exaggerated colours, the effect his word or deed would have upon men. Of himself, it was certainly true as he once wrote: that the craving for fame has less sharp spurs than the fear of ignominy. Erasmus is with Rousseau among those who cannot bear the consciousness of guilt, out of a sort of mental cleanliness. Not to be able to repay a benefit with interest, makes him ashamed and sad. He cannot abide 'dunning creditors, unperformed duty, neglect of the need of a friend'. If he cannot discharge the obligation, he explains it away. The Dutch historian Fruin has quite correctly observed: 'Whatever Erasmus did contrary to his duty and his rightly understood interests was the fault of circumstances or wrong advice; he is never to blame himself'. And what he has thus justified for himself becomes with him universal law: 'God relieves people of pernicious vows, if only they repent of them,' says the man who himself had broken a vow.

There is in Erasmus a dangerous fusion between inclination and conviction. The correlations between his idiosyncrasies and his precepts are undeniable. This has special reference to his point of view in the matter of fasting and abstinence from meat. He too frequently vents his own aversion to fish, or talks of his inability to postpone meals, not to make this connection

clear to everybody. In the same way his personal experience in
the monastery passes into his disapproval, on principle, of
monastic life.

The distortion of the image of his youth in his memory, to
which we have referred, is based on that need of self-justification. It is all unconscious interpretation of the undeniable facts
to suit the ideal which Erasmus had made of himself and to
which he honestly thinks he answers. The chief features of
that self-conceived picture are a remarkable, simple sincerity
and frankness, which make it impossible to him to dissemble;
inexperience and carelessness in the ordinary concerns of life
and a total lack of ambition. All this is true in the first instance:
there is a superficial Erasmus who answers to that image, but
it is not the whole Erasmus; there is a deeper one who is almost
the opposite and whom he himself does not know because he
will not know him. Possibly because behind this there is a still
deeper being, which is truly good.

Does he not ascribe weaknesses to himself? Certainly. He is,
in spite of his self-coddling, ever dissatisfied with himself and
his work. *Putidulus*, he calls himself, meaning the quality of
never being content with himself. It is that peculiarity which
makes him dissatisfied with any work of his directly after it
has appeared, so that he always keeps revising and supple-
menting. 'Pusillanimous' he calls himself in writing to Colet.
But again he cannot help giving himself credit for acknow-
ledging that quality, nay, converting that quality itself into a
virtue: it is modesty, the opposite of boasting and self-love.

This bashfulness about himself is the reason that he does not
love his own physiognomy, and is only persuaded with difficulty by his friends to sit for a portrait. His own appearance is
not heroic or dignified enough for him, and he is not duped
by an artist who flatters him: 'Heigh-ho,' he exclaims, on
seeing Holbein's thumbnail sketch illustrating the *Moria*:
'if Erasmus still looked like that, he would take a wife at
once'. It is that deep trait of dissatisfaction that suggests the
inscription on his portraits: 'his writings will show you a
better image'.

Erasmus's modesty and the contempt which he displays of the fame that fell to his lot are of a somewhat rhetorical character. But in this we should not so much see a personal trait of Erasmus as a general form common to all humanists. On the other hand, this mood cannot be called altogether artificial. His books, which he calls his children, have not turned out well. He does not think they will live. He does not set store by his letters: he publishes them because his friends insist upon it. He writes his poems to try a new pen. He hopes that geniuses will soon appear who will eclipse him, so that Erasmus will pass for a stammerer. What is fame? A pagan survival. He is fed up with it to repletion and would do nothing more gladly than cast it off.

Sometimes another note escapes him. If Lee would help him in his endeavours, Erasmus would make him immortal, he had told the former in their first conversation. And he threatens an unknown adversary, 'If you go on so impudently to assail my good name, then take care that my gentleness does not give way and I cause you to be ranked, after a thousand years, among the venomous sycophants, among the idle boasters, among the incompetent physicians'.

The self-centred element in Erasmus must needs increase accordingly as he in truth became a centre and objective point of ideas and culture. There really was a time when it must seem to him that the world hinged upon him, and that it awaited the redeeming word from him. What a widespread enthusiastic following he had, how many warm friends and venerators! There is something naïve in the way in which he thinks it requisite to treat all his friends, in an open letter, to a detailed, rather repellent account of an illness that attacked him on the way back from Basle to Louvain. *His* part, *his* position, *his* name, this more and more becomes the aspect under which he sees world-events. Years will come in which his whole enormous correspondence is little more than one protracted self-defence.

Yet this man who has so many friends is nevertheless solitary at heart. And in the depth of that heart he desires to be alone. He is of a most retiring disposition; he is *a recluse*. 'I have always wished to be alone, and there is nothing I hate so much as sworn partisans.' Erasmus is one of those whom contact with others weakens. The less he has to address and to consider others, friends or enemies, the more truly he utters his deepest soul. Intercourse with particular people always causes little scruples in him, intentional amenities, coquetry, reticences, reserves, spiteful hits, evasions. Therefore it should not be thought that we get to know him to the core from his letters. Natures like his, which all contact with men unsettles, give their best and deepest when they speak impersonally and to all.

After the early effusions of sentimental affection he no longer opens his heart unreservedly to others. At bottom he feels separated from all and on the alert towards all. There is a great fear in him that others will touch his soul or disturb the image he has made of himself. The attitude of warding off reveals itself as fastidiousness and as bashfulness. Budaeus hit the mark when he exclaimed jocularly: '*Fastidiosule!* You little fastidious person!' Erasmus himself interprets the dominating trait of his being as maidenly coyness. The excessive sensitiveness to the stain attaching to his birth results from it. But his friend Ammonius speaks of his *subrustica verecundia*, his somewhat rustic *gaucherie*. There is, indeed, often something of the small man about Erasmus, who is hampered by greatness and therefore shuns the great, because, at bottom, they obsess him and he feels them to be inimical to his being.

It seems a hard thing to say that genuine loyalty and fervent gratefulness were strange to Erasmus. And yet such was his nature. In characters like his a kind of mental cramp keeps back the effusions of the heart. He subscribes to the adage: 'Love so, as if you may hate one day, and hate so, as if you may love one day'. He cannot bear benefits. In his inmost soul he continually retires before everybody. He who considers himself the pattern of simple unsuspicion, is indeed in the highest degree suspicious towards all his friends. The dead Ammonius, who had helped him so zealously in the most

delicate concerns, is not secure from it. 'You are always un-
fairly distrustful towards me,' Budaeus complains. 'What!'
exclaims Erasmus, 'you will find few people who are so little
distrustful in friendship as myself.'

When at the height of his fame the attention of the world
was indeed fixed on all he spoke or did, there was some
ground for a certain feeling on his part of being always
watched and threatened. But when he was yet an unknown
man of letters, in his Parisian years, we continually find traces
in him of a mistrust of the people about him that can only be
regarded as a morbid feeling. During the last period of his life
this feeling attaches especially to two enemies, Eppendorf and
Aleander. Eppendorf employs spies everywhere who watch
Erasmus's correspondence with his friends. Aleander continually sets people to combat him, and lies in wait for him wherever he can. His interpretation of the intentions of his assailants
has the ingenious self-centred element which passes the
borderline of sanity. He sees the whole world full of calumny
and ambuscades threatening his peace: nearly all those who
once were his best friends have become his bitterest enemies;
they wag their venomous tongues at banquets, in conversation, in the confessional, in sermons, in lectures, at court, in
vehicles and ships. The minor enemies, like troublesome
vermin, drive him to weariness of life, or to death by in-
somnia. He compares his tortures to the martyrdom of Saint
Sebastian, pierced by arrows. But his is worse, for there is no end
to it. For years he has daily been dying a thousand deaths and
that alone; for his friends, if such there are, are deterred by envy.

He mercilessly pillories his patrons in a row for their stingi-
ness. Now and again there suddenly comes to light an undercurrent of aversion and hatred which we did not suspect.
Where had more good things fallen to his lot than in England?
Which country had he always praised more? But suddenly
a bitter and unfounded reproach escapes him. England is
responsible for his having become faithless to his monastic
vows, 'for no other reason do I hate Britain more than for this,
though it has always been pestilent to me'.

He seldom allows himself to go so far. His expressions of hatred or spite are, as a rule, restricted to the feline. They are aimed at friends and enemies, Budaeus, Lypsius, as well as Hutten and Beda. Occasionally we are struck by the expression of coarse pleasure at another's misfortune. But in all this, as regards malice, we should not measure Erasmus by our ideas of delicacy and gentleness. Compared with most of his contemporaries he remains moderate and refined.

Erasmus never felt happy, was never content. This may perhaps surprise us for a moment, when we think of his cheerful, never-failing energy, of his gay jests and his humour. But upon reflection this unhappy feeling tallies very well with his character. It also proceeds from his general attitude of warding off. Even when in high spirits he considers himself in all respects an unhappy man. 'The most miserable of all men, the thrice-wretched Erasmus,' he calls himself in fine Greek terms. His life 'is an Iliad of calamities, a chain of misfortunes. How can anyone envy *me*?' To no one has Fortune been so constantly hostile as to him. She has sworn his destruction, thus he sang in his youth in a poetical complaint addressed to Gaguin: from earliest infancy the same sad and hard fate has been constantly pursuing him. Pandora's whole box seems to have been poured out over him.

This unhappy feeling takes the special form of his having been charged by unlucky stars with Herculean labour, without profit or pleasure to himself:[1] troubles and vexations without end. His life might have been so much easier if he had taken his chances. He should never have left Italy; or he ought to have stayed in England. 'But an immoderate love of liberty caused me to wrestle long with faithless friends and inveterate poverty.' Elsewhere he says more resignedly: 'But we are driven by fate'.

That immoderate love of liberty had indeed been as fate to

---

[1] Ad. 2001 LB. II, 717B, 77 c. 58A. On the book which Erasmus holds in his hand in Holbein's portrait at Longford Castle, we read in Greek: The Labours of Hercules.

him. He had always been the great seeker of quiet and liberty who found liberty late and quiet never. By no means ever to bind himself, to incur no obligations which might become fetters—again that fear of the entanglements of life. Thus he remained the great restless one. He was never truly satisfied with anything, least of all with what he produced himself. 'Why, then, do you overwhelm us with so many books', someone at Louvain objected, 'if you do not really approve of any of them?' And Erasmus answers with Horace's word: 'In the first place, because I cannot sleep'.

A sleepless energy, it was that indeed. He cannot rest. Still half seasick and occupied with his trunks, he is already thinking about an answer to Dorp's letter, just received, censuring the *Moria*. We should fully realize what it means that time after time Erasmus, who, by nature, loved quiet and was fearful, and fond of comfort, cleanliness and good fare, undertakes troublesome and dangerous journeys, even voyages, which he detests, for the sake of his work and of that alone.

He is not only restless, but also precipitate. Helped by an incomparably retentive and capacious memory he writes at haphazard. He never becomes anacoluthic; his talent is too refined and sure for that; but he does repeat himself and is unnecessarily circumstantial. 'I rather pour out than write everything,' he says. He compares his publications to parturitions, nay, to abortions. He does not select his subjects, he tumbles into them, and having once taken up a subject he finishes without intermission. For years he has read only *tumultuarie*, up and down all literature; he no longer finds time really to refresh his mind by reading, and to work so as to please himself. On that account he envied Budaeus.

'Do not publish too hastily,' More warns him: 'you are watched to be caught in inexactitudes.' Erasmus knows it: he will correct all later, he will ever have to revise and to polish everything. He hates the labour of revising and correcting, but he submits to it, and works passionately, 'in the treadmill of Basle', and, he says, finishes the work of six years in eight months.

In that recklessness and precipitation with which Erasmus labours there is again one of the unsolved contradictions of his being. He *is* precipitate and careless; he *wants* to be careful and cautious; his mind drives him to be the first, his nature restrains him, but usually only after the word has been written and published. The result is a continual intermingling of explosion and reserve.

The way in which Erasmus always tries to shirk definite statements irritates us. How carefully he always tries to represent the *Colloquies*, in which he had spontaneously revealed so much of his inner convictions, as mere trifling committed to paper to please his friends. They are only meant to teach correct Latin! And if anything is said in them touching matters of faith, it is not I who say it, is it? As often as he censures classes or offices in the *Adagia*, princes above all, he warns the readers not to regard his words as aimed at particular persons.

Erasmus was a master of reserve. He knew, even when he held definite views, how to avoid direct decisions, not only from caution, but also because he saw the eternal ambiguity of human issues.

Erasmus ascribes to himself an unusual horror of lies. On seeing a liar, he says, he was corporeally affected. As a boy he already violently disliked mendacious boys, such as the little braggart of whom he tells in the *Colloquies*. That this reaction of aversion is genuine is not contradicted by the fact that we catch Erasmus himself in untruths. Inconsistencies, flattery, pieces of cunning, white lies, serious suppression of facts, simulated sentiments of respect or sorrow—they may all be pointed out in his letters. He once disavowed his deepest conviction for a gratuity from Anne of Borselen by flattering her bigotry. He requested his best friend Batt to tell lies in his behalf. He most sedulously denied his authorship of the Julius dialogue, for fear of the consequences, even to More, and always in such a way as to avoid saying outright, 'I did not write it'. Those who know other humanists, and know how frequently and impudently they lied, will perhaps think more lightly of Erasmus's sins.

For the rest, even during his lifetime he did not escape punishment for his eternal reserve, his proficiency in semi-conclusions and veiled truths, insinuations and slanderous allusions. The accusation of perfidy was often cast in his teeth, sometimes in serious indignation. 'You are always engaged in bringing suspicion upon others,' Edward Lee exclaims. 'How dare you usurp the office of a general censor, and condemn what you have hardly ever tasted? How dare you despise all but yourself? Falsely and insultingly do you expose your antagonist in the *Colloquia*.' Lee quotes the spiteful passage referring to himself, and then exclaims: 'Now from these words the world may come to know its divine, its censor, its modest and sincere author, that Erasmian diffidence, earnest, decency and honesty! Erasmian modesty has long been proverbial. You are always using the words "false accusations". You say: if I was consciously guilty of the smallest of all his (Lee's) false accusations, I should not dare to approach the Lord's table!—O man, who are you, to judge another, a servant who stands or falls before his Lord?'

This was the first violent attack from the conservative side, in the beginning of 1520, when the mighty struggle which Luther's action had unchained kept the world in ever greater suspense. Six months later followed the first serious reproaches on the part of radical reformers. Ulrich von Hutten, the impetuous, somewhat foggy-headed knight, who wanted to see Luther's cause triumph as the national cause of Germany, turns to Erasmus, whom, at one time, he had enthusiastically acclaimed as the man of the new weal, with the urgent appeal not to forsake the cause of the reformation or to compromise it. 'You have shown yourself fearful in the affair of Reuchlin; now in that of Luther you do your utmost to convince his adversaries that you are altogether averse from it, though we know better. Do not disown us. You know how triumphantly certain letters of yours are circulated, in which, to protect yourself from suspicion, you rather meanly fasten it on others . . . If you are now afraid to incur a little hostility for *my* sake, concede me at least that you will not allow yourself, out of fear for another, to be tempted to renounce me; rather be silent about me.'

Those were bitter reproaches. In the man who had to swallow them there was a puny Erasmus who deserved those reproaches, who took offence at them, but did not take them to heart, who continued to act with prudent reserve till Hutten's friendship was turned to hatred. In him was also a great Erasmus who knew how, under the passion and infatuation with which the parties combated each other, the Truth he sought, and the Love he hoped would subdue the world, were obscured; who knew the God whom he professed too high to take sides. Let us try ever to see of that great Erasmus as much as the petty one permits.

CHAPTER XV

AT LOUVAIN

1517–18

Erasmus at Louvain, 1517—He expects the renovation of the Church as the fruit of good learning—Controversy with Lefèvre d'Étaples—Second journey to Basle, 1518—He revises the edition of the New Testament—Controversies with Latomus, Briard and Lee—Erasmus regards the opposition of conservative theology merely as a conspiracy against good learning

W HEN Erasmus established himself at Louvain in the summer of 1517 he had a vague presentiment that great changes were at hand. 'I fear', he writes in September, 'that a great subversion of affairs is being brought about here, if God's favour and the piety and wisdom of princes do not concern themselves about human matters.' But the forms which that great change would assume he did not in the least realize.

He regarded his removal as merely temporary. It was only to last 'till we shall have seen which place of residence is best fit for old age, which is already knocking'. There is something pathetic in the man who desires nothing but quiet and liberty, and who through his own restlessness, and his inability not to concern himself about other people, never found a really fixed abode or true independence. Erasmus is one of those people who always seem to say: tomorrow, tomorrow! I must first deal with this, and then . . . As soon as he shall be ready with the new edition of the New Testament and shall have extricated himself from troublesome and disagreeable theological controversies, in which he finds himself entangled against his wish, he will sleep, hide himself, 'sing for himself and the Muses'. But that time never came.

Where to live when he shall be free? Spain, to which Cardinal Ximenes called him, did not appeal to him. From Germany, he says, the stoves and the insecurity deter him. In England the servitude which was required of him there revolted him. But in the Netherlands themselves, he did not feel at his ease, either: 'Here I am barked at a great deal, and there is no remuneration; though I desired it ever so much, I could not bear to stay there long'. Yet he remained for four years.

Erasmus had good friends in the University of Louvain. At first he put up with his old host Johannes Paludanus, Rhetor of the University, whose house he exchanged that summer for quarters in the College of the Lily. Martin Dorp, a Dutchman like himself, had not been estranged from him by their polemics about the *Moria*; his good will was of great importance to Erasmus, because of the important place Dorp occupied in the theological faculty. And lastly, though his old patron, Adrian of Utrecht, afterwards Pope, had by that time been called away from Louvain to higher dignities, his influence had not diminished in consequence, but rather increased; for just about that time he had been made a cardinal.

Erasmus was received with great complaisance by the Louvain divines. Their leader, the vice-chancellor of the University, Jean Briard of Ath, repeatedly expressed his approval of the edition of the New Testament, to Erasmus's great satisfaction. Soon Erasmus found himself a member of the theological faculty. Yet he did not feel at his ease among the Louvain theologians. The atmosphere was a great deal less congenial to him than that of the world of the English scholars. Here he felt a spirit which he did not understand and distrusted in consequence.

In the years in which the Reformation began, Erasmus was the victim of a great misunderstanding, the result of the fact that his delicate, aesthetic, hovering spirit understood neither the profoundest depths of the faith nor the hard necessities of human society. He was neither mystic nor realist. Luther was both. To Erasmus the great problem of Church and State and society, seemed simple. Nothing was required but restoration and purification by a return to the original, unspoilt sources of Christianity. A number of accretions to the faith, rather ridiculous than revolting, had to be cleared away. All should be reduced to the nucleus of faith, Christ and the Gospel. Forms, ceremonies, speculations should make room for the practice of true piety. The Gospel was easily intelligible to everybody and within everybody's reach. And the means to reach all this was good learning, *bonae literae*. Had he not himself, by his editions of the New Testament and of Jerome, and even earlier by the now famous *Enchiridion*, done most of what had to be done? 'I hope that what now pleases the upright, will soon please all.' As early as the beginning of 1517 Erasmus had written to Wolfgang Fabricius Capito, in the tone of one who has accomplished the great task. 'Well then, take you the torch from us. The work will henceforth be a great deal easier and cause far less hatred and envy. *We* have lived through the first shock.'

Budaeus writes to Tunstall in May 1517: 'Was anyone born under such inauspicious Graces that the dull and obscure discipline (scholasticism) does not revolt him, since sacred literature, too, cleansed by Erasmus's diligence, has regained its ancient purity and brightness? But it is still much greater that he should have effected by the same labour the emergence of sacred truth itself out of that Cimmerian darkness, even though divinity is not yet quite free from the dirt of the sophist school. If that should occur one day, it will be owing to the beginnings made in our times.' The philologist Budaeus believed even more firmly than Erasmus that faith was a matter of erudition.

It could not but vex Erasmus that not everyone accepted the cleansed truth at once. How could people continue to oppose themselves to what, to him, seemed as clear as daylight and so simple? He, who so sincerely would have liked to live in peace with all the world, found himself involved in a series of polemics. To let the opposition of opponents pass unnoticed was forbidden not only by his character, for ever striving to justify himself in the eyes of the world, but also by the custom of his time, so eager for dispute.

There were, first of all, his polemics with Jacques Lefèvre d'Étaples, or in Latinized form, Faber Stapulensis, the Parisian theologian, who as a preparer of the Reformation may, more than anyone else, be ranked with Erasmus. At the moment when Erasmus got into the travelling cart which was to take him to Louvain, a friend drew his attention to a passage in the new edition of Faber's commentary on St. Paul's epistles, in which he controverted Erasmus's note on the Second Epistle to the Hebrews, verse 7. Erasmus at once bought Faber's book, and soon published an *Apologia*. It concerned Christ's relation to God and the angels, but the dogmatic point at issue hinged, after all, on a philological interpretation of Erasmus.

Not yet accustomed to much direct wrangling, Erasmus was violently agitated by the matter, the more as he esteemed Faber highly and considered him a congenial spirit. 'What on earth has occurred to the man? Have others set him on against me? All theologians agree that I am right,' he asserts. It makes him nervous that Faber does not reply again at once. Badius has told Peter Gilles that Faber is sorry about it. Erasmus in a dignified letter appeals to their friendship; he will suffer himself to be taught and censured. Then again he growls: Let him be careful. And he thinks that his controversy with Faber keeps the world in suspense: there is not a meal at which the guests do not side with one or the other of them. But finally the combat abated and the friendship was preserved.

Towards Easter 1518, Erasmus contemplated a new journey to Basle, there to pass through the press, during a few months of hard labour, the corrected edition of the New Testament. He did not fail to request the chiefs of conservative divinity at Louvain beforehand to state their objections to his work. Briard of Ath declared he had found nothing offensive in it, after he had first been told all sorts of bad things about it. 'Then the new edition will please you much better,' Erasmus had said. His friend Dorp and James Latomus, also one of the chief divines, had expressed themselves in the same sense, and the Carmelite Nicholas of Egmond had said that he had never read Erasmus's work. Only a young Englishman, Edward Lee, who was studying Greek at Louvain, had summarized a number of criticisms into ten conclusions. Erasmus had got rid of the matter by writing to Lee that he had not been able to get hold of his conclusions and therefore could not make use of them. But his youthful critic had not put up with being slighted so, and worked out his objections in a more circumstantial treatise.

Thus Erasmus set out for Basle once more in May 1518. He had been obliged to ask all his English friends (of whom Ammonius had been taken from him by death in 1517) for support to defray the expenses of the journey; he kept holding out to them the prospect that, after his work was finished, he would return to England. In a letter to Martin Lypsius, as he was going up the Rhine, he answered Lee's criticism, which had irritated him extremely. In revising his edition he not only took it but little into account, but ventured, moreover, this time to print his own translation of the New Testament of 1506 without any alterations. At the same time he obtained for the new edition a letter of approval from the Pope, a redoubtable weapon against his cavillers.

At Basle Erasmus worked again like a horse in a treadmill. But he was really in his element. Even before the second edition of the New Testament, the *Enchiridion* and the *Institutio Principis Christiani* were reprinted by Froben. On his return journey, Erasmus, whose work had been hampered all through the summer by indisposition, and who had, on that account, been unable to finish it, fell seriously ill. He reached Louvain with difficulty (21 September 1518). It might be the pestilence, and Erasmus, ever much afraid of contagion himself, now took all precautions to safeguard his friends against it. He avoided his quarters in the College of the Lily, and found shelter with his most trusted friend, Dirck Maertensz, the printer. But in spite of rumours of the plague and his warnings, first Dorp and afterwards also Ath came, at once, to visit him. Evidently the Louvain professors did not mean so badly by him, after all.

But the differences between Erasmus and the Louvain faculty were deeply rooted. Lee, hurt by the little attention paid by Erasmus to his objections, prepared a new critique, but kept it from Erasmus, for the present, which irritated the

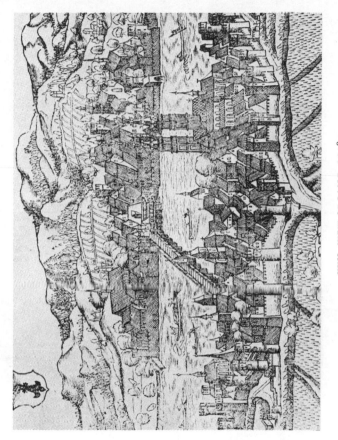

XVII. VIEW OF BASLE, 1548

XVIII. Title-page of the New Testament printed by Froben in 1520

latter and made him nervous. In the meantime a new oppo-
nent arose. Directly after his return to Louvain, Erasmus had
taken much trouble to promote the establishment of the
Collegium Trilingue, projected and endowed by Jerome
Busleiden, in his testament, to be founded in the university.
The three biblical languages, Hebrew, Greek and Latin, were
to be taught there. Now when James Latomus, a member of
the theological faculty and a man whom he esteemed, in a
dialogue about the study of those three languages and of
theology, doubted the utility of the former, Erasmus judged
himself concerned, and answered Latomus in an *Apologia*.
About the same time (spring 1519) he got into trouble with
the vice-chancellor himself. Erasmus thought that Ath had
publicly censured him with regard to his 'Praise of Marriage',
which had recently appeared. Though Ath withdrew at once,
Erasmus could not abstain from writing an *Apologia*, however moderate. Meanwhile the smouldering quarrel with Lee
assumed ever more hateful forms. In vain did Erasmus's
English friends attempt to restrain their young, ambitious
compatriot. Erasmus on his part irritated him furtively. He
reveals in this whole dispute a lack of self-control and dignity
which shows his weakest side. Usually so anxious as to decorum he now lapses into invectives: The British adder, Satan,
even the old taunt ascribing a tail to Englishmen has to serve
once more. The points at issue disappear altogether behind
the bitter mutual reproaches. In his unrestrained anger,
Erasmus avails himself of the most unworthy weapons. He
eggs his German friends on to write against Lee and to ridicule
him in all his folly and brag, and then he assures all his English
friends: 'All Germany is literally furious with Lee; I have the
greatest trouble in keeping them back'.

Alack! Germany had other causes of disturbance: it is 1520
and the three great polemics of Luther were setting the world
on fire.

Though one may excuse the violence and the petty spite-
fulness of Erasmus in this matter, as resulting from an
over-sensitive heart falling somewhat short in really manly

qualities, yet it is difficult to deny that he failed completely to understand both the arguments of his adversaries and the great movements of his time.

It was very easy for Erasmus to mock the narrow-mindedness of conservative divines who thought that there would be an end to faith in Holy Scripture as soon as the emendation of the text was attempted. ' "They correct the Holy Gospel, nay, the Pater Noster itself!" the preacher exclaims indignantly in the sermon before his surprised congregation. As if I cavilled at Matthew and Luke, and not at those who, out of ignorance and carelessness, have corrupted them. What do people wish? That the Church should possess Holy Scripture as correct as possible, or not?' This reasoning seemed to Erasmus, with his passionate need of purity, a conclusive refutation. But instinct did not deceive his adversaries, when it told them that doctrine itself was at stake if the linguistic judgement of a single individual might decide as to the correct version of a text. And Erasmus wished to avoid the inferences which assailed doctrine. He was not aware of the fact that his conceptions of the Church, the sacraments and the dogmas were no longer purely Catholic, because they had become subordinated to his philological insight. He could not be aware of it because, in spite of all his natural piety and his fervent ethical sentiments, he lacked the mystic insight which is the foundation of every creed.

It was this personal lack in Erasmus which made him unable to understand the real grounds of the resistance of Catholic orthodoxy. How was it possible that so many, and among them men of high consideration, refused to accept what to him seemed so clear and irrefutable! He interpreted the fact in a highly personal way. He, the man who would so gladly have lived in peace with all the world, who so yearned for sympathy and recognition, and bore enmity with difficulty, saw the ranks of haters and opponents increase about him. He did not understand how they feared his mocking acrimony, how many wore the scar of a wound that the *Moria* had made. That real and supposed hatred troubled Erasmus. He sees his enemies as a sect. It is especially the Dominicans and the Carmelites who are ill-affected towards the new scientific theology. Just then a new adversary had arisen at Louvain in the person of his compatriot Nicholas of Egmond, prior of the Carmelites, henceforth an object of particular abhorrence to him. It is remarkable that at Louvain Erasmus found his fiercest opponents in some compatriots, in the narrower sense of the word: Vincent Dirks of Haarlem, William of Vianen, Ruurd Tapper. The persecution increases: the venom of slander spreads more and more every day and becomes more deadly; the greatest untruths are impudently preached about him; he calls in the help of Ath, the vice-chancellor, against them. But it is no use; the hidden enemies laugh; let him write for the erudite, who are few; we shall bark to stir up the people. After 1520 he writes again and again: 'I am stoned every day'.

But Erasmus, however much he might see himself, not without reason, at the centre, could, in 1519 and 1520, no longer be blind to the fact that the great struggle did not concern him alone. On all sides the battle was being fought. What is it, that great commotion about matters of spirit and of faith?

The answer which Erasmus gave himself was this: it is a great and wilful conspiracy on the part of the conservatives to suffocate good learning and make the old ignorance triumph. This idea recurs innumerable times in his letters after the middle of 1518. 'I know quite certainly', he writes on 21 March 1519 to one of his German friends, 'that the barbarians on all sides have conspired to leave no stone unturned till they have suppressed *bonae literae*.' 'Here we are still fighting with the protectors of the old ignorance'; cannot Wolsey persuade the Pope to stop it here? All that appertains to ancient and cultured literature is called 'poetry' by those narrow-minded fellows. By that word they indicate everything that savours of a more elegant doctrine, that is to say all that they have not learned themselves. All the tumult, the whole tragedy—under these terms he usually refers to the great theological struggle—

originates in the hatred of *bonae literae*. 'This is the source and hot-bed of all this tragedy; incurable hatred of linguistic study and the *bonae literae*.' 'Luther provokes those enemies, whom it is impossible to conquer, though their cause is a bad one. And meanwhile envy harasses the *bonae literae*, which are attacked at his (Luther's) instigation by these gadflies. They are already nearly insufferable, when things do not go well with them; but who can stand them when they triumph? Either I am blind, or they aim at something else than Luther. They are preparing to conquer the phalanx of the Muses.'

This was written by Erasmus to a member of the University of Leipzig in December 1520. This one-sided and academic conception of the great events, a conception which arose in the study of a recluse bending over his books, did more than anything else to prevent Erasmus from understanding the true nature and purport of the Reformation.

CHAPTER XVI

FIRST YEARS OF THE REFORMATION

Beginning of the relations between Erasmus and Luther—Archbishop Albert of Mayence, 1517—Progress of the Reformation—Luther tries to bring about a rapprochement with Erasmus, March 1519—Erasmus keeps aloof; fancies he may yet act as a conciliator—His attitude becomes ambiguous—He denies ever more emphatically all relations with Luther and resolves to remain a spectator—He is pressed by either camp to take sides—Aleander in the Netherlands—The Diet of Worms, 1521—Erasmus leaves Louvain to safeguard his freedom, October 1521

ABOUT the close of 1516, Erasmus received a letter from the librarian and secretary of Frederick, elector of Saxony, George Spalatinus, written in the respectful and reverential tone in which the great man was now approached. 'We all esteem you here most highly; the elector has all your books in his library and intends to buy everything you may publish in future.' But the object of Spalatinus's letter was the execution of a friend's commission. An Augustinian ecclesiastic, a great admirer of Erasmus, had requested him to direct his attention to the fact that in his interpretation of St. Paul, especially in that of the epistle to the Romans, Erasmus had failed to conceive the idea of *justitia* correctly, had paid too little attention to original sin: he might profit by reading Augustine.

The nameless Austin Friar was Luther, then still unknown outside the circle of the Wittenberg University, in which he was a professor, and the criticism regarded the cardinal point of his hardly acquired conviction: justification by faith.

Erasmus paid little attention to this letter. He received so many of that sort, containing still more praise and no criticism. If he answered it, the reply did not reach Spalatinus, and later Erasmus completely forgot the whole letter.

Nine months afterwards, in September 1517, when Erasmus had been at Louvain for a short time, he received an honourable invitation, written by the first prelate of the Empire, the young Archbishop of Mayence, Albert of Brandenburg. The archbishop would be pleased to see him on an occasion: he greatly admired his work (he knew it so little as to speak of Erasmus's emendation of the Old Testament, instead of the New) and hoped that he would one day write some lives of saints in elegant style.

The young Hohenzoller, advocate of the new light of classical studies, whose attention had probably been drawn to Erasmus by Hutten and Capito, who sojourned at his court, had recently become engaged in one of the boldest political and financial transactions of his time. His elevation to the see of Mayence, at the age of twenty-four, had necessitated a papal dispensation, as he also wished to keep the archbishopric of Magdeburg and the see of Halberstadt. This accumulation of ecclesiastical offices had to be made subservient to the Branden-burg policy which opposed the rival house of Saxony. The Pope granted the dispensation in return for a great sum of money, but to facilitate its payment he accorded to the arch-bishop a liberal indulgence for the whole archbishopric of Mayence, Magdeburg and the Brandenburg territories. Albert, to whom half the proceeds were tacitly left, raised a loan with the house of Fugger, and this charged itself with the indulgence traffic.

When in December 1517, Erasmus answered the arch-bishop, Luther's propositions against indulgences, provoked by the Archbishop of Mayence's instructions regarding their colportage, had already been posted up (31 October 1517), and were circulated throughout Germany, rousing the whole Church. They were levelled at the same abuses which Erasmus combated, the mechanical, atomistical, and juridical concep-tion of religion. But how different was their practical effect, as compared with Erasmus's pacific endeavour to purify the Church by lenient means!

'Lives of saints?' Erasmus asked replying to the archbishop. 'I have tried in my poor way to add a little light to the prince of saints himself. For the rest, your endeavour, in addition to so many difficult matters of government, and at such an early age, to get the lives of the saints purged of old women's tales and disgusting style, is extremely laudable. For nothing should be suffered in the Church that is not perfectly pure or refined.' And he concludes with a magnificent eulogy of the excellent prelate.

During the greater part of 1518, Erasmus was too much occupied by his own affairs—the journey to Basle and his red-hot labours there, and afterwards his serious illness—to concern himself much with Luther's business. In March he sends Luther's theses to More, without comment, and, in passing, complains to Colet about the impudence with which Rome disseminates indulgences. Luther, now declared a heretic and summoned to appear at Augsburg, stands before the legate Cajetanus and refuses to recant. Seething enthusiasm surrounds him. Just about that time Erasmus writes to one of Luther's partisans, John Lang, in very favourable terms about his work. The theses have pleased everybody. 'I see that the monarchy of the Pope at Rome, as it is now, is a pestilence to Christendom, but I do not know if it is expedient to touch that sore openly. That would be a matter for princes, but I fear that these will act in concert with the Pope to secure part of the spoils. I do not understand what possessed Eck to take up arms against Luther.' The letter did not find its way into any of the collections.

The year 1519 brought the struggle attending the election of an emperor, after old Maximilian had died in January, and the attempt of the curia to regain ground with lenity. Germany was expecting the long-projected disputation between Johannes Eck and Andreas Karlstadt which, in truth, would concern Luther. How could Erasmus, who himself was involved that year in so many polemics, have foreseen that the Leipzig disputation, which was to lead Luther to the consequence of rejecting the highest ecclesiastical authority, would remain of lasting importance in the history of the world, whereas his quarrel with Lee would be forgotten?

On 28 March 1519 Luther addressed himself personally to Erasmus for the first time. 'I speak with you so often, and you with me, Erasmus, our ornament and our hope; and we do not know each other as yet.' He rejoices to find that Erasmus displeases many, for this he regards as a sign that God has blessed him. Now that his, Luther's, name begins to get known too, a longer silence between them might be wrongly interpreted. 'Therefore, my Erasmus, amiable man, if you think fit, acknowledge also this little brother in Christ, who really admires you and feels friendly disposed towards you, and for the rest would deserve no better, because of his ignorance, than to lie, unknown, buried in a corner.'

There was a very definite purpos in this somewhat rustically cunning and half ironical le Luther wanted, if possible, to make Erasmus show his colours, to win him, the powerful authority, touchstone of science and culture, for the cause which he advocated. In his heart Luther had long been aware of the deep gulf separating him from Erasmus. As early as March 1517, six months before his public appearance, he wrote about Erasmus to John Lang: 'human matters weigh heavier with him than divine,' an opinion that so many have pronounced about Erasmus—obvious, and yet unfair.

The attempt, on the part of Luther, to effect a *rapprochement* was a reason for Erasmus to retire at once. Now began that extremely ambiguous policy of Erasmus to preserve peace by his authority as a light of the world and to steer a middle course without committing himself. In that attitude the great and the petty side of his personality are inextricably intertwined. The error because of which most historians have seen Erasmus's attitude towards the Reformation either in far too unfavourable a light or—as for instance the German historian Kalkoff—much too heroic and far-seeing, is that they erroneously regard him as psychologically homogeneous. Just that he is not. His double-sidedness roots in the depths of his being. Many of his utterances during the struggle proceed directly from his fear and lack of character, also from his inveterate dislike of siding with a person or a cause; but behind that is always his deep and fervent conviction that neither of the conflicting opinions can completely express the truth, that human hatred and purblindness infatuate men's minds. And with that conviction is allied the noble illusion that it might yet be possible to preserve the peace by moderation, insight, and kindliness.

In April 1519 Erasmus addressed himself by letter to the elector Frederick of Saxony, Luther's patron. He begins by alluding to his dedication of Suetonius two years before; but his real purpose is to say something about Luther. Luther's writings, he says, have given the Louvain obscurants plenty of reason to inveigh against the *bonae literae*, to decry all scholars. He himself does not know Luther and has glanced through his writings only cursorily as yet, but everyone praises his life. How little in accordance with theological gentleness it is to condemn him offhand, and that before the indiscreet vulgar! For has he not proposed a dispute, and submitted himself to everybody's judgement? No one has, so far, admonished, taught, convinced him. Every error is not at once heresy.

The best of Christianity is a life worthy of Christ. Where we find that, we should not rashly suspect people of heresy. Why do we so uncharitably persecute the lapses of others, though none of us is free from error? Why do we rather want to conquer than cure, suppress than instruct?

But he concludes with a word that could not but please Luther's friends, who so hoped for his support. 'May the duke prevent an innocent man from being surrendered under the cloak of piety to the impiety of a few. This is also the wish of Pope Leo, who has nothing more at heart than that innocence be safe.'

At this same time Erasmus does his best to keep Froben back from publishing Luther's writings, 'that they may not fan the hatred of the *bonae literae* still more'. And he keeps repeating: I do not know Luther, I have not read his writings. He makes this declaration to Luther himself, in his reply to the latter's epistle of 28 March. This letter of Erasmus, dated 30 May 1519, should be regarded as a newspaper leader,[1] to acquaint the public with his attitude towards the Luther question. Luther does not know the tragedies which his writings have caused at Louvain. People here think that Erasmus has helped him in

[1] Translation on pp. 229 ff.

composing them and call him the standard bearer of the party! That seemed to them a fitting pretext to suppress the *bonae literae*. 'I have declared that you are perfectly unknown to me, that I have not yet read your books and therefore neither approve nor disapprove anything.' 'I reserve myself, so far as I may, to be of use to the reviving studies. Discreet moderation seems likely to bring better progress than impetuosity. It was by this that Christ subjugated the world.'

On the same day he writes to John Lang, one of Luther's friends and followers, a short note, not meant for publication: 'I hope that the endeavours of yourself and your party will be successful. Here the Papists rave violently. . . . All the best minds are rejoiced at Luther's boldness: I do not doubt he will be careful that things do not end in a quarrel of parties! . . . We shall never triumph over feigned Christians unless we first abolish the tyranny of the Roman see, and of its satellites, the Dominicans, the Franciscans and the Carmelites. But no one could attempt that without a serious tumult.'

As the gulf widens, Erasmus's protestations that he has nothing to do with Luther become much more frequent. Relations at Louvain grow ever more disagreeable and the general sentiment about him ever more unkind. In August 1519 he turns to the Pope himself for protection against his opponents. He still fails to see how wide the breach is. He still takes it all to be quarrels of scholars. King Henry of England and King Francis of France in their own countries have imposed silence upon the quarrellers and slanderers; if only the Pope would do the same!

In October he was once more reconciled with the Louvain faculty. It was just at this time that Colet died in London, the man who had, better perhaps than anyone else, understood Erasmus's standpoint. Kindred spirits in Germany still looked up to Erasmus as the great man who was on the alert to interpose at the right moment and who had made moderation the watchword, until the time should come to give his friends the signal.

But in the increasing noise of the battle his voice already sounded less powerfully than before. A letter to Cardinal

Albert of Mayence, 19 October 1519, of about the same
content as that of Frederick of Saxony written in the preced-
ing spring, was at once circulated by Luther's friends; and by
the advocates of conservatism, in spite of the usual protestation,
'I do not know Luther', it was made to serve against Erasmus.

It became more and more clear that the mediating and conciliatory position which Erasmus wished to take up would
soon be altogether untenable. The inquisitor Jacob Hoog-
straten had come from Cologne, where he was a member of
the University, to Louvain, to work against Luther there, as
he had worked against Reuchlin. On 7 November 1519 the
Louvain faculty, following the example of that of Cologne,
proceeded to take the decisive step: the solemn condemnation
of a number of Luther's opinions. In future no place could be
less suitable to Erasmus than Louvain, the citadel of action
against reformers. It is surprising that he remained there
another two years.

The expectation that he would be able to speak the conciliating word was paling. For the rest he failed to see the true
proportions. During the first months of 1520 his attention was
almost entirely taken up by his own polemics with Lee, a
paltry incident in the great revolution. The desire to keep aloof
got more and more the upper hand of him. In June he writes
to Melanchthon: 'I see that matters begin to look like sedition.
It is perhaps necessary that scandals occur, but I should prefer
not to be the author.' He has, he thinks, by his influence with
Wolsey, prevented the burning of Luther's writings in
England, which had been ordered. But he was mistaken. The
burning had taken place in London, as early as 12 May.

The best proof that Erasmus had practically given up his
hope to play a conciliatory part may be found in what follows.
In the summer of 1520 the famous meeting between the three
monarchs, Henry VIII, Francis I and Charles V, took place
at Calais. Erasmus was to go there in the train of his prince.
How would such a congress of princes—where in peaceful
conclave the interests of France, England, Spain, the German
Empire, and a considerable part of Italy, were represented

together—have affected Erasmus's imagination, if his ideal had remained unshaken! But there are no traces of this. Erasmus was at Calais in July 1520, had some conversation with Henry VIII there, and greeted More, but it does not appear that he attached any other importance to the journey than that of an opportunity, for the last time, to greet his English friends.

It was awkward for Erasmus that just at this time, when the cause of faith took so much harsher forms, his duties as counsellor to the youthful Charles, now back from Spain to be crowned as emperor, circumscribed his liberty more than before. In the summer of 1520 appeared, based on the incriminating material furnished by the Louvain faculty, the papal bull declaring Luther to be a heretic, and, unless he should speedily recant, excommunicating him. 'I fear the worst for the unfortunate Luther,' Erasmus writes, 9 September 1520, 'so does conspiracy rage everywhere, so are princes incensed with him on all sides, and, most of all, Pope Leo. Would Luther had followed my advice and abstained from those hostile and seditious actions! . . . They will not rest until they have quite subverted the study of languages and the good learning. . . . Out of the hatred against these and the stupidity of monks did this tragedy first arise. . . . I do not meddle with it. For the rest, a bishopric is waiting for me if I choose to write against Luther.'

Indeed, Erasmus had become, by virtue of his enormous celebrity, as circumstances would have it, more and more a valuable asset in the great policy of emperor and pope. People wanted to use his name and make him choose sides. And that he would not do for any consideration. He wrote evasively to the Pope about his relations with Luther without altogether disavowing him. How zealously he defends himself from the suspicion of being on Luther's side as noisy monks make out in their sermons, who summarily link the two in their scoffing disparagement.

But by the other side also he is pressed to choose sides and to speak out. Towards the end of October 1520 the coronation of the emperor took place at Aix-la-Chapelle. Erasmus was perhaps present; in any case he accompanied the Emperor to Cologne. There, on 5 November, he had an interview about Luther with the Elector Frederick of Saxony. He was persuaded to write down the result of that discussion in the form of twenty-two *Axiomata concerning Luther's cause.* Against his intention they were printed at once.

Erasmus's hesitation in those days between the repudiation and the approbation of Luther is not discreditable to him. It is the tragic defect running through his whole personality: his refusal or inability ever to draw ultimate conclusions. Had he only been a calculating and selfish nature, afraid of losing his life, he would long since have altogether forsaken Luther's cause. It is his misfortune affecting his fame, that he continually shows his weaknesses, whereas what is great in him lies deep.

At Cologne Erasmus also met the man with whom, as a promising young humanist, fourteen years younger than himself, he had, for some months, shared a room in the house of Aldus's father-in-law, at Venice: Hieronymus Aleander, now sent to the Emperor as a papal nuncio, to persuade him to conform his imperial policy to that of the Pope, in the matter of the great ecclesiastical question, and give effect to the papal excommunication by the imperial ban.

It must have been somewhat painful for Erasmus that his friend had so far surpassed him in power and position, and was now called to bring by diplomatic means the solution which he himself would have liked to see achieved by ideal harmony, good will and toleration. He had never trusted Aleander, and was more than ever on his guard against him. As a humanist, in spite of brilliant gifts, Aleander was by far Erasmus's inferior, and had never, like him, risen from literature to serious theological studies; he had simply prospered in the service of Church magnates (whom Erasmus had given up early). This man was now invested with the highest mediating powers.

To what degree of exasperation Erasmus's most violent antagonists at Louvain had now been reduced is seen from the witty and slightly malicious account he gives Thomas

More of his meeting with Egmondanus before the Rector of the university, who wanted to reconcile them. Still things did not look so black as Ulrich von Hutten thought, when he wrote to Erasmus: 'Do you think that you are still safe, now that Luther's books are burned? Fly, and save yourself for us!'

Ever more emphatic do Erasmus's protestations become that he has nothing to do with Luther. Long ago he had already requested him not to mention his name, and Luther promised it: 'Very well, then, I shall not again refer to you, neither will other good friends, since it troubles you'. Ever louder, too, are Erasmus's complaints about the raving of the monks at him, and his demands that the mendicant orders be deprived of the right to preach.

In April 1521 comes the moment in the world's history to which Christendom has been looking forward: Luther at the Diet of Worms, holding fast to his opinions, confronted by the highest authority in the Empire. So great is the rejoicing in Germany that for a moment it may seem that the Emperor's power is in danger rather than Luther and his adherents. 'If I had been present', writes Erasmus, 'I should have endeavoured that this tragedy would have been so tempered by moderate arguments that it could not afterwards break out again to the still greater detriment of the world.'

The imperial sentence was pronounced: within the Empire (as in the Burgundian Netherlands before that time) Luther's books were to be burned, his adherents arrested and their goods confiscated, and Luther was to be given up to the authorities. Erasmus hopes that now relief will follow. 'The Luther tragedy is at an end with us here; would it had never appeared on the stage.' In these days Albrecht Dürer, on hearing the false news of Luther's death, wrote in the diary of his journey that passionate exclamation: 'O Erasmus of Rotterdam, where will you be? Hear, you knight of Christ, ride forth beside the Lord Christ, protect the truth, obtain the martyr's crown. For you are but an old manikin. I have heard you say that you have allowed yourself two more years, in which you are still fit to do some work; spend them well, in behalf of the Gospel and the true Christian faith. . . . O Erasmus, be on this side, that God may be proud of you.'

It expresses confidence in Erasmus's power, but at bottom is the expectation that he will not do all this. Dürer had rightly understood Erasmus.

The struggle abated nowise, least of all at Louvain. Latomus, the most dignified and able of Louvain divines, had now become one of the most serious opponents of Luther and, in so doing, touched Erasmus, too, indirectly. To Nicholas of Egmond, the Carmelite, another of Erasmus's compatriots had been added as a violent antagonist, Vincent Dirks of Haarlem, a Dominican. Erasmus addresses himself to the faculty, to defend himself against the new attacks, and to explain why he has never written against Luther. He will read him, he will soon take up something to quiet the tumult. He succeeds in getting Aleander, who arrived at Louvain in June, to prohibit preaching against him. The Pope still hopes that Aleander will succeed in bringing back Erasmus, with whom he is again on friendly terms, to the right track.

But Erasmus began to consider the only exit which was now left to him: to leave Louvain and the Netherlands to regain his menaced independence. The occasion to depart had long ago presented itself: the third edition of his New Testament called him to Basle once more. It would not be a permanent departure, and he purposed to return to Louvain. On 28 October (his birthday) he left the town where he had spent four difficult years. His chambers in the College of the Lily were reserved for him and he left his books behind. On 15 November he reached Basle.

Soon the rumour spread that out of fear of Aleander he had saved himself by flight. But the idea, revived again in our days in spite of Erasmus's own painstaking denial, that Aleander should have cunningly and expressly driven him from the Netherlands, is inherently improbable. So far as the Church was concerned, Erasmus would at almost any point be more dangerous than at Louvain, in the headquarters of conservatism, under immediate control of the strict Burgundian government, where, it seemed, he could sooner or later be pressed into the service of the anti-Lutheran policy.

It was this contingency, as Dr. Allen has correctly pointed out, which he feared and evaded. Not for his bodily safety did he emigrate; Erasmus would not have been touched—he was far too valuable an asset for such measures. It was his mental independence, so dear to him above all else, that he felt to be threatened; and, to safeguard that, he did not return to Louvain.

XIX. THE HOUSE AT ANDERLECHT WHERE ERASMUS LIVED FROM MAY TO NOVEMBER 1521

XX. ERASMUS'S STUDY AT ANDERLECHT

CHAPTER XVII

ERASMUS AT BASLE

1521–9

Basle his dwelling-place for nearly eight years: 1521–9 — Political thought of Erasmus — Concord and peace — Anti-war writings — Opinions concerning princes and government — New editions of several Fathers—The Colloquia *— Controversies with Stunica, Beda, etc. — Quarrel with Hutten — Eppendorff*

IT is only towards the evening of life that the picture of Erasmus acquires the features with which it was to go down to posterity. Only at Basle—delivered from the troublesome pressure of parties wanting to enlist him, transplanted from an environment of haters and opponents at Louvain to a circle of friends, kindred spirits, helpers and admirers, emancipated from the courts of princes, independent of the patronage of the great, unremittingly devoting his tremendous energy to the work that was dear to him—did he become Holbein's Erasmus. In those late years he approaches most closely to the ideal of his personal life.

He did not think that there were still fifteen years in store for him. Long before, in fact, since he became forty years old in 1506, Erasmus had been in an old-age mood. 'The last act of the play has begun,' he keeps saying after 1517.

He now felt practically independent as to money matters. Many years had passed before he could say that. But peace of mind did not come with competence. It never came. He never became truly placid and serene, as Holbein's picture seems to represent him. He was always too much concerned about what people said or thought of him. Even at Basle he did not feel thoroughly at home. He still speaks repeatedly of a removal in the near future to Rome, to France, to England, or back to the Netherlands. Physical rest, at any rate, which was not in him, was granted him by circumstances: for nearly eight years he now remained at Basle, and then he lived at Freiburg for six.

Erasmus at Basle is a man whose ideals of the world and society have failed him. What remains of that happy expectation of a golden age of peace and light, in which he had believed as late as 1517? What of his trust in good will and rational insight, in which he wrote the *Institutio Principis Christiani* for the youthful Charles V? To Erasmus all the weal of state and society had always been merely a matter of personal morality and intellectual enlightenment. By recommending and spreading those two he at one time thought he had introduced the great renovation himself. From the moment when he saw that the conflict would lead to an exasperated struggle he refused any longer to be anything but a spectator. As an actor in the great ecclesiastical combat Erasmus had voluntarily left the stage.

But he does not give up his ideal. 'Let us resist,' he concludes an Epistle about gospel philosophy, 'not by taunts and threats, not by force of arms and injustice, but by simple discretion, by benefits, by gentleness and tolerance.' Towards the close of his life, he prays: 'If Thou, O God, deignst to renew that Holy Spirit in the hearts of all, then also will those external disasters cease. . . . Bring order to this chaos, Lord Jesus, let Thy Spirit spread over these waters of sadly troubled dogmas.'

Concord, peace, sense of duty and kindliness, were all valued highly by Erasmus; yet he rarely saw them realized in practical life. He becomes disillusioned. After the short spell of political optimism he never speaks of the times any more but in bitter terms—a most criminal age, he says—and again, the most unhappy and most depraved age imaginable. In vain had he always written in the cause of peace: *Querela pacis*, the complaint of peace, the adage *Dulce bellum inexpertis*, war is sweet to those who have not known it, *Oratio de pace et discordia*, and more still. Erasmus thought rather highly of his pacifistic labours: 'that polygraph, who never leaves off persecuting war by means of his pen', thus he makes a character of the *Colloquies* designate himself. According to a tradition noted by Melanchthon, Pope Julius is said to have called him before him in connection with his advice about the war with

Venice,[1] and to have remarked to him angrily that he should stop writing on the concerns of princes: 'You do not understand those things!'

Erasmus had, in spite of a certain innate moderation, a wholly non-political mind. He lived too much outside of practical reality, and thought too naïvely of the corrigibility of mankind, to realize the difficulties and necessities of government. His ideas about a good administration were extremely primitive, and, as is often the case with scholars of a strong ethical bias, very revolutionary at bottom, though he never dreamed of drawing the practical inferences. His friendship with political and juridical thinkers, as More, Budaeus and Zasius, had not changed him. Questions of forms of government, law or right, did not exist for him. Economic problems he saw in idyllic simplicity. The prince should reign gratuitously and impose as few taxes as possible. 'The good prince has all that loving citizens possess.' The unemployed should be simply driven away. We feel in closer contact with the world of facts when he enumerates the works of peace for the prince: the cleaning of towns, building of bridges, halls, and streets, draining of pools, shifting of river-beds, the diking and reclamation of moors. It is the Netherlander who speaks here, and at the same time the man in whom the need of cleansing and clearing away is a fundamental trait of character.

Vague politicians like Erasmus are prone to judge princes very severely, since they take them to be responsible for all wrongs. Erasmus praises them personally, but condemns them in general. From the kings of his time he had for a long time expected peace in Church and State. They had disappointed him. But his severe judgement of princes he derived rather from classical reading than from political experience of his own times. In the later editions of the *Adagia* he often reverts to princes, their task and their neglect of duty, without ever mentioning special princes. 'There are those who sow the seeds of

[1] Melanchthon, *Opera, Corpus Reformatorum*, XII 266, where he refers to *Querela pacis*, which, however, was not written before 1517; *vide* A. 603 and I p. 37.10.

dissension between their townships in order to fleece the poor unhindered and to satisfy their gluttony by the hunger of innocent citizens.' In the adage *Scarabeus aquilam quaerit* he represents the prince under the image of the Eagle as the great cruel robber and persecutor. In another, *Aut regem aut fatuum nasci oportere*, and in *Dulce bellum inexpertis* he utters his frequently quoted dictum: 'The people found and develop towns, the folly of princes devastates them.' 'The princes conspire with the Pope, and perhaps with the Turk, against the happiness of the people,' he writes to Colet in 1518.

He was an academic critic writing from his study. A revolutionary purpose was as foreign to Erasmus as it was to More when writing the *Utopia*. 'Bad monarchs should perhaps be suffered now and then. The remedy should not be tried.' It may be doubted whether Erasmus exercised much real influence on his contemporaries by means of his diatribes against princes. One would fain believe that his ardent love of peace and bitter arraignment of the madness of war had some effect. They have undoubtedly spread pacific sentiments in the broad circles of intellectuals who read Erasmus, but unfortunately the history of the sixteenth century shows little evidence that such sentiments bore fruit in actual practice. However this may be, Erasmus's strength was not in these political declamations. He could never be a leader of men with their passions and their harsh interests.

His life-work lay elsewhere. Now, at Basle, though tormented more and more frequently by his painful complaint which he had already carried for so many years, he could devote himself more fully than ever before to the great task he had set himself: the opening up of the pure sources of Christianity, the exposition of the truth of the Gospel in all the simple comprehensibility in which he saw it. In a broad stream flowed the editions of the Fathers, of classic authors, the new editions of the New Testament, of the *Adagia*, of his own Letters, together with Paraphrases of the New Testament, Commentaries on Psalms, and a number of new theological, moral and philological treatises. In 1522 he was ill for months on end; yet in that year Arnobius and the third edition of the New Testament succeeded Cyprian, whom he had already annotated at Louvain and edited in 1520, closely followed by Hilary in 1523 and next by a new edition of Jerome in 1524. Later appeared Irenaeus, 1526; Ambrose, 1527; Augustine, 1528–9, and a Latin translation of Chrysostom in 1530. The rapid succession of these comprehensive works proves that the work was done as Erasmus always worked: hastily, with an extraordinary power of concentration and a surprising command of his mnemonic faculty, but without severe criticism and the painful accuracy that modern philology requires in such editions.

Neither the polemical Erasmus nor the witty humorist had been lost in the erudite divine and the disillusioned reformer. The paper-warrior we would further gladly have dispensed with, but not the humorist, for many treasures of literature. But the two are linked inseparably as the *Colloquies* prove.

What was said about the *Moria* may be repeated here: if in the literature of the world only the *Colloquies* and the *Moria* have remained alive, that choice of history is right. Not in the sense that in literature only Erasmus's pleasantest, lightest and most readable works were preserved, whereas the ponderous theological erudition was silently relegated to the shelves of libraries. It was indeed Erasmus's best work that was kept alive in the *Moria* and the *Colloquies*. With these his sparkling wit has charmed the world. If only we had space here to assign to the Erasmus of the *Colloquies* his just and lofty place in that brilliant constellation of sixteenth-century followers of Democritus: Rabelais, Ariosto, Montaigne, Cervantes, and Ben Jonson!

When Erasmus gave the *Colloquies* their definite form at Basle, they had already had a long and curious genesis. At first they had been no more than *Familiarium colloquiorum formu-lae*, models of colloquial Latin conversation, written at Paris before 1500, for the use of his pupils. Augustine Caminade, the shabby friend who was fond of living on young Erasmus's genius, had collected them and had turned them to advantage within a limited compass. He had long been dead when one Lambert Hollonius of Liége sold the manuscript that he had got from Caminade to Froben at Basle. Beatus Rhenanus, although then already Erasmus's trusted friend, had it printed at once without the latter's knowledge. That was in 1518. Erasmus was justly offended at it, the more so as the book was full of slovenly blunders and solecisms. So he at once prepared a better edition himself, published by Maertensz at Louvain in 1519. At that time the work really contained but one true dialogue, the nucleus of the later *Convivium profanum*. The rest were formulae of etiquette and short talks. But already in this form it was, apart from its usefulness to latinists, so full of happy wit and humorous invention that it became very popular. Even before 1522 it had appeared in twenty-five editions, mostly reprints, at Antwerp, Paris, Strassburg, Cologne, Cracow, Deventer, Leipzig, London, Vienna, Mayence.

At Basle Erasmus himself revised an edition which was published in March 1522 by Froben, dedicated to the latter's six-year-old son, the author's godchild, Johannes Erasmius Froben. Soon after he did more than revise. In 1523 and 1524 first ten new dialogues, afterwards four, and again six, were added to the *Formulae*, and at last in 1526 the title was changed to *Familiarium colloquiorum opus*. It remained dedicated to the boy Froben and went on growing with each new edition: a rich and motley collection of dialogues, each a masterpiece of literary form, well-knit, spontaneous, convincing, unsurpassed in lightness, vivacity and fluent Latin; each one a finished one-act play. From that year on, the stream of editions and translations flowed almost uninterruptedly for two centuries.

Erasmus's mind had lost nothing of its acuteness and freshness when, so many years after the *Moria*, he again set foot in the field of satire. As to form, the *Colloquies* are less confessedly satirical than the *Moria*. With its telling subject, the *Praise of Folly*, the latter at once introduces itself as a satire: whereas, at first sight, the *Colloquies* might seem to be mere innocent genre-pieces. But as to the contents, they are more satirical, at least more directly so. The *Moria*, as a satire, is philo-sophical and general; the *Colloquia* are up to date and special. At the same time they combine more the positive and negative elements. In the *Moria* Erasmus's own ideal dwells unexpressed behind the representation; in the *Colloquia* he continually and clearly puts it in the foreground. On this account they form, notwithstanding all the jests and mockery, a profoundly serious moral treatise and are closely akin to the *Enchiridion militis Christiani*. What Erasmus really demanded of the world and of mankind, how he pictured to himself that passionately desired, purified Christian society of good morals, fervent faith, simplicity and moderation, kindliness, toleration and peace—this we can nowhere else find so clearly and well-expressed as in the *Colloquia*. In these last fifteen years of his life Erasmus resumes, by means of a series of moral-dogmatic disquisitions, the topics he broached in the *Enchiridion:* the exposition of simple, general Christian conduct; untram-melled and natural ethics. That is his message of redemption. It came to many out of *Exomologesis, De esu carnium, Lingua, Institutio christiani matrimonii, Vidua christiana, Ecclesiastes*. But, to far larger numbers, the message was contained in the *Colloquies*.

The *Colloquia* gave rise to much more hatred and contest than the *Moria*, and not without reason, for in them Erasmus attacked persons. He allowed himself the pleasure of ridiculing his Louvain antagonists. Lee had already been introduced as a sycophant and braggart into the edition of 1519, and when the quarrel was assuaged, in 1522, the reference was expunged. Vincent Dirks was caricatured in *The Funeral* (1526) as a covetous friar, who extorts from the dying testaments in favour of his order. He remained. Later sarcastic observations were added about Beda and numbers of others. The adherents of Oecolampadius took a figure with a long nose in the *Colloquies* for their leader: 'Oh, no,' replied Erasmus, 'it is meant for quite another person.' Henceforth all those who were at loggerheads with Erasmus, and they were many, ran the risk of being pilloried in the *Colloquia*. It was no wonder that this work, especially with its scourging mockery of the monastic orders, became the object of controversy.

Erasmus never emerged from his polemics. He was, no doubt, serious when he said that, in his heart, he abhorred and had never desired them; but his caustic mind often got the better of his heart, and having once begun to quarrel he undoubtedly enjoyed giving his mockery the rein and wielding his facile dialectic pen. For understanding his personality it is unnecessary here to deal at large with all those fights on paper. Only the most important ones need be mentioned.

Since 1516 a pot had been boiling for Erasmus in Spain. A theologian of the University at Alcalá, Diego Lopez Zuñiga, or, in Latin, Stunica, had been preparing Annotations to the edition of the New Testament: 'a second Lee', said Erasmus. At first Cardinal Ximenes had prohibited the publication, but in 1520, after his death, the storm broke. For some years Stunica kept persecuting Erasmus with his criticism, to the latter's great vexation; at last there followed a *rapprochement*, probably as Erasmus became more conservative, and a kindly attitude on the part of Stunica.

No less long and violent was the quarrel with the syndic of the Sorbonne, Noël Bedier or Beda, which began in 1522. The Sorbonne was prevailed upon to condemn several of Erasmus's dicta as heretical in 1526. The effort of Beda to implicate Erasmus in the trial of Louis de Berquin, who had translated the condemned writings and who was eventually burned at the stake for faith's sake in 1529, made the matter still more disagreeable for Erasmus.

It is clear enough that both at Paris and at Louvain in the circles of the theological faculties the chief cause of exasperation was in the *Colloquia*. Egmondanus and Vincent Dirks did not forgive Erasmus for having acridly censured their station and their personalities.

More courteous than the aforementioned polemics was the fight with a high-born Italian, Alberto Pio, prince of Carpi;

AETHERNA IPSE SVAE MENTIS SIMVLACHRA LVTHERVS
EXPRIMIT·AT VVLTVS CERA LVCAE OCCIDVOS·

·M·D·X·X·

XXI. MARTIN LUTHER AS A MONK

XXII. ULRICH VON HUTTEN

acrid and bitter was one with a group of Spanish monks, who brought the Inquisition to bear upon him. In Spain 'Erasmistas' was the name of those who inclined to more liberal conceptions of the creed.

In this way the matter accumulated for the volume of Erasmus's works which contains, according to his own arrangement, all his *Apologiae*: not 'excuses', but 'vindications'. 'Miserable man that I am; they just fill a volume,' exclaimed Erasmus.

Two of his polemics merit a somewhat closer examination: that with Ulrich von Hutten and that with Luther.

Hutten, knight and humanist, the enthusiastic herald of a national German uplift, the ardent hater of papacy and supporter of Luther, was certainly a hot-head and perhaps somewhat of a muddle-head. He had applauded Erasmus when the latter still seemed to be the coming man and had afterwards besought him to take Luther's side. Erasmus had soon discovered that this noisy partisan might compromise him. Had not one of Hutten's rash satires been ascribed to him, Erasmus? There came a time when Hutten could no longer abide Erasmus. His knightly instinct reacted on the very weaknesses of Erasmus's character: the fear of committing himself and the inclination to repudiate a supporter in time of danger. Erasmus knew that weakness himself: 'Not all have strength enough for martyrdom,' he writes to Richard Pace in 1521. 'I fear that I shall, in case it results in a tumult, follow St. Peter's example.' But this acknowledgement does not discharge him from the burden of Hutten's reproaches which he flung at him in fiery language in 1523. In this quarrel Erasmus's own fame pays the penalty of his fault. For nowhere does he show himself so undignified and puny as in that 'Sponge against Hutten's mire', which the latter did not live to read. Hutten, disillusioned and forsaken, died at an early age in 1523, and Erasmus did not scruple to publish the venomous pamphlet against his former friend after his demise.

Hutten, however, was avenged upon Erasmus living. One of his adherents, Henry of Eppendorff, inherited Hutten's bitter disgust with Erasmus and persecuted him for years. Getting hold of one of Erasmus's letters in which he was denounced, he continually threatened him with an action for defamation of character. Eppendorff's hostility so thoroughly exasperated Erasmus that he fancied he could detect his machinations and spies everywhere even after the actual persecution had long ceased.

CHAPTER XVIII

CONTROVERSY WITH LUTHER AND
GROWING CONSERVATISM
1524–6

*Erasmus persuaded to write against Luther—De Libero Arbitrio: 1524 —
Luther's answer:* De Servo Arbitrio *—Erasmus's indefiniteness contrasted
with Luther's extreme rigour—Erasmus henceforth on the side of conservatism—The Bishop of Basle and Oecolampadius—Erasmus's half-
hearted dogmatics: confession, ceremonies, worship of the Saints, Eucharist —*
Institutio Christiani Matrimonii: *1526—He feels surrounded by enemies*

AT length Erasmus was led, in spite of all, to do what he had
always tried to avoid: he wrote against Luther. But it did not
in the least resemble the *geste* Erasmus at one time contemplated, in the cause of peace in Christendom and uniformity
of faith, to call a halt to the impetuous Luther, and thereby to
recall the world to its senses. In the great act of the Reformation their polemics were merely an after-play. Not Erasmus
alone was disillusioned and tired—Luther too was past his
heroic prime, circumscribed by conditions, forced into the
world of affairs, a disappointed man.

Erasmus had wished to persevere in his resolution to remain
a spectator of the great tragedy. 'If, as appears from the
wonderful success of Luther's cause, God wills all this'—thus
did Erasmus reason—'and He has perhaps judged such a
drastic surgeon as Luther necessary for the corruption of
these times, then it is not my business to withstand him.' But
he was not left in peace. While he went on protesting that he
had nothing to do with Luther and differed widely from him,
the defenders of the old Church adhered to the standpoint
urged as early as 1520 by Nicholas of Egmond before the
rector of Louvain: 'So long as he refuses to write against
Luther, we take him to be a Lutheran'. So matters stood.
'That you are looked upon as a Lutheran here is certain,'
Vives writes to him from the Netherlands in 1522.

Ever stronger became the pressure to write against Luther. From Henry VIII came a call, communicated by Erasmus's old friend Tunstall, from George of Saxony, from Rome itself, whence Pope Adrian VI, his old patron, had urged him shortly before his death.

Erasmus thought he could refuse no longer. He tried some dialogues in the style of the *Colloquies*, but did not get on with them; and probably they would not have pleased those who were desirous of enlisting his services. Between Luther and Erasmus himself there had been no personal correspondence, since the former had promised him, in 1520: 'Well then, Erasmus, I shall not mention your name again.' Now that Erasmus had prepared to attack Luther, however, there came an epistle from the latter, written on 15 April 1524, in which the reformer, in his turn, requested Erasmus in his own words: 'Please remain now what you have always professed yourself desirous of being: a mere spectator of our tragedy'. There is a ring of ironical contempt in Luther's words, but Erasmus called the letter 'rather humane; I had not the courage to reply with equal humanity, because of the sycophants'.

In order to be able to combat Luther with a clear conscience Erasmus had naturally to choose a point on which he differed from Luther in his heart. It was not one of the more superficial parts of the Church's structure. For these he either, with Luther, cordially rejected, such as ceremonies, observances, fasting, etc., or, though more moderately than Luther, he had his doubts about them, as the sacraments or the primacy of St. Peter. So he naturally came to the point where the deepest gulf yawned between their natures, between their conceptions of the essence of faith, and thus to the central and eternal problem of good and evil, guilt and compulsion, liberty and bondage, God and man. Luther confessed in his reply that here indeed the vital point had been touched.

De libero arbitrio diatribe (*A Disquisition upon Free Will*) appeared in September 1524. Was Erasmus qualified to write about such a subject? In conformity with his method and with his evident purpose to vindicate authority and tradition, this time, Erasmus developed the argument that Scripture teaches, doctors affirm, philosophers prove, and human reason testifies man's will to be free. Without acknowledgement of free will the terms of God's justice and God's mercy remain without meaning. What would be the sense of the teachings, reproofs, admonitions of Scripture (Timothy iii.) if all happened according to mere and inevitable necessity? To what purpose is obedience praised, if for good and evil works we are equally but tools to God, as the hatchet to the carpenter? And if this were so, it would be dangerous to reveal such a doctrine to the multitude, for morality is dependent on the consciousness of freedom.

Luther received the treatise of his antagonist with disgust and contempt. In writing his reply, however, he suppressed these feelings outwardly and observed the rules of courtesy. But his inward anger is revealed in the contents itself of *De servo arbitrio* (*On the Will not free*). For here he really did what Erasmus had just reproached him with—trying to heal a dislocated member by tugging at it in the opposite direction. More fiercely than ever before, his formidable boorish mind drew the startling inferences of his burning faith. Without any reserve he now accepted all the extremes of absolute determinism. In order to confute indeterminism in explicit terms, he was now forced to have recourse to those primitive metaphors of exalted faith striving to express the inexpressible: God's two wills, which do not coincide, God's 'eternal hatred of mankind, a hatred not only on account of demerits and the works of free will, but a hatred that existed even before the world was created', and that metaphor of the human will, which, as a riding beast, stands in the middle between God and the devil and which is mounted by one or the other without being able to move towards either of the two contending riders. If anywhere, Luther's doctrine in *De Servo Arbitrio* means a recrudescence of faith and a straining of religious conceptions.

But it was Luther who here stood on the rockbed of a profound and mystic faith in which the absolute conscience of the eternal pervades all. In him all conceptions, like dry straw, were consumed in the glow of God's majesty, for him each human co-operation to attain to salvation was a profanation of God's glory. Erasmus's mind after all did not truly *live* in the ideas which were here disputed, of sin and grace, of redemption and the glory of God as the final cause of all that is.

Was, then, Erasmus's cause in all respects inferior? Was Luther right at the core? Perhaps. Dr. Murray rightly reminds us of Hegel's saying that tragedy is not the conflict between right and wrong, but the conflict between right and right. The combat of Luther and Erasmus proceeded beyond the point at which our judgement is forced to halt and has to accept an equivalence, nay, a compatibility of affirmation and negation. And this fact, that they here were fighting with words and metaphors in a sphere beyond that of what may be known and expressed, was understood by Erasmus. Erasmus, the man of the fine shades, for whom ideas eternally blended into each other and interchanged, called a Proteus by Luther; Luther the man of over-emphatic expression about all matters. The Dutchman, who sees the sea, was opposed to the German, who looks out on mountain tops.

'This is quite true that we cannot speak of God but with inadequate words.' 'Many problems should be deferred, not to the oecumenical Council, but till the time when, the glass and the darkness having been taken away, we shall see God face to face.' 'What is free of error?' 'There are in sacred literature certain sanctuaries into which God has not willed that we should penetrate further.'

The Catholic Church had on the point of free will reserved to itself some slight proviso, left a little elbow-room to the consciousness of human liberty *under* grace. Erasmus conceived that liberty in a considerably broader spirit. Luther absolutely denied it. The opinion of contemporaries was at first too much dominated by their participation in the great struggle as such: they applauded Erasmus, because he struck boldly at Luther, or the other way about, according to their sympathies. Not only Vives applauded Erasmus, but also more orthodox Catholics such as Sadolet. The German humanists, unwilling, for the most part, to break with the ancient Church, were moved by Erasmus's attack to turn their backs still more upon Luther: Mutianus, Zasius, and Pirckheimer. Even Melanchthon inclined to Erasmus's standpoint. Others, like Capito, once a zealous supporter, now washed their hands of him. Soon Calvin with the iron cogency of his argument was completely to take Luther's side.

It is worth while to quote the opinion of a contemporary Catholic scholar about the relations of Erasmus and Luther. 'Erasmus,' says F. X. Kiefl,[1] 'with his concept of free, unspoiled human nature was intrinsically much more foreign to the Church than Luther. He only combated it, however, with haughty scepticism: for which reason Luther with subtle psychology upbraided him for liking to speak of the shortcomings and the misery of the Church of Christ in such a way that his readers could not help laughing, instead of bringing his charges, with deep sighs, as beseemed before God.'

The *Hyperaspistes*, a voluminous treatise in which Erasmus again addressed Luther, was nothing but an epilogue, which need not be discussed here at length.

Erasmus had thus, at last, openly taken sides. For, apart from the dogmatical point at issue itself, the most important part about *De libero arbitrio* was that in it he had expressly turned against the individual religious conceptions and had spoken in favour of the authority and tradition of the Church. He always regarded himself as a Catholic. 'Neither death nor life shall draw me from the communion of the Catholic Church,' he writes in 1522, and in the *Hyperaspistes* in 1526: 'I have never been an apostate from the Catholic Church. I know that in this Church, which you call the Papist Church, there are many who displease me, but such I also see in your Church. One bears more easily the evils to which one is accustomed. Therefore I bear with this Church, until I shall see a better, and it cannot help bearing with me, until I shall myself be better. And he does not sail badly who steers a middle course between two several evils.'

[1] *Luther's religiöse Psyche*, Hochland XV, 1917, p. 21.

But was it possible to keep to that course? On either side people turned away from him. 'I who, formerly, in countless letters was addressed as thrice great hero, Prince of letters, Sun of studies, Maintainer of true theology, am now ignored, or represented in quite different colours,' he writes. How many of his old friends and congenial spirits had already gone!

A sufficient number remained, however, who thought and hoped as Erasmus did. His untiring pen still continued to propagate, especially by means of his letters, the moderating and purifying influence of his mind throughout all the countries of Europe. Scholars, high church dignitaries, nobles, students, and civil magistrates were his correspondents. The Bishop of Basle himself, Christopher of Utenheim, was a man after Erasmus's heart. A zealous advocate of humanism, he had attempted, as early as 1503, to reform the clergy of his bishopric by means of synodal statutes, without much success; afterwards he had called scholars like Oecolampadius, Capito and Wimpfeling to Basle. That was before the great struggle began, which was soon to carry away Oecolampadius and Capito much further than the Bishop of Basle or Erasmus approved. In 1522 Erasmus addressed the bishop in a treatise *De interdicto esu carnium* (*On the Prohibition of eating Meat*). This was one of the last occasions on which he directly opposed the established order.

The bishop, however, could no longer control the movement. A considerable number of the commonalty of Basle and the majority of the council, were already on the side of radical Reformation. About a year after Erasmus, Johannes Oecolampadius, whose first residence at Basle had also coincided with his (at that time he had helped Erasmus with Hebrew for the edition of the New Testament), returned to the town with the intention of organizing the resistance to the old order there. In 1523 the council appointed him professor of Holy Scripture in the University; at the same time four Catholic professors lost their places. He succeeded in obtaining general permission for unlicensed preaching. Soon a far more hot-headed agitator, the impetuous Guillaume Farel, also arrived for active work at Basle and in the environs. He is the man who will afterwards reform Geneva and persuade Calvin to stay there.

Though at first Oecolampadius began to introduce novelties into the church service with caution, Erasmus saw these innovations with alarm. Especially the fanaticism of Farel, whom he hated bitterly. It was these men who retarded what he still desired and thought possible: a compromise. His lambent spirit, which never fully decided in favour of a definite opinion, had, with regard to most of the disputed points, gradually fixed on a half-conservative midway standpoint, by means of which, without denying his deepest conviction, he tried to remain faithful to the Church. In 1524 he had expressed his sentiments about confession in the treatise *Exomologesis* (*On the Way to confess*). He accepts it halfway: if not instituted by Christ or the Apostles, it was, in any case, by the Fathers. It should be piously preserved. Confession is of excellent use, though, at times, a great evil. In this way he tries 'to admonish either party', 'neither to agree with nor to assail' the deniers, 'though inclining to the side of the believers'.

In the long list of his polemics he gradually finds opportunities to define his views somewhat; circumstantially, for instance, in the answers to Alberto Pio, of 1525 and 1529. Subsequently it is always done in the form of an *Apologia*, whether he is attacked for the *Colloquia*, for the *Moria*, Jerome, the *Paraphrases* or anything else. At last he recapitulates his views to some extent in *De amabili Ecclesiae concordia* (*On the Amiable Concord of the Church*), of 1533, which, however, ranks hardly any more among his reformatory endeavours.

On most points Erasmus succeeds in finding moderate and conservative formulae. Even with regard to ceremonies he no longer merely rejects. He finds a kind word to say even for fasting, which he had always abhorred, for the veneration of relics and for Church festivals. He does not want to abolish the worship of the Saints: it no longer entails danger of idolatry. He is even willing to admit the images: 'He who takes the imagery out of life deprives it of its highest pleasure; we often discern more in images than we conceive from the written word'. Regarding Christ's substantial presence in the sacrament of the altar he holds fast to the Catholic view, but without fervour, only on the ground of the Church's consensus, and because he cannot believe that Christ, who is truth and love, would have suffered His bride to cling so long to so horrid an error as to worship a crust of bread instead of Him. But for these reasons he might, at need, accept Oecolampadius's view.

From the period at Basle dates one of the purest and most beneficent moral treatises of Erasmus's, the *Institutio Christiani matrimonii* (*On Christian Marriage*) of 1526, written for Catherine of Aragon, Queen of England, quite in the spirit of the *Enchiridion*, save for a certain diffuseness betraying old age. Later follows *De vidua Christiana*, *The Christian Widow*, for Mary of Hungary, which is as impeccable but less interesting.

All this did not disarm the defenders of the old Church. They held fast to the clear picture of Erasmus's creed that arose from the *Colloquies* and that could not be called purely Catholic. There it appeared only too clearly that, however much Erasmus might desire to leave the letter intact, his heart was not in the convictions which were vital to the Catholic Church. Consequently the *Colloquies* were later, when Erasmus's works were expurgated, placed on the index in the lump, with the *Moria* and a few other works. The rest is *caute legenda*, to be read with caution. Much was rejected of the Annotations to the New Testament, of the *Paraphrases* and the *Apologiae*, very little of the *Enchiridion*, of the *Ratio verae theologiae*, and even of the *Exomologesis*. But this was after the fight against the living Erasmus had long been over.

So long as he remained at Basle, or elsewhere, as the centre of a large intellectual group whose force could not be estimated, just because it did not stand out as a party—it was not known what turn he might yet take, what influence his mind might yet have on the Church. He remained a king of minds in his quiet study. The hatred that was felt for him, the watching of all his words and actions, were of a nature as only falls to the lot of the acknowledged great. The chorus of enemies who laid the fault of the whole Reformation on Erasmus was not silenced. 'He laid the eggs which Luther and Zwingli have hatched.' With vexation Erasmus quoted ever new specimens of narrow-minded, malicious and stupid controversy. At Constance there lived a doctor who had hung his portrait on the wall merely to spit at it as often as he passed it. Erasmus jestingly compares his fate to that of Saint Cassianus, who was stabbed to death by his pupils with pencils. Had he not been pierced to the quick for many years by the pens and tongues of countless people and did he not live in that torment without death bringing the end? The keen sensitiveness to opposition was seated very deeply with Erasmus. And he could never forbear irritating others into opposing him.

CHAPTER XIX

AT WAR WITH HUMANISTS AND REFORMERS

1528–9

Erasmus turns against the excesses of humanism: its paganism and pedantic classicism—Ciceronianus: *1528—It brings him new enemies—The Reformation carried through at Basle—He emigrates to Freiburg: 1529 — His view concerning the results of the Reformation*

NOTHING is more characteristic of the independence which Erasmus reserved for himself regarding all movements of his time than the fact that he also joined issue in the camp of the humanists. In 1528 there were published by Froben (the chief of the firm of Johannes Froben had just died) two dialogues in one volume from Erasmus's hand: one about the correct pronunciation of Latin and Greek, and one entitled *Ciceronianus* or *On the Best Diction*, i.e. in writing and speaking Latin. Both were proofs that Erasmus had lost nothing of his liveliness and wit. The former treatise was purely philological, and as such has had great influence; the other was satirical as well. It had a long history.

Erasmus had always regarded classical studies as the panacea of civilization, provided they were made serviceable to pure Christianity. His sincere ethical feeling made him recoil from the obscenity of a Poggio and the immorality of the early Italian humanists. At the same time his delicate and natural taste told him that a pedantic and servile imitation of antique models could never produce the desired result. Erasmus knew Latin too well to be strictly classical; his Latin was alive and required freedom. In his early works we find taunts about the over-precise Latin purists: one had declared a newly found fragment of Cicero to be thoroughly barbaric; 'among all sorts of authors none are so insufferable to me as those apes of Cicero'.

In spite of the great expectations he cherished of classical studies for pure Christianity, he saw one danger: 'that under the cloak of reviving ancient literature paganism tries to rear its head, as there are those among Christians who acknowledge Christ only in name but inwardly breathe heathenism'. This he writes in 1517 to Capito. In Italy scholars devote themselves too exclusively and in too pagan guise to *bonae literae*. He considered it his special task to assist in bringing it about that those *bonae literae* 'which with the Italians have thus far been almost pagan, shall get used to speaking of Christ'.

How it must have vexed Erasmus that in Italy of all countries he was, at the same time and in one breath, charged with heresy and questioned in respect to his knowledge and integrity as a scholar. Italians accused him of plagiarism and trickery. He complained of it to Aleander, who, he thought, had a hand in it.

In a letter of 13 October 1527, to a professor at Toledo, we find the *ébauche* of the *Ciceronianus*. In addition to the haters of classic studies for the sake of orthodox belief, writes Erasmus, 'lately another and new sort of enemies has broken from their ambush. These are troubled that the *bonae literae* speak of Christ, as though nothing can be elegant but what is pagan. To their ears *Jupiter optimus maximus* sounds more pleasant than *Jesus Christus redemptor mundi*, and *patres conscripti* more agreeable than *sancti apostoli*. . . . They account it a greater dishonour to be no Ciceronian than no Christian, as if Cicero, if he should now come to life again, would not speak of Christian things in other words than in his time he spoke of his own religion! . . . What is the sense of this hateful swaggering with the name Ciceronian? I will tell you briefly, in your ear. With that pearl-powder they cover the paganism that is dearer to them than the glory of Christ.' To Erasmus Cicero's style is by no means the ideal one. He prefers something more solid, succinct, vigorous, less polished, more manly. He who sometimes has to write a book in a day has no time to polish his style, often not even to read it over. . . . 'What do I care for an empty dish of words, ten words here and there mumped from Cicero: I want all Cicero's spirit.' These are apes at whom one may laugh, for far more serious than these things are the tumults of the so-called new Gospel, to which he next proceeds in this letter.

And so, in the midst of all his polemics and bitter vindication, he allowed himself once more the pleasure of giving the reins to his love of scoffing, but, as in the *Moria* and *Colloquia*, ennobled by an almost passionate sincerity of Christian disposition and a natural sense of measure. The *Ciceronianus* is a masterpiece of ready, many-sided knowledge, of convincing eloquence, and of easy handling of a wealth of arguments. With splendid, quiet and yet lively breadth flows the long conversation between Bulephorus, representing Erasmus's opinions, Hypologus, the interested inquirer, and Nosoponus, the zealous Ciceronian, who, to preserve a perfect purity of mind, breakfasts off ten currants.

Erasmus in drawing Nosoponus had evidently, in the main, alluded to one who could no longer reply: Christopher Longolius, who had died in 1522.

The core of the *Ciceronianus* is where Erasmus points out the danger to Christian faith of a too zealous classicism. He exclaims urgently: 'It is paganism, believe me, Nosoponus, it is paganism that charms our ear and our soul in such things. We are Christians in name alone.' Why does a classic proverb sound better to us than a quotation from the Bible: *corchorum inter olera*, 'chick-weed among the vegetables', better than 'Saul among the prophets'? As a sample of the absurdity of Ciceronianism, he gives a translation of a dogmatic sentence in classical language: 'Optimi maximique Jovis interpres ac filius, servator, rex, juxta vatum responsa, ex Olympo devolavit in terras,' for: Jesus Christ, the Word and the Son of the eternal Father, came into the world according to the prophets. Most humanists wrote indeed in that style.

Was Erasmus aware that he here attacked his own past? After all, was it not exactly the same thing which he had done, to the indignation of his opponents, when translating *Logos* by *Sermo* instead of by *Verbum*? Had he not himself desired that in the church hymns the metre should be corrected, not to mention his own classical odes and paeans to Mary and the

Saints? And was his warning against the partiality for classic proverbs and turns applicable to anything more than to the *Adagia*?

We here see the aged Erasmus on the path of reaction, which might eventually have led him far from humanism. In his combat with humanistic purism he foreshadows a Christian puritanism.

As always his mockery procured him a new flood of invectives. Bembo and Sadolet, the masters of pure Latin, could afford to smile at it, but the impetuous Julius Caesar Scaliger violently inveighed against him, especially to avenge Longolius's memory. Erasmus's perpetual feeling of being persecuted got fresh food: he again thought that Aleander was at the bottom of it. 'The Italians set the imperial court against me,' he writes in 1530. A year later all is quiet again. He writes jestingly: 'Upon my word, I am going to change my style after Budaeus's model and to become a Ciceronian according to the example of Sadolet and Bembo'. But even near the close of his life he was engaged in a new contest with Italians, because he had hurt their national pride; 'they rage at me on all sides with slanderous libels, as at the enemy of Italy and Cicero'.

There were, as he had said himself, other difficulties touching him more closely. Conditions at Basle had for years been developing in a direction which distressed and alarmed him. When he established himself there in 1521, it might still have seemed to him as if the bishop, old Christopher of Utenheim, a great admirer of Erasmus and a man after his heart, would succeed in effecting a reformation at Basle, as he desired it; abolishing acknowledged abuses, but remaining within the fold of the Church. In that very year, 1521, however, the emancipation of the municipality from the bishop's power—it had been in progress since Basle, in 1501, had joined the Swiss Confederacy—was consummated. Henceforth the council was number one, now no longer exclusively made up of aristocratic elements. In vain did the bishop ally himself with his colleagues of Constance and Lausanne to maintain

Catholicism. In the town the new creed got more and more the upper hand. When, however, in 1525, it had come to open tumults against the Catholic service, the council became more cautious and tried to reform more heedfully.

Oecolampadius desired this, too. Relations between him and Erasmus were precarious. Erasmus himself had at one time directed the religious thought of the impulsive, sensitive, restless young man. When he had, in 1520, suddenly sought refuge in a convent, he had expressly justified that step towards Erasmus, the condemner of binding vows. And now they saw each other again at Basle, in 1522: Oecolampadius having left the monastery, a convinced adherent and apostle of the new doctrine; Erasmus, the great spectator which he wished to be. Erasmus treated his old coadjutor coolly, and as the latter progressed, retreated more and more. Yet he kept steering a middle course and in 1525 gave some moderate advice to the council, which meanwhile had turned more Catholic again.

The old bishop, who for some years had no longer resided in his town, in 1527 requested the chapter to relieve him of his office, and died shortly afterwards. Then events moved very quickly. After Berne had, meanwhile, reformed itself in 1528, Oecolampadius demanded a decision also for Basle. Since the close of 1528 the town had been on the verge of civil war. A popular rising put an end to the resistance of the Council and cleared it of Catholic members; and in February 1529 the old service was prohibited, the images were removed from the churches, the convents abolished, and the University suspended. Oecolampadius became the first minister in the 'Münster' and leader of the Basle church, for which he soon drew up a reformatory ordinance. The new bishop remained at Porrentruy, and the chapter removed to Freiburg.

The moment of departure had now come for Erasmus. His position at Basle in 1529 somewhat resembled, but in a reversed sense, the one at Louvain in 1521. Then the Catholics wanted to avail themselves of his services against Luther, now the Evangelicals would fain have kept him at Basle. For his

XXIII. ERASMUS'S RESIDENCE AT FREIBURG, 1529-31

XXIV. CARDINAL JEROME ALEANDER

name was still as a banner. His presence would strengthen the position of reformed Basle; on the one hand, because, as people reasoned, if he were not of the same mind as the reformers, he would have left the town long ago; on the other hand, because his figure seemed to guarantee moderation and might attract many hesitating minds.

It was, therefore, again to safeguard his independence that Erasmus changed his residence. It was a great wrench this time. Old age and invalidism had made the restless man a stay-at-home. As he foresaw trouble from the side of the municipality, he asked Archduke Ferdinand—who for his brother Charles V governed the German empire and just then presided over the Diet of Speyer—to send him a safe conduct for the whole empire and an invitation, moreover, to come to court, which he did not dream of accepting. As place of refuge he had selected the not far distant town of Freiburg im Breisgau, which was directly under the strict government of the Austrian house, and where he, therefore, need not be afraid of such a turn of affairs as that at Basle. It was, moreover, a juncture at which the imperial authority and the Catholic cause in Germany seemed again to be gaining ground rapidly.

Erasmus would not or could not keep his departure a secret. He sent the most precious of his possessions in advance, and when this had drawn attention to his plan, he purposely invited Oecolampadius to a farewell talk. The reformer declared his sincere friendship for Erasmus, which the latter did not decline, provided he granted him to differ on certain points of dogma. Oecolampadius tried to keep him from leaving the town, and, when it proved too late for that, to persuade him to return later. They took leave with a handshake. Erasmus had desired to join his boat at a distant landing-stage, but the Council would not allow this: he had to start from the usual place near the Rhine bridge. A numerous crowd witnessed his embarkation, 13 April 1529. Some friends were there to see him off. No unfavourable demonstration occurred.

His reception at Freiburg convinced him that, in spite of all, he was still the celebrated and admired prince of letters. The

Council placed at his disposal the large, though unfinished, house built for the Emperor Maximilian himself; a professor of theology offered him his garden. Anthony Fugger had tried to draw him to Augsburg by means of a yearly allowance. For the rest he considered Freiburg by no means a permanent place of abode. 'I have resolved to remain here this winter and then to fly with the swallows to the place whither God shall call me.' But he soon recognized the great advantage which Freiburg offered. The climate, to which he was so sensitive, turned out better than he expected, and the position of the town was extremely favourable for emigrating to France, should circumstances require this, or for dropping down the Rhine back to the Netherlands, whither many always called him. In 1531 he bought a house at Freiburg.

The old Erasmus at Freiburg, ever more tormented by his painful malady, much more disillusioned than when he left Louvain in 1521, of more confirmed views as to the great ecclesiastical strife, will only be fully revealed to us when his correspondence with Boniface Amerbach, the friend whom he left behind at Basle—a correspondence not found complete in the older collections—has been edited by Dr. Allen's care. From no period of Erasmus's life, it seems, may so much be gleaned, in point of knowledge of his daily habits and thoughts, as from these very years. Work went on without a break in that great scholar's workshop where he directs his famuli, who hunt manuscripts for him, and then copy and examine them, and whence he sends forth his letters all over Europe. In the series of editions of the Fathers followed Basil and new editions of Chrysostom and Cyprian; his editions of classic authors were augmented by the works of Aristotle. He revised and republished the *Colloquies* three more times, the *Adages* and the New Testament once more. Occasional writings of a moral or politico-theological nature kept flowing from his pen.

From the cause of the Reformation he was now quite estranged. 'Pseudevangelici', he contumeliously calls the reformed. 'I might have been a corypheus in Luther's church,' he writes in 1528, 'but I preferred to incur the hatred of all Germany to being separate from the community of the Church.' The authorities should have paid a little less attention at first to Luther's proceedings; then the fire would never have spread so violently. He had always urged theologians to let minor concerns which only contain an appearance of piety rest, and to turn to the sources of Scripture. Now it was too late. Towns and countries united ever more closely for or against the Reformation. 'If, what I pray may never happen,' he writes to Sadolet in 1530, 'you should see horrible commotions of the world arise, not so fatal for Germany as for the Church, then remember Erasmus prophesied it.' To Beatus Rhenanus he frequently said that, had he known that an age like theirs was coming, he would never have written many things, or would not have written them as he had.

'Just look,' he exclaims, 'at the Evangelical people, have they become any better? Do they yield less to luxury, lust and greed? Show me a man whom that Gospel has changed from a toper to a temperate man, from a brute to a gentle creature, from a miser into a liberal person, from a shameless to a chaste being. I will show you many who have become even worse than they were.' Now they have thrown the images out of the churches and abolished mass (he is thinking of Basle especially): has anything better come instead? 'I have never entered their churches, but I have seen them return from hearing the sermon, as if inspired by an evil spirit, the faces of all showing a curious wrath and ferocity, and there was no one except one old man who saluted me properly, when I passed in the company of some distinguished persons.'

He hated that spirit of absolute assuredness so inseparably bound up with the reformers. 'Zwingli and Bucer may be inspired by the Spirit, Erasmus from himself is nothing but a man and cannot comprehend what is of the Spirit.'

There was a group among the reformed to whom Erasmus in his heart of hearts was more nearly akin than to the Lutherans or Zwinglians with their rigid dogmatism: the Anabaptists. He rejected the doctrine from which they derived their name, and abhorred the anarchic element in them. He remained far too much the man of spiritual decorum to identify himself with these irregular believers. But he was not blind to the sincerity of their moral aspirations and sympathized with their dislike of brute force and the patience with which they bore persecution. 'They are praised more than all others for the innocence of their life,' he writes in 1529. Just in the last part of his life came the episode of the violent revolutionary proceedings of the fanatic Anabaptists; it goes without saying that Erasmus speaks of it only with horror.

One of the best historians of the Reformation, Walter Köhler, calls Erasmus one of the spiritual fathers of Anabaptism. And certain it is that in its later, peaceful development it has important traits in common with Erasmus: a tendency to acknowledge free will, a certain rationalistic trend, a dislike of an exclusive conception of a Church. It seems possible to prove that the South German Anabaptist Hans Denk derived opinions directly from Erasmus. For a considerable part, however, this community of ideas must, no doubt, have been based on peculiarities of religious consciousness in the Netherlands, whence Erasmus sprang, and where Anabaptism found such a receptive soil. Erasmus was certainly never aware of these connections.

Some remarkable evidence regarding Erasmus's altered attitude towards the old and the new Church is shown by what follows.

The reproach he had formerly so often flung at the advocates of conservatism that they hated the *bonae literae*, so dear to him, and wanted to stifle them, he now uses against the evangelical party. 'Wherever Lutherism is dominant the study of literature is extinguished. Why else,' he continues, using a remarkable sophism, 'are Luther and Melanchthon compelled to call back the people so urgently to the love of letters?' 'Just compare the University of Wittenberg with that of Louvain or Paris! . . . Printers say that before this Gospel came they used to dispose of 3,000 volumes more quickly than now of 600. A sure proof that studies flourish!'

CHAPTER XX

LAST YEARS

Religious and political contrasts grow sharper—The coming strife in Germany still suspended—Erasmus finishes his Ecclesiastes*—Death of Fisher and More—Erasmus back at Basle: 1535—Pope Paul III wants to make him write in favour of the cause of the Council—Favours declined by Erasmus—De* Puritate Ecclesiae*—The end: 12 July 1536*

DURING the last years of Erasmus's life all the great issues which kept the world in suspense were rapidly taking threatening forms. Wherever compromise or reunion had before still seemed possible, sharp conflicts, clearly outlined party-groupings, binding formulae were now barring the way to peace. While in the spring of 1529 Erasmus prepared for his departure from Basle, a strong Catholic majority of the Diet at Speyer got the 'recess' of 1526, favourable for the Evangelicals, revoked, only the Lutherans among them keeping what they had obtained; and secured a prohibition of any further changes or novelties. The Zwinglians and Anabaptists were not allowed to enjoy the least tolerance. This was immediately followed by the Protest of the chief evangelical princes and towns, which henceforth was to give the name to all anti-Catholics together (19 April 1529). And not only between Catholics and Protestants in the Empire did the rupture become complete. Even before the end of that year the question of the Lord's supper proved an insuperable stumbling-block in the way of a real union of Zwinglians and Lutherans. Luther parted from Zwingli at the colloquy of Marburg with the words, 'Your spirit differs from ours'.

In Switzerland civil war had openly broken out between the Catholic and the Evangelical cantons, only calmed for a short time by the first peace of Kappel. The treaties of Cambray and Barcelona, which in 1529 restored at least political peace in Christendom for the time being, could no longer draw from old Erasmus jubilations about a coming golden age, like those with which the concord of 1516 had inspired him. A month later the Turks appeared before Vienna.

All these occurrences could not but distress and alarm Erasmus. But he was outside them. When reading his letters of that period we are more than ever impressed by the fact that, for all the width and liveliness of his mind, he is remote from the great happenings of his time. Beyond a certain circle of interests, touching his own ideas or his person, his perceptions are vague and weak. If he still meddles occasionally with questions of the day, he does so in the moralizing manner, by means of generalities, without emphasis: his 'Advice about declaring war on the Turks' (March 1530) is written in the form of an interpretation of Psalm 28, and so vague that, at the close, he himself anticipates that the reader may exclaim: 'But now say clearly: do you think that war should be declared or not?'

In the summer of 1530 the Diet met again at Augsburg under the auspices of the Emperor himself to try once more 'to attain to a good peace and Christian truth'. The Augsburg Confession, defended all too weakly by Melanchthon, was read here, disputed, and declared refuted by the Emperor.

Erasmus had no share in all this. Many had exhorted him in letters to come to Augsburg; but he had in vain expected a summons from the Emperor. At the instance of the Emperor's counsellors he had postponed his proposed removal to Brabant in that autumn till after the decision of the Diet. But his services were not needed for the drastic resolution of repression with which the Emperor closed the session in November.

The great struggle in Germany seemed to be approaching: the resolutions of Augsburg were followed by the formation of the League of Schmalkalden uniting all Protestant territories and towns of Germany in their opposition to the Emperor. In the same year (1531) Zwingli was killed in the battle of Kappel against the Catholic cantons, soon to be followed by Oecolampadius, who died at Basle. 'It is right', writes Erasmus, 'that those two leaders have perished. If

Mars had been favourable to them, we should now have been done for.'

In Switzerland a sort of equilibrium had set in; at any rate matters had come to a standstill; in Germany the inevitable struggle was postponed for many years. The Emperor had understood that, to combat the German Protestants effectively, he should first get the Pope to hold the Council which would abolish the acknowledged abuses of the Church. The religious peace of Nuremberg (1532) put the seal upon this turn of imperial policy.

It might seem as if before long the advocates of moderate reform and of a compromise might after all get a chance of being heard. But Erasmus had become too old to actively participate in the decisions (if he had ever seriously considered such participation). He does write a treatise, though, in 1533, 'On the sweet concord of the Church', like his 'Advice on the Turks' in the form of an interpretation of a psalm (83). But it would seem as if the old vivacity of his style and his power of expression, so long unimpaired, now began to flag. The same remark applies to an essay 'On the preparation for death', published the same year. His voice was growing weaker.

During these years he turned his attention chiefly to the completion of the great work which more than any other represented for him the summing up and complete exposition of his moral-theological ideas: *Ecclesiastes* or, *On the Way to preach*. Erasmus had always regarded preaching as the most dignified part of an ecclesiastic's duties. As preachers, he had most highly valued Colet and Vitrarius. As early as 1519 his friend, John Becar of Borselen, urged him to follow up the *Enchiridion* of the Christian soldier and the *Institutio* of the Christian prince, by the true instruction of the Christian preacher. 'Later, later,' Erasmus had promised him, 'at present I have too much work, but I hope to undertake it soon.' In 1523 he had already made a sketch and some notes for it. It was meant for John Fisher, the Bishop of Rochester, Erasmus's great friend and brother-spirit, who eagerly looked forward to it and urged the author to finish it. The work gradually grew into the most voluminous of Erasmus's original writings: a forest of a work, *operis sylvam*, he calls it himself. In four books he treated his subject, the art of preaching well and decorously, with an inexhaustible abundance of examples, illustrations, schemes, etc. But was it possible that a work, conceived already by the Erasmus of 1519, and upon which he had been so long engaged, while he himself had gradually given up the boldness of his earlier years, could still be a revelation in 1533, as the *Enchiridion* had been in its day?

Ecclesiastes is the work of a mind fatigued, which no longer sharply reacts upon the needs of his time. As the result of a correct, intellectual, tasteful instruction in a suitable manner of preaching, in accordance with the purity of the Gospel, Erasmus expects to see society improve. 'The people become more obedient to the authorities, more respectful towards the law, more peaceable. Between husband and wife comes greater concord, more perfect faithfulness, greater dislike of adultery. Servants obey more willingly, artisans work better, merchants cheat no more.'

At the same time that Erasmus took this work to Froben, at Basle, to print, a book of a young Frenchman, who had recently fled from France to Basle, passed through the press of another Basle printer, Thomas Platter. It too was to be a manual of the life of faith: the *Institution of the Christian Religion*, by Calvin.

Even before Erasmus had quite completed the *Ecclesiastes*, the man for whom the work had been meant was no more. Instead of to the Bishop of Rochester, Erasmus dedicated his voluminous work to the Bishop of Augsburg, Christopher of Stadion. John Fisher, to set a seal on his spiritual endeavours, resembling those of Erasmus in so many respects, had left behind, as a testimony to the world, for which Erasmus knew himself too weak, that of martyrdom. On 22 June 1535, he was beheaded by command of Henry VIII. He died for being faithful to the old Church. Together with More he had steadfastly refused to take the oath to the Statute of Supremacy.

Not two weeks after Fisher, Thomas More mounted the scaffold. The fate of those two noblest of his friends grieved Erasmus. It moved him to do what for years he had no longer done: to write a poem. But rather than in the fine Latin measure of that *Carmen heroïcum* one would have liked to hear his emotion in language of sincere dismay and indignation in his letters. They are hardly there. In the words devoted to Fisher's death in the preface to the *Ecclesiastes* there is no heartfelt emotion. Also in his letters of those days, he speaks with reserve. 'Would More had never meddled with that dangerous business, and left the theological cause to the theologians.' As if More had died for aught but simply for his conscience!

When Erasmus wrote these words, he was no longer at Freiburg. He had in June 1535 gone to Basle, to work in Froben's printing-office, as of old; the *Ecclesiastes* was at last going to press and still required careful supervision and the final touches during the process; the *Adagia* had to be reprinted, and a Latin edition of Origenes was in preparation. The old, sick man was cordially received by the many friends who still lived at Basle. Hieronymus Froben, Johannes's son, who after his father's death managed the business with two relatives, sheltered him in his house *Zum Luft*. In the hope of his return a room had been built expressly for him and fitted up as was convenient for him. Erasmus found that at Basle the ecclesiastical storms which had formerly driven him away had subsided. Quiet and order had returned. He did feel a spirit of distrust in the air, it is true, 'but I think that, on account of my age, of habit, and of what little erudition I possess, I have now got so far that I may live in safety anywhere'. At first he had regarded the removal as an experiment. He did not mean to stay at Basle. If his health could not stand the change of air, he would return to his fine, well-appointed, comfortable house at Freiburg. If he should prove able to bear it, then the choice was between the Netherlands (probably Brussels, Malines or Antwerp, perhaps Louvain) or Burgundy, in particular Besançon. Towards the end of his life he clung to the illusion which he had been cherishing for a long time that Burgundy wine alone was good for him and kept his malady in check. There is something pathetic in the proportions which this wine-question gradually assumes: that it is so dear at Basle might be overlooked, but the thievish wagoners drink up or spoil what is imported.

In August he doubted greatly whether he will return to Freiburg. In October he sold his house and part of his furniture and had the rest transported to Basle. After the summer he hardly left his room, and was mostly bedridden.

Though the formidable worker in him still yearned for more years and time to labour, his soul was ready for death. Happy he had never felt; only during the last years he utters his longing for the end. He was still, curiously enough, subject to the delusion of being in the thick of the struggle. 'In this arena I shall have to fall,' he writes in 1533. 'Only this consoles me, that near at hand already, the general haven comes in sight, which, if Christ be favourable, will bring the end of all labour and trouble.' Two years later his voice sounds more urgent: 'That the Lord might deign to call me out of this raving world to His rest'.

Most of his old friends were gone. Warham and Mountjoy had passed away before More and Fisher; Peter Gilles, so many years younger than he, had departed in 1533; also Pirckheimer had been dead for years. Beatus Rhenanus shows him to us, during the last months of his life, re-perusing his friends' letters of the last few years, and repeating: 'This one, too, is dead'. As he grew more solitary, his suspiciousness and his feeling of being persecuted became stronger. 'My friends decrease, my enemies increase,' he writes in 1532, when Warham has died and Aleander has risen still higher. In the autumn of 1535 he thinks that all his former servant-pupils betray him, even the best beloved ones like Quirin Talesius and Charles Utenhove. They do not write to him, he complains.

In October 1534, Pope Clement VII was succeeded by Paul III, who at once zealously took up the Council-question.

The meeting of a Council was, in the eyes of many, the only means by which union could be restored to the Church, and now a chance of realizing this seemed nigh. At once the most learned theologians were invited to help in preparing the great work. Erasmus did not omit, in January 1535, to address to the new Pope a letter of congratulation, in which he professed his willingness to co-operate in bringing about the pacification of the Church, and warned the Pope to steer a cautious middle course. On 31 May followed a reply full of kindliness and acknowledgement. The Pope exhorted Erasmus, 'that you too, graced by God with so much laudable talent and learning, may help Us in this pious work, which is so agreeable to your mind, to defend, with Us, the Catholic religion, by the spoken and the written word, before and during the Council, and in this manner by this last work of piety, as by the best act to close a life of religion and so many writings, to refute your accusers and rouse your admirers to fresh efforts.'

Would Erasmus in years of greater strength have seen his way to co-operate actively in the council of the great? Undoubtedly, the Pope's exhortation correctly represented his inclination. But once faced by the necessity of hard, clear resolutions, what would he have effected? Would his spirit of peace and toleration, of reserve and compromise, have brought alleviation and warded off the coming struggle? He was spared the experiment.

He knew himself too weak to be able to think of strenuous church-political propaganda any more. Soon there came proofs that the kindly feelings at Rome were sincere. There had been some question also of numbering Erasmus among the cardinals who were to be nominated with a view to the Council; a considerable benefice connected with the church of Deventer was already offered him. But Erasmus urged the Roman friends who were thus active in his behalf to cease their kind offices; he would accept nothing, he a man who lived from day to day in expectation of death and often hoping for it, who could hardly ever leave his room—would people instigate *him* to hunt for deaneries and cardinals' hats! He had subsistence enough to last him. He wanted to die independent. Yet his pen did not rest. The *Ecclesiastes* had been printed and published and *Origenes* was still to follow. Instead of the important and brilliant task to which Rome called him, he devoted his last strength to a simple deed of friendly cordiality. The friend to whose share the honour fell to receive from the old, death-sick author a last composition prepared expressly for him, amidst the most terrible pains, was the most modest of the number who had not lost their faith in him. No prelate or prince, no great wit or admired divine, but Christopher Eschenfelder, customs officer at Boppard on the Rhine. On his passage in 1518 Erasmus had, with glad surprise, found him to be a reader of his work and a man of culture.[1] That friendship had been a lasting one. Eschenfelder had asked Erasmus to dedicate the interpretation of some psalm to him (a form of composition often preferred by Erasmus of late). About the close of 1535 he remembered that request. He had forgotten whether Eschenfelder had indicated a particular psalm and chose one at haphazard, Psalm 14, calling the treatise 'On the purity of the Christian Church'. He expressly dedicated it to 'the publican' in January 1536. It is not remarkable among his writings as to contents and form, but it was to be his last.

On 12 February 1536, Erasmus made his final preparations. In 1527 he had already made a will with detailed clauses for the printing of his complete works by Froben. In 1534 he drew up an accurate inventory of his belongings. He sold his library to the Polish nobleman Johannes a Lasco. The arrangements of 1536 testify to two things which had played an important part in his life: his relations with the house of Froben and his need of friendship. Boniface Amerbach is his heir. Hieronymus Froben and Nicholas Episcopius, the managers of the business, are his executors. To each of the good friends left to him he bequeathed one of the trinkets which spoke of his fame with princes and the great ones of the earth, in the first place to Louis Ber and Beatus Rhenanus. The poor and the sick were

[1] See Erasmus's letter, p. 224.

not forgotten, and he remembered especially girls about to marry and youths of promise. The details of this charity he left to Amerbach.

In March 1536, he still thinks of leaving for Burgundy. Money matters occupy him and he speaks of the necessity of making new friends, for the old ones leave him: the Bishop of Cracow, Zasius at Freiburg. According to Beatus Rhenanus, the Brabant plan stood foremost at the end of Erasmus's life. The Regent, Mary of Hungary, did not cease to urge him to return to the Netherlands. Erasmus's own last utterance leaves us in doubt whether he had made up his mind. 'Though I am living here with the most sincere friends, such as I did not possess at Freiburg, I should yet, on account of the differences of doctrine, prefer to end my life elsewhere. If only Brabant were nearer.'

This he writes on 28 June 1536. He had felt so poorly for some days that he had not even been able to read. In the letter we again trace the delusion that Aleander persecutes him, sets on opponents against him, and even lays snares for his friends. Did his mind at last give way too?

On 12 July the end came. The friends around his couch heard him groan incessantly: 'O Jesu, misericordia; Domine libera me; Domine miserere mei!' And at last in Dutch: 'Lieve God.'

CHAPTER XXI

CONCLUSION

Conclusion—Erasmus and the spirit of the sixteenth century—His weak points—A thorough idealist and yet a moderate mind—The enlightener of a century—He anticipates tendencies of two centuries later—His influence affects both Protestantism and Catholic reform—The Erasmian spirit in the Netherlands

LOOKING back on the life of Erasmus the question still arises: why has he remained so great? For ostensibly his endeavours ended in failure. He withdraws in alarm from that tremendous struggle which he rightly calls a tragedy; the sixteenth century, bold and vehement, thunders past him, disdaining his ideal of moderation and tolerance. Latin literary erudition, which to him was the epitome of all true culture, has gone out as such. Erasmus, so far as regards the greater part of his writings, is among the great ones who are no longer read. He has become a name. But why does that name still sound so clear and articulate? Why does he keep regarding us, as if he still knew a little more than he has ever been willing to utter?

What has he been to his age, and what was he to be for later generations? Has he been rightly called a precursor of the modern spirit?

Regarded as a child of the sixteenth century, he does seem to differ from the general tenor of his times. Among those vehemently passionate, drastically energetic and violent natures of the great ones of his day, Erasmus stands as the man of too few prejudices, with a little too much delicacy of taste, with a deficiency, though not, indeed, in every department, of that *stultitia* which he had praised as a necessary constituent of life. Erasmus is the man who is too sensible and moderate for the heroic.

What a surprising difference there is between the *accent* of Erasmus and that of Luther, Calvin, and Saint Teresa! What a difference, also, between his accent, that is, the accent of humanism, and that of Albrecht Dürer, of Michelangelo, or of Shakespeare.

Erasmus seems, at times, the man who was not strong enough for his age. In that robust sixteenth century it seems as if the oaken strength of Luther was necessary, the steely edge of Calvin, the white heat of Loyola; not the velvet softness of Erasmus. Not only were their force and their fervour necessary, but also their depth, their unsparing, undaunted consistency, sincerity and outspokenness.

They cannot bear that smile which makes Luther speak of the guileful being looking out of Erasmus's features. His piety is too even for them, too limp. Loyola has testified that the reading of the *Enchiridion militis Christiani* relaxed his fervour and made his devotion grow cold. He saw that warrior of Christ differently, in the glowing colours of the Spanish-Christian, medieval ideal of chivalry.

Erasmus had never passed through those depths of self-reprobation and that consciousness of sin which Luther had traversed with toil; he saw no devil to fight with, and tears were not familiar to him. Was he altogether unaware of the deepest mystery? Or did it rest in him too deep for utterance?

Let us not suppose too quickly that we are more nearly allied to Luther or Loyola because their figures appeal to us more. If at present our admiration goes out again to the ardently pious, and to spiritual extremes, it is partly because our unstable time requires strong stimuli. To appreciate Erasmus we should begin by giving up our admiration of the extravagant, and for many this requires a certain effort at present. It is extremely easy to break the staff over Erasmus. His faults lie on the surface, and though he wished to hide many things, he never hid his weaknesses.

He was too much concerned about what people thought, and he could not hold his tongue. His mind was *too* rich and facile, always suggesting a superfluity of arguments, cases, examples, quotations. He could never let things slide. All his life he grudged himself leisure to rest and collect himself, to see how unimportant after all was the commotion round about him, if only he went his own way courageously. Rest and independence he desired most ardently of all things; there was no more restless and dependent creature. Judge him as one of a too delicate constitution who ventures out in a storm. His will-power was great enough. He worked night and day, amidst the most violent bodily suffering, with a great ideal steadfastly before him, never satisfied with his own achievements. He was not self-sufficient.

As an intellectual type Erasmus was one of a rather small group: the absolute idealists who, at the same time, are thoroughly moderate. They can not bear the world's imperfections; they feel constrained to oppose. But extremes are uncongenial to them; they shrink back from action, because they know it pulls down as much as it erects, and so they withdraw themselves, and keep calling that everything should be different; but when the crisis comes, they reluctantly side with tradition and conservatism. Here too is a fragment of Erasmus's life-tragedy: he was the man who saw the new and coming things more clearly than anyone else—who must needs quarrel with the old and yet could not accept the new. He tried to remain in the fold of the old Church, after having damaged it seriously, and renounced the Reformation, and to a certain extent even Humanism, after having furthered both with all his strength.

Our final opinion about Erasmus has been concerned with negative qualities, so far. What was his positive importance?

Two facts make it difficult for the modern mind to understand Erasmus's positive importance: first that his influence was extensive rather than intensive, and therefore less historically discernible at definite points, and second, that his influence has ceased. He has done his work and will speak to the world no more. Like Saint Jerome, his revered model, and Voltaire, with whom he has been occasionally compared, 'he has his reward'. But like them he has been the enlightener of an age from whom a broad stream of culture emanated.

XXV. ERASMUS AT THE AGE OF 65

XXVI. ERASMUS DICTATING TO HIS SECRETARY, 1530

As historic investigation of the French Revolution is becoming more and more aware that the true history of France during that period should be looked for in those groups which as 'Centre' or 'Marais' seemed for a long time but a drove of supernumeraries, and understands that it should occasionally protect its eyes a little from the lightning flashes of the Gironde and Mountain thunderstorm; so the history of the Reformation period should pay attention—and it has done so for a long time—to the broad central sphere permeated by the Erasmian spirit. One of his opponents said: 'Luther has drawn a large part of the Church to himself, Zwingli and Oecolampadius also some part, but Erasmus the largest'. Erasmus's public was numerous and of high culture. He was the only one of the Humanists who really wrote for all the world, that is to say, for all educated people. He accustomed a whole world to another and more fluent mode of expression: he shifted the interest, he influenced by his perfect clarity of exposition, even through the medium of Latin, the style of the vernacular languages, apart from the numberless translations of his works. For his contemporaries Erasmus put on many new stops, one might say, of the great organ of human expression, as Rousseau was to do two centuries later.

He might well think with some complacency of the influence he had exerted on the world. 'From all parts of the world'—he writes towards the close of his life—'I am daily thanked by many, because they have been kindled by my works, whatever may be their merit, into zeal for a good disposition and sacred literature; and they who have never seen Erasmus, yet know and love him from his books.' He was glad that his translations from the Greek had become superfluous; he had everywhere led many to take up Greek and Holy Scripture, 'which otherwise they would never have read'. He had been an introducer and an initiator. He might leave the stage after having said his say.

His word signified something beyond a classical sense and biblical disposition. It was at the same time the first enunciation of the creed of education and perfectibility, of warm social feeling and of faith in human nature, of peaceful kindliness and toleration. 'Christ dwells everywhere; piety is practised under every garment, if only a kindly disposition is not wanting.'

In all these ideas and convictions Erasmus really heralds a later age. In the sixteenth and seventeenth centuries those thoughts remained an undercurrent: in the eighteenth Erasmus's message of deliverance bore fruit. In this respect he has most certainly been a precursor and preparer of the modern mind: of Rousseau, Herder, Pestalozzi and of the English and American thinkers. It is only part of the modern mind which is represented by all this. To a number of its developments Erasmus was wholly a stranger, to the evolution of natural science, of the newer philosophy, of political economy. But in so far as people still believe in the ideal that moral education and general tolerance may make humanity happier, humanity owes much to Erasmus.

This does not imply that Erasmus's mind did not directly and fruitfully influence his own times. Although Catholics regarded him in the heat of the struggle as the corrupter of the Church, and Protestants as the betrayer of the Gospel, yet his word of moderation and kindliness did not pass by unheard or unheeded on either side. Eventually neither camp finally rejected Erasmus. Rome did not brand him as an archheretic, but only warned the faithful to read him with caution. Protestant history has been studious to reckon him as one of the Reformers. Both obeyed in this the pronouncement of a public opinion which was above parties and which continued to admire and revere Erasmus.

To the reconstruction of the Catholic Church and the erection of the evangelical churches not only the names of Luther and Loyola are linked. The moderate, the intellectual, the conciliating have also had their share of the work; figures like Melanchthon here, Sadolet there, both nearly allied to Erasmus and sympathetically disposed towards him. The frequently repeated attempts to arrive at some compromise in the great religious conflict, though they might be doomed to end in failure, emanated from the Erasmian spirit.

Nowhere did that spirit take root so easily as in the country that gave Erasmus birth. A curious detail shows us that it was not the exclusive privilege of either great party. Of his two most favoured pupils of later years, both Netherlanders, whom as the actors of the colloquy *Astragalismus* (*The Game of Knucklebones*), he has immortalized together, the one, Quirin Talesius, died for his attachment to the Spanish cause and the Catholic faith: he was hanged in 1572 by the citizens of Haarlem, where he was a burgomaster. The other, Charles Utenhove, was sedulous on the side of the revolt and the Reformed religion. At Ghent, in concert with the Prince of Orange, he turned against the narrow-minded Protestant terrorism of the zealots.

A Dutch historian recently tried to trace back the opposition of the Dutch against the king of Spain to the influence of Erasmus's political thought in his arraignment of bad princes—wrongly as I think. Erasmus's political diatribes were far too academic and too general for that. The desire of resistance and revolt arose from quite other causes. The 'Gueux' were not Erasmus's progeny. But there is much that is Erasmian in the spirit of their great leader, William of Orange, whose vision ranged so widely beyond the limitations of religious hatred. Thoroughly permeated by the Erasmian spirit, too, was that class of municipal magistrates who were soon to take the lead and to set the fashion in the established Republic. History is wont, as always with an aristocracy, to take their faults very seriously. After all, perhaps no other aristocracy, unless it be that of Venice, has ruled a state so long, so well and with so little violence. If in the seventeenth century the institutions of Holland, in the eyes of foreigners, were the admired models of prosperity, charity and social discipline, and patterns of gentleness and wisdom, however defective they may seem to us—then the honour of all this is due to the municipal aristocracy. If in the Dutch patriciate of that time those aspirations lived and were translated into action, it was Erasmus's spirit of social responsibility which inspired them. The history of Holland is far less bloody and cruel than that of any of the surrounding countries. Not for naught did Erasmus praise as truly Dutch those qualities which we might also call truly Erasmian: gentleness, kindliness, moderation, a generally diffused moderate erudition. Not romantic virtues, if you like; but are they the less salutary?

One more instance. In the Republic of the Seven Provinces the atrocious executions of witches and wizards ceased more than a century before they did in all other countries. This was not owing to the merit of the Reformed pastors. They shared the popular belief which demanded persecution. It was the magistrates whose enlightenment even as early as the beginning of the seventeenth century no longer tolerated these things. Again, we are entitled to say, though Erasmus was not one of those who combated this practice: the spirit which breathes from this is that of Erasmus.

Cultured humanity has cause to hold Erasmus's memory in esteem, if for no other reason than that he was the fervently sincere preacher of that general kindliness which the world still so urgently needs.

SELECTION FROM THE
LETTERS OF ERASMUS

SELECTION FROM THE LETTERS OF ERASMUS

This selection from the vast correspondence of Erasmus is intended to exhibit him at a few points in his strenuous and rather comfortless life, always overworked, often ill, and perpetually hurried—many of his letters have the postscript 'In haste' or 'I had no time to read this over'—but holding always tenaciously to his aim of steering a middle course; in religion between the corruption and fossilization of the old and the uncompromising violence of the new: in learning between neo-paganism on the one hand and the indolent refusal, under the pretext of piety, to apply critical methods to sacred texts on the other. The first letter has been included because it may provide a clue to his later reluctance to trust his feelings when self-committal to any cause seemed to be required of him, a reluctance not unnaturally interpreted by his enemies as an arrogant refusal to 'yield to any'.

The notes have been compiled from P. S. and H. M. Allen's Opus epistolarum Des. Erasmi Roterodami, *Oxford, 1906–47, by the kind permission of the Delegates of the Clarendon Press, and references are to the numbers of the letters in that edition.*

I. TO SERVATIUS ROGER[1]

[Steyn, *c.* 1487]

To his friend Servatius, greetings:

. . . You say there is something which you take very hard, which torments you wretchedly, which in short makes life a misery to you. Your looks and your carriage betray this, even if you were silent. Where is your wonted and beloved cheerful countenance gone, your former beauty, your lively glance? Whence come these sorrowful downcast eyes, whence this perpetual silence, so unlike you, whence the look of a sick man in your expression? Assuredly as the poet says, 'the sick body betrays the torments of the lurking soul, likewise its joys: it is to the mind that the face owes its looks, well or ill'.[2]

It is certain then, my Servatius, that there is something which troubles you, which is destroying your former good health. But what

---

[1] Servatius Roger (d. 1540), whom Erasmus came to know as a young monk soon after his entry into Steyn, became eighth Prior of Steyn; it was as Prior that he wrote to Erasmus in 1514 to urge him to return to the monastery, see pp. 11, 87 f., 212 ff.

[2] Juvenal, IX. 18–20.

am I to do now? Must I comfort you or scold you? Why do you hide your pain from me as if we did not know each other by this time? You are so deep that you do not believe your closest friend, or trust even the most trustworthy; or do you not know that the hidden fire burns stronger? . . . And for the rest, my Servatius, what is it makes you draw in and hide yourself like a snail? I suspect what the matter is: you have not yet convinced yourself that I love you very much. So I entreat you by the things sweetest to you in life, by our great love, if you have any care for your safety, if you want me to live unharmed, not to be at such pains to hide your feelings, but whatever it is, entrust it to my safe ears. I will assist you in whatever way I can with help or counsel. But if I cannot provide either, still it will be sweet to rejoice with you, to weep with you, to live and die with you. Farewell, my Servatius, and look after your health.

II. TO NICHOLAS WERNER[1]

Paris, 13 September [1496]

To the religious Father Nicholas Werner, greetings:

If you are all well there, things are as I wish and hope; I myself am very well, the gods be thanked. I have now made clear by my actions —if it was not clear to anyone before this—how much theology is coming to mean to me. A somewhat arrogant claim; but it ill becomes Erasmus to hide anything from his most loving Father. Lately I had fallen in with certain Englishmen, of noble birth, and all of them wealthy. Very recently I was approached by a young priest,[2] very rich, who said he had refused a bishopric offered him, as he knew that he was not well educated; nevertheless he is to be recalled by the King to take a bishopric within a year, although, apart from any bishopric even, he has a yearly income of more than 2000 *scudi*. As soon as he heard of my learning he proceeded in unbelievably affectionate fashion to devote himself to me, to frequent and revere me—he lived for a while in my house. He offered 100 *scudi*, if I would teach him for a year; he offered a benefice in a few months' time; he offered to lend me 300 *scudi*, if I should need them to procure the office, until I could pay them back out of the benefice. By this service I could have laid all the English in this city under an obligation to me—they are

---

[1] N. Werner (d. 5 September 1504), later Prior of Steyn.

[2] Probably James Stuart, brother of James IV of Scotland, Archbishop of St. Andrews, 1497, aged about twenty-one at this time.

all of the first families—and through them all England, had I so
wished. But I cared nothing for the splendid income and the far more
splendid prospects; I cared nothing for their entreaties and the tears
which accompanied them. I am telling the truth, exaggerating not at
all; the English realize that the money of all England means nothing
to me. This refusal, which I still maintain, was not made without due
consideration; not for any reward will I let myself be drawn away
from theological studies. I did not come here to teach or to pile up
gold, but to learn. Indeed I shall seek a Doctorate in Theology, if the
gods so will it.

The Bishop of Cambrai is marvellously fond of me: he makes
liberal promises; the remittances are not so liberal, to tell the truth. I
wish you good health, excellent Father. I beg and entreat you to commend me in your prayers to God: I shall do likewise for you. From my
library in Paris.

III. TO ROBERT FISHER[1]

London, 5 December [1499]

To Robert Fisher, Englishman, abiding in Italy, greetings:

I hesitated not a little to write to you, beloved Robert, not that I
feared lest so great a sunderance in time and place had worn away
anything of your affection towards me, but because you are in a
country where even the house-walls are more learned and more
eloquent than are our men here, so that what is here reckoned
polished, fine and delectable cannot there appear anything but crude,
mean and insipid. Wherefore your England assuredly expects you to
return not merely very learned in the law but also equally eloquent
in both the Greek and the Latin tongues. You would have seen me
also there long since, had not my friend Mountjoy carried me off to
his country when I was already packed for the journey into Italy.
Whither indeed shall I not follow a youth so polite, so kindly, so
lovable? I swear I would follow him even into Hades. You indeed
had most handsomely commended him and, in a word, precisely
delineated him; but believe me, he every day surpasses both your
commendation and my opinion of him.

But you ask how England pleases me. If you have any confidence
in me, dear Robert, I would have you believe me when I say that I
have never yet liked anything so well. I have found here a climate as

---

[1] Relative of John Fisher, Bishop of Rochester. Took his doctor's degree in
Italy, returned to England 1507.

delightful as it is wholesome; and moreover so much humane learning, not of the outworn, commonplace sort, but the profound,
accurate, ancient Greek and Latin learning, that I now scarcely miss
Italy, but for the sight of it. When I listen to my friend Colet, I seem
to hear Plato himself. Who would not marvel at the perfection of
encyclopaedic learning in Grocyn?[1] What could be keener or nobler
or nicer than Linacre's[2] judgement? What has Nature ever fashioned
gentler or sweeter or happier than the character of Thomas More?
But why should I catalogue the rest? It is marvellous how thick upon
the ground the harvest of ancient literature is here everywhere
flowering forth: all the more should you hasten your return hither.
Your friend's affection and remembrance of you is so strong that he
speaks of none so often or so gladly. Farewell. Written in haste in
London on the 5th of December.

IV. TO JAMES BATT[3]

Orleans [c. 12 December] 1500

. . . If you care sincerely what becomes of your Erasmus, do you
act thus: plead my shyness before my Lady[4] in pleasant phrases, as if
I had not been able to bring myself to reveal my poverty to her in
person. But you must write that I am now in a state of extreme
poverty, owing to the great expense of this flight to Orleans, as I had
to leave people from whom I was making some money. Tell her that
Italy is by far the most suitable place in which to take the Degree of
Doctor, and that it is impossible for a fastidious man to go to Italy
without a large sum of money; particularly because I am not even
at liberty to live meanly, on account of my reputation, such as it is,
for learning. You will explain how much greater fame I am likely to
bring my Lady by my learning than are the other theologians main-
tained by her. They compose commonplace harangues: I write works
destined to live for ever. Their ignorant triflings are heard by one or
two persons in church: my books will be read by Latins, Greeks, by

---

[1] William Grocyn (c. 1446–1519), Fellow of New College, one of the first
to teach Greek in Oxford.

[2] Thomas Linacre (c. 1460–1524), Fellow of All Souls College, Oxford,
1484. Translator of Galen. Helped to found the College of Physicians, 1518.

[3] James Batt (1464?–1502), secretary to the council of the town of Bergen.

[4] Anne of Burgundy, the Lady of Veere (1469?–1518), patroness of Erasmus
until 1501–2, when she remarried.

every race all over the world. Tell her that this kind of unlearned theologian is to be found in hordes everywhere, whereas a man like myself is hardly to be found once in many centuries; unless indeed you are so superstitious that you scruple to employ a few harmless lies to help a friend. Then you must point out that she will not be a whit the poorer if, with a few gold pieces, she helps to restore the corrupt text of St. Jerome and the true Theology, when so much of her wealth is being shamelessly dissipated. After dilating on this with your customary ingenuity and writing at length on my character, my expectations, my affection for my Lady and my shyness, you must then add that I have written to say that I need 200 francs in all, and request her to grant me next year's payment now; I am not inventing this, my dear Batt; to go to Italy with 100 francs, no, less than 100 francs, seems to me a hazardous enterprise, unless I want to enslave myself to someone once more; may I die before I do this. Then how little difference it will make to her whether she gives me the money this year or next, and how much it means to me! Next urge her to look out for a benefice for me, so that on my return I may have some place where I can pursue learning in peace. Do not stop at this, but devise on your own the most convenient method of indicating to her that she should promise me, before all the other candidates, at least a reasonable, if not a splendid, benefice which I can change as soon as a better one appears. I am well aware that there are many candidates for benefices; but you must say that I am the one man, whom, compared with the rest, etc., etc. You know your old way of lying profusely about Erasmus . . . You will add at the end that I have made the same complaint in my letter which Jerome makes more than once in his letters, that study is tearing my eyes out, that things look as if I shall have to follow his example and begin to study with my ears and tongue only; and persuade her, in the most amusing words at your command, to send me some sapphire or other gem wherewith to fortify my eyesight. I would have told you myself which gems have this virtue, but I have not Pliny at hand; get the information out of your doctor . . . Let me tell you what else I want you to attempt still further—to extract a grant from the Abbot. You know him— invent some modest and persuasive argument for making this request. Tell him that I have a great design in hand—to constitute in its entirety the text of Jerome, which has been corrupted, mutilated, and thrown into disorder through the ignorance of the theologians (I have detected many false and spurious pieces among his writings), and to restore the Greek.¹ I shall reveal [in him] an ingenuity and a knowledge of antiquities which no one, I venture to claim, has yet realized. Explain that for this undertaking many books are needed, also Greek works, so that I may receive a grant. Here you will not be lying, Batt; I am wholly engaged on this work. Farewell, my best and dearest Batt, and put all of Batt into this business. I mean Batt the friend, not Batt the slowcoach.

V. TO ANTONY OF BERGEN²

[Paris?] [16 March? 1501]

To the most illustrious prelate Antony, Abbot of St. Bertin, greetings:

. . . I have accidentally happened upon some Greek books, and am busy day and night secretly copying them out. I shall be asked why I am so delighted with Cato the Censor's example that I want to turn Greek at my age. Indeed, most excellent Father, if in my boyhood I had been of this mind, or rather if time had not been wanting, I should be the happiest of men. As things are, I think it better to learn, even if a little late, than not to know things which it is of the first importance to have at one's command. I have already tasted of Greek literature in the past, but merely (as the saying goes) sipped at it; however, having lately gone a little deeper into it, I perceive—as one has often read in the best authorities—that Latin learning, rich as it is, is defective and incomplete without Greek; for we have but a few small streams and muddy puddles, while they have pure springs and rivers rolling gold. I see that it is utter madness even to touch the branch of theology which deals chiefly with the mysteries unless one is also provided with the equipment of Greek, as the translators of the Scriptures, owing to their conscientious scruples, render Greek forms in such a fashion that not even the primary sense (what our theologians call the *literal* sense) can be understood by persons ignorant of Greek. Who could understand the sentence in the Psalm [Ps. 50.4

---

¹ i.e. to replace Greek words either corrupted or omitted. Erasmus is here referring probably to the text of the *Letters* of Jerome; he uses the same expression in his letter of 21 May 1515 to Leo X (Allen 335, v. 268 ff.): 'I have purified the text of the Letters . . . and carefully restored the Greek, which was either missing altogether or inserted incorrectly'.

² Brother of Henry of Bergen (Bishop of Cambrai) and by this time Abbot of St. Bertin at St. Omer, where he was forcibly installed by his brother the bishop in 1493.

(51.3)] *Et peccatum meum contra me est semper,*[1] unless he has read the Greek? This runs as follows: καὶ ἡ ἁμαρτία μου ἐνώπιόν μου ἐστὶ διαπαντός. At this point some theologian will spin a long story of how the flesh is perpetually in conflict with the spirit, having been misled by the double meaning of the preposition, that is, *contra,* when the word ἐνώπιον refers not to *conflict* but to *position,* as if you were to say *opposite,* i.e., *in sight:* so that the Prophet's meaning was that his fault was so hateful to him that the memory of it never left him, but floated always before his mind as if it were present. Further in a passage elsewhere [Ps. 91 (92. 14)], *Bene patientes erunt ut annuncient,* everyone will be misled by the deceptive form, unless he has learned from the Greek that, just as according to Latin usage we say *bene facere* of those who *do good to* someone, so the Greeks call εὐπαθοῦντας (*bene patientes*) those who *suffer good to be done them.* So that the sense is, 'They will be well treated and will be helped by my benefactions, so that they will make mention of my beneficence towards them'. But why do I pick out a few trifling examples from so many important ones, when I have on my side the venerable authority of the papal Curia? There is a Curial Decree[2] still extant in the Decretals, ordaining that persons should be appointed in the chief academies (as they were then) capable of giving accurate instruction in Hebrew, Greek, and Latin literature, since, as they believed, the Scriptures could not be understood, far less discussed, without this knowledge. This most sound and most holy decree we so far neglect that we are perfectly satisfied with the most elementary knowledge of the Latin language, being apparently convinced that everything can be extracted from Duns Scotus, as it were from a cornucopia.

For myself I do not fight with men of this sort; each man to his taste, as far as I am concerned; let the old man marry the old woman. It is my delight to set foot on the path into which Jerome and the splendid host of so many ancients summon me; so help me God, I would sooner be mad with them than as sane as you like with the mob of modern theologians. Besides I am attempting an arduous and,

---

[1] 'And my sin is ever before me,' where *contra* could be rendered as either 'before' or 'against'; the ambiguity is resolved by referring to the Greek, where ἐνώπιον = face to face with.

[2] Apparently a loose statement of the *Constitutions* of Clement V, promulgated after the Council of Vienne, 1311–12, Bk. 5, tit. 1, cap. 1, in which for the better conversion of infidels it was ordained that two teachers for each of the three languages, Hebrew, Arabic, and Chaldaean be appointed in each of the four Universities, Paris, Oxford, Bologna and Salamanca. Greek was included in the original list, but afterwards omitted.

so to say, Phaethontean task—to do my best to restore the works of Jerome, which have been partly corrupted by those half-learned persons, and are partly—owing to the lack of knowledge of antiquities and of Greek literature—forgotten or mangled or mutilated or at least full of mistakes and monstrosities; not merely to restore them but to elucidate them with commentaries, so that each reader will acknowledge to himself that the great Jerome, considered by the ecclesiastical world as the most perfect in both branches of learning, the sacred and the profane, can indeed be read by all, but can only be understood by the most learned. As I am working hard on this design and see that I must in the first place acquire Greek, I have decided to study for some months under a Greek teacher,[1] a real Greek, no, twice a Greek, always hungry,[2] who charges an immoderate fee for his lessons. Farewell.

VI. TO WILLIAM WARHAM[3]

London, 24 January [1506]

To the Reverend Father in Christ, William, Archbishop of Canterbury, Primate of England, many greetings from Erasmus of Rotterdam, Canon of the Order of St. Augustine:

Having made up my mind, most illustrious prelate, to translate the Greek authors and by so doing to revive or, if you will, promote as far as I could theological studies—and God immortal, how miserably they have been corrupted by sophistical nonsensicalities!—I did not wish to give the impression that I was attempting forthwith to learn the potter's art on a winejar[4] (as the Greek adage goes) and rushing in with unwashen feet, as they say, on so vast an undertaking; so I decided to begin by testing how far I had profited by my studies in both languages, and that in a material difficult indeed, but not sacred; so that the difficulty of the undertaking might be useful for practice and at the same time if I made any mistakes these mistakes should

---

[1] Probably George Hermonymus of Sparta.

[2] Cf. Juvenal, III.78. (*Graeculus esuriens*.)

[3] William Warham (1450?–1532) became Archbishop of Canterbury in 1503, Lord Chancellor of England, 1504–15, Chancellor of Oxford University from 1506. This letter forms the preface to Hecuba in *Euripidis. . . . Hecuba et Iphigenia; Latinae factae Erasmo Roterodamo interprete*, Paris, J. Badius, September 1506.

[4] ἐν τῷ πίθῳ τὴν κεραμείαν, i.e., to run before one can walk, to make a winejar being the most advanced job in pottery.

involve only the risk of my talent and leave the Holy Scriptures un-
damaged. And so I endeavoured to render in Latin two tragedies of
Euripides, the *Hecuba* and the *Iphigeneia in Aulis,* in the hope that
perchance some god might favour so bold a venture with fair breezes.
Then, seeing that a specimen of the work begun found favour with
persons excellently well versed in both tongues (assuredly England by
now possesses several of these, if I may acknowledge the truth without
envy, men deserving of the admiration even of all Italy in any branch
of learning), I brought the work to a finish, with the good help of
the Muses, within a few short months. At what a cost in exertion,
those will best feel who enter the same lists.

Why so? Because the mere task of putting real Greek into real
Latin is such that it requires an extraordinary artist, and not only a
man with a rich store of scholarship in both languages at his finger-
tips, but one exceedingly alert and observant; so that for several
centuries now none has appeared whose efforts in this field were
unanimously approved by scholars. It is surely easy then to conjecture what a heavy task it has proved to render verse in verse, particularly verse so varied and unfamiliar, and to do this from a writer not
merely so remote in time, and withal a tragedian, but also marvellously concise, taut and unadorned, in whom there is nothing
otiose, nothing which it would not be a crime to alter or remove; and
besides, one who treats rhetorical topics so frequently and so acutely
that he appears to be everywhere declaiming. Add to all this the
choruses, which through I know not what striving after effect are so
obscure that they need not so much a translator as an Oedipus or
priest of Apollo to interpret them. In addition there is the corrupt
state of the manuscripts, the dearth of copies, the absence of any
translators to whom one can have recourse. So I am not so much
surprised that even in this most prolific age none of the Italians has
ventured to attempt the task of translating any tragedy or comedy,
whereas many have set their hand to Homer (among these even
Politian[1] failed to satisfy himself); one man[2] has essayed Hesiod, and
that without much success; another[3] has attempted Theocritus,
but with even far more unfortunate results: and finally Francesco
Filelfo has translated the first scene of the Hecuba in one of his funeral

[1] Politian translated parts of Iliad, 2–5 into Latin hexameters, dedicating the
work to Lorenzo dei Medici. Published by A. Mai, Spicilegium Romanum, ii.

[2] Nicholas de Valle translated the *Works and Days (Georgica),* Bonninus
Mombritius the *Theogonia.*

[3] Martin Phileticus.

orations.[1] (I first learned this after I had begun my version), but in such a way that, great as he is, his work gave me courage enough to proceed, overprecise as I am in other respects.

Then for me the lure of this poet's more than honeyed eloquence, which even his enemies allow him, proved stronger than the deterrent of these great examples and the many difficulties of the work, so that I have been bold to attack a task never before attempted, in the hope that, even if I failed, my honest readers would consider even this poor effort of mine not altogether unpraiseworthy, and the more grudging would at least be lenient to an inexperienced translator of a work so difficult: in particular because I have deliberately added no light burden to my other difficulties through my conscientiousness as a translator, in attempting so far as possible to reproduce the shape and as it were contours of the Greek verse, by striving to render line for line and almost word for word, and everywhere seeking with the utmost fidelity to convey to Latin ears the force and value of the sentence: whether it be that I do not altogether approve of the freedom in translation which Cicero allows others and practised himself (I would almost say to an immoderate degree), or that as an inexperienced translator I preferred to err on the side of seeming overscrupulous rather than over-free—hesitating on the sandy shore instead of wrecking my ship and swimming in the midst of the billows; and I preferred to run the risk of letting scholars complain of lack of brilliance and poetic beauty in my work rather than of lack of fidelity to the original. Finally I did not want to set myself up as a paraphraser, thus securing myself that retreat which many use to cloak their ignorance, wrapping themselves like the cuttle-fish in darkness of their own making to avoid detection. Now, if readers do not find here the grandiloquence of Latin tragedy, 'the bombast and the words half a yard long,' as Horace calls it, they must not blame me if in performing my function of translator I have preferred to reproduce the concise simplicity and elegance of my original, and not the bombast to which he is a stranger, and which I do not greatly admire at any time.

Furthermore, I am encouraged to hope with all certainty that these labours of mine will be most excellently protected against the calumnies of the unjust, as their publication will be most welcome to the honest and just, if you, most excellent Father, have voted them your approval. For me it was not difficult to select you from the great host

---

[1] No. 3; his Funeral Orations were printed *c.* 1481 at Milan.

XXVII. PORTRAIT MEDAL OF ERASMUS AT THE AGE OF 53
On the reverse his device and motto

XXVIII. ERASMUS AT THE AGE OF ABOUT 57

of illustrious and distinguished men to be the recipient of this product of my vigils, as the one man I have observed to be—aside from the brilliance of your fortune—so endowed, adorned and showered with learning, eloquence, good sense, piety, modesty, integrity, and lastly with an extraordinary liberality towards those who cultivate good letters, that the word Primate suits none better than yourself, who hold the first place not solely by reason of your official dignity, but far more because of all your virtues, while at the same time you are the principal ornament of the Court and the sole head of the ecclesiastical hierarchy. If I have the fortune to win for this my work the commendation of a man so highly commended I shall assuredly not repent of the exertions I have so far expended, and will be forward to promote theological studies with even more zeal for the future.

Farewell, and enrol Erasmus in the number of those who are wholeheartedly devoted to Your Fathership.

VII. TO ALDUS MANUTIUS[1]

Bologna, 28 October [1507]

To Aldus Manutius of Rome, many greetings:

I have often wished, most learned Manutius, that the light you have cast on Greek and Latin literature, not by your printing alone and your splendid types, but by your brilliance and your uncommon learning, could have been matched by the profit you in your turn drew from them. So far as *fame* is concerned, the name of Aldus Manutius will without doubt be on the lips of all devotees of sacred literature unto all posterity; and your memory will be—as your fame now is—not merely illustrious but loved and cherished as well, because you are engaged, as I hear, in reviving and disseminating the good authors with extreme diligence but not at a commensurate profit—undergoing truly Herculean labours, labours splendid indeed and destined to bring you immortal glory, but meanwhile more profitable to others than to yourself. I hear that you are printing Plato[2] in Greek types; very many scholars eagerly await the book. I should like to know what medical authors you have printed; I wish you would give us Paul of Aegina.[3] I wonder what has prevented you from

---

[1] Aldus Manutius (1449–1515) founded the Aldine Press at Venice, 1494.

[2] Published by Aldus, 1513.

[3] Published by Aldus, 1528.

publishing the New Testament[1] long since—a work which would delight even the common people (if I conjecture aright) but particularly my own class, the theologians.

I send you two tragedies[2] which I have been bold enough to translate, whether with success you yourself shall judge. Thomas Linacre, William Grocyn, William Latimer, Cuthbert Tunstall, friends of yours as well as of mine, thought highly of them; you know yourself that they are too learned to be deceived in their judgement, and too sincere to want to flatter a friend—unless their affection for me has somewhat blinded them; the Italians to whom I have so far shown my attempt do not condemn it. It has been printed by Badius, successfully as far as he is concerned, so he writes, for he has now sold all the copies to his satisfaction. But my reputation has not been enhanced thereby, so full is it all of mistakes, and in fact he offers his services to repair the first edition by printing a second. But I am afraid of his mending ill with ill, as the Sophoclean saying goes. I should consider my labours to have been immortalized if they could come out printed in your types, particularly the smaller types, the most beautiful of all. This will result in the volume being very small and the business being concluded at little expense. If you think it convenient to undertake the affair, I will supply you with a corrected copy, which I send by the bearer, *gratis*, except that you may wish to send me a few volumes as gifts for my friends.

I should not have hesitated to attempt the publication at my own risk and expense, were it not that I have to leave Italy within a few months: so I should much like to have the business concluded as soon as possible; in fact it is hardly ten days' work. If you insist on my taking a hundred or two hundred volumes, though the god of gain does not usually favour me and it will be most inconvenient to transport the package, I shall not refuse, if only you fix a horse as the price. Farewell, most learned Aldus, and reckon Erasmus as one of your well-wishers.

If you have any rare authors in your press, I shall be obliged if you will indicate this—my learned British friends have asked me to search for them. If you decide not to print the *Tragedies*, will you return the copy to the bearer to bring back to me?

[1] Published by Aldus, 1518, although projected in 1499.

[2] *Euripidis . . . Hecuba et Iphigenia* [in Aulide]; *Latinae factae Erasmo Roterodamo interprete*, Paris, J. Badius, 13 September 1506. Reprinted by Aldus at Venice, December 1507 (and by Froben at Basle in 1518 and 1524).

VIII. TO THOMAS MORE[1]

[Paris?] 9 June [1511]

To his friend Thomas More, greetings:

In days gone by, on my journey back from Italy into England, in order not to waste all the time that must needs be spent on horseback in dull and unlettered gossiping, I preferred at times either to turn over in my mind some topic of our common studies or to give myself over to the pleasing recollection of the friends, as learned as they are beloved, whom I had left behind me in England. You were among the very first of these to spring to mind, my dear More; indeed I used to enjoy the memory of you in absence even as I was wont to delight in your present company, than which I swear I never in my life met anything sweeter. Therefore, since I thought that I must at all hazards do *something*, and that time seemed ill suited to serious meditation, I determined to amuse myself with the *Praise of Folly*. You will ask what goddess put this into my mind. In the first place it was your family name of More, which comes as near to the word *moria* [folly] as you yourself are far from the reality—everyone agrees that you are far removed from it. Next I suspected that you above all would approve this *jeu d'esprit* of mine, in that you yourself do greatly delight in jests of this kind, that is, jests learned (if I mistake not) and at no time insipid, and altogether like to play in some sort the Democritus[2] in the life of society. Although you indeed, owing to your incredibly sweet and easy-going character, are both able and glad to be all things to all men, even as your singularly penetrating intellect causes you to dissent widely from the opinions of the herd. So you will not only gladly accept this little declamation as a memento of your comrade, but will also take it under your protection, inasmuch as it is dedicated to you and is now no longer mine but yours.

And indeed there will perhaps be no lack of brawlers to represent that trifles are more frivolous than becomes a theologian, or more mordant than suits with Christian modesty, and they will be crying out that I am reviving the Old Comedy or Lucian and assailing everything with biting satire. But I would have those who are offended by the levity and sportiveness of my theme reflect that it was not I that began this, but that the same was practised by great writers in

[1] Thomas More (1478–1535). This letter is the preface to the *Moriae Encomium*, published by Gilles Gourmont at Paris without date, reprinted by Schürer at Strasbourg, August 1511.

[2] The Greek 'laughing philosopher'.

former times; seeing that so many centuries ago Homer made his trifle *The Battle of Frogs and Mice*, Virgil his *Gnat* and *Dish of Herbs* and Ovid his *Nut*; seeing that Busiris was praised by Polycrates and his critic Isocrates, Injustice by Glaucon, Thersites and the Quartan Fever by Favorinus, Baldness by Synesius, the Fly and the Art of Being a Parasite by Lucian; and that Seneca devised the Apotheosis of the Emperor Claudius, Plutarch the Dialogue of Gryllus and Ulysses, Lucian and Apuleius the Ass, and someone unknown the Testament of Grunnius Corocotta the Piglet, mentioned even by St. Jerome.

So, if they will, let my detractors imagine that I have played an occasional game of draughts for a pastime or, if they prefer, taken a ride on a hobby-horse. How unfair it is truly, when we grant every calling in life its amusements, not to allow the profession of learning any amusement at all, particularly if triflings bring serious thoughts in their train and frivolous matters are so treated that a reader not altogether devoid of perception wins more profit from these than from the glittering and portentous arguments of certain persons—as when for instance one man eulogizes rhetoric or philosophy in a painfully stitched-together oration, another rehearses the praises of some prince, another urges us to begin a war with the Turks, another foretells the future, and another proposes a new method of splitting hairs. Just as there is nothing so trifling as to treat serious matters triflingly, so there is nothing so delightful as to treat trifling matters in such fashion that it appears that you have been doing anything but trifle. As to me, the judgement is in other hands—and yet, unless I am altogether misled by self-love, I have sung the praise of Folly and that not altogether foolishly.

And now to reply to the charge of mordacity. It has ever been the privilege of wits to satirize the life of society with impunity, provided that licence does not degenerate into frenzy. Wherefore the more do I marvel at the fastidiousness of men's ears in these times, who by now can scarce endure anything but solemn appellations. Further, we see some men so perversely religious that they will suffer the most hideous revilings against Christ sooner than let prince or pope be sullied by the lightest jest, particularly if this concerns monetary gain. But if a man censures men's lives without reproving anyone at all by name, pray do you think this man a satirist, and not rather a teacher and admonisher? Else on how many counts do I censure myself? Moreover he who leaves no class of men unmentioned is clearly foe to no man but to all vices. Therefore anyone who rises up and cries out that he is insulted will be revealing a bad conscience, or at all events fear. St. Jerome wrote satire in this kind far more free and biting, not always abstaining from the mention of names, whereas I myself, apart from not mentioning anyone by name, have moreover so tempered my pen that the sagacious reader will easily understand that my aim has been to give pleasure, not pain; for I have at no point followed Juvenal's example in 'stirring up the murky bilge of crime', and I have sought to survey the laughable, not the disgusting. If there is anyone whom even this cannot appease, at least let him remember that it is a fine thing to be reviled by Folly; in bringing her upon the stage I had to suit the words to the character. But why need I say all this to you, an advocate so remarkable that you can defend excellently even causes far from excellent? Farewell, most eloquent More, and be diligent in defending your *moria*.

IX. TO JOHN COLET[1]

Cambridge, 29 October [1511]

To his friend Colet, greetings:

. . . Something came into my mind which I know will make you laugh. In the presence of several Masters [of Arts] I was putting forward a view on the Assistant Teacher, when one of them, a man of some repute, smiled and said: 'Who could bear to spend his life in that school among boys, when he could live anywhere in any way he liked?' I answered mildly that it seemed to me a very honourable task to train young people in manners and literature, that Christ himself did not despise the young, that no age had a better right to help, and that from no quarter was a richer return to be expected, seeing that young people were the harvest-field and raw material of the nation. I added that all truly religious people felt that they could not better serve God in any other duty than the bringing of children to Christ. He wrinkled his nose and said with a scornful gesture: 'If any man wishes to serve Christ altogether, let him go into a monastery and enter a religious order.' I answered that St. Paul said that true religion consisted in the offices of charity—charity consisting in doing our best to help our neighbours. This he rejected as an ignorant remark. 'Look,' said he, 'we have forsaken everything: in this is perfection.' 'That man has not forsaken everything,' said I, 'who, when he could

---

[1] John Colet (1466?–1519), Dean of St. Paul's 1504, had founded St. Paul's School in the previous year (1510).

help very many by his labours, refuses to undertake a duty because it is regarded as humble.' And with that, to prevent a quarrel arising, I let the man go. There you have the dialogue. You see the Scotist philosophy! Once again, farewell.

X. TO SERVATIUS ROGER

Hammes Castle [near Calais],
8 July 1514

To the Reverend Father Servatius, many greetings:

Most humane father, your letter has at last reached me, after passing through many hands, when I had already left England, and it has afforded me unbelievable delight, as it still breathes your old affection for me. However, I shall answer briefly, as I am writing just after the journey, and shall reply in particular on those matters which are, as you write, strictly to the point. Men's thoughts are so varied, 'to each his own bird-song', that it is impossible to satisfy everyone. My own feelings are that I want to follow what is best to do, God is my witness. Those feelings which I had in my youth have been corrected partly by age, partly by experience of the world. I have never intended to change my mode of life or my habit—not that I liked them, but to avoid scandal. You are aware that I was not so much led as driven to this mode of life by the obstinate determination of my guardians and the wrongful urgings of others, and that afterwards, when I realized that this kind of life was quite unsuited to me (for not all things suit all men), I was held back by Cornelius of Woerden's reproaches and by a certain boyish sense of shame. I was never able to endure fasting, through some peculiarity of my constitution. Once roused from sleep I could never fall asleep again for several hours. I was so drawn towards literature, which is not practised in the monastery, that I do not doubt that if I had chanced on some free mode of life I could have been numbered not merely among the happy but even among the good.

So, when I realized that I was by no means fit for this mode of life, that I had taken it up under compulsion and not of my own free will, nevertheless, as public opinion in these days regards it as a crime to break away from a mode of life once taken up, I had resolved to endure with fortitude this part of my unhappiness also—you know that I am in many things unfortunate. But I have always regarded this one thing as harder than all the rest, that I had been forced into a mode of life for which I was totally unfit both in body and in mind: in mind, because I abhorred ritual and loved liberty; in body, because even had I been perfectly satisfied with the life, my constitution could not endure such labours. One may object that I had a year of probation, as it is called, and that I was of ripe age. Ridiculous! As if anyone could expect a boy of sixteen, particularly one with a literary training, to know himself (an achievement even for an old man), or to have succeeded in learning in a single year what many do not yet understand in their grey hairs. Though I myself never liked the life, still less after I had tried it, but was trapped in the way I have mentioned; although I confess that the truly good man will live a good life in any calling. And I do not deny that I was prone to grievous vices, but not of so utterly corrupt a nature that I could not have come to some good, had I found a kindly guide, a true Christian, not one given to Jewish scruples.

Meanwhile I looked about to find in what kind of life I could be least bad, and I believe indeed that I have attained this. I have spent my life meantime among sober men, in literary studies, which have kept me off many vices. I have been able to associate with true followers of Christ, whose conversation has made me a better man. I do not now boast of my books, which you at Steyn perhaps despise. But many confess that they have become not merely more knowledgeable, but even better men through reading them. Passion for money has never affected me. I am quite untouched by the thirst for fame. I have never been a slave to pleasures, although I was formerly inclined to them. Over-indulgence and drunkenness I have ever loathed and avoided. But whenever I thought of returning to your society, I remembered the jealousy of many, the contempt of all, the conversations how dull, how foolish, how un-Christlike, the feasts how unclerical! In short the whole way of life, from which if you remove the ritual, I do not see what remains that one could desire. Lastly I remembered my frail constitution, now weakened by age, disease and hard work, as a result of which I should fail to satisfy you and kill myself. For several years now I have been subject to the stone, a severe and deadly illness, and for several years I have drunk nothing but wine, and not all kinds of wine at that, owing to my disease; I cannot endure all kinds of food nor indeed all climates. The illness is very liable to recur and demands a very careful regimen; and I know the climate in Holland and your style of living, not to mention your ways. So, had I come back to you, all I would have achieved would have been to bring trouble on you and death on myself.

But perhaps you think it a great part of happiness to die amid one's fellow-brethren? This belief deceives and imposes not on you alone but on nearly everyone. We make Christian piety depend on place, dress, style of living and on certain little rituals. We think a man lost who changes his white dress for black, or his cowl for a cap, or occasionally moves from place to place. I should dare to say that Christian piety has suffered great damage from these so-called religious practices, although it may be that their first introduction was due to pious zeal. They then gradually increased and divided into thousands of distinctions; this was helped by a papal authority which was too lax and easy-going in many cases. What more defiled or more impious than these lax rituals? And if you turn to those that are commended, no, to the most highly commended, apart from some dreary Jewish rituals, I know not what image of Christ one finds in them. It is these on which they preen themselves, these by which they judge and condemn others. How much more in conformity with the spirit of Christ to consider the whole Christian world one home and as it were one monastery, to regard all men as one's fellow-monks and fellow-brethren, to hold the sacrament of Baptism as the supreme rite, and not to consider where one lives but how well one lives! You want me to settle on a permanent abode, a course which my very age also suggests. But the travellings of Solon, Pythagoras and Plato are praised; and the Apostles, too, were wanderers, in particular Paul. St. Jerome also was a monk now in Rome, now in Syria, now in Antioch, now here, now there, and even in his old age pursued literary studies.

But I am not to be compared with St. Jerome—I agree; yet I have never moved unless forced by the plague or for reasons of study or health, and wherever I have lived (I shall say this of myself, arrogantly perhaps, but truthfully) I have been commended by the most highly commended and praised by the most praised. There is no land, neither Spain nor Italy nor Germany nor France nor England nor Scotland, which does not summon me to partake of its hospitality. And if I am not liked by all (which is not my aim), at all events I am liked in the highest places of all. At Rome there was no cardinal who did not welcome me like a brother; in particular the Cardinal of St. George,[1] the Cardinal of Bologna,[2] Cardinal Grimani, the Cardinal

---

[1] Raffaele Riario (1461–1521), Leo X's most formidable rival in the election of 1513.

[2] Francesco Alidosi of Imola, d. 1511.

of Nantes,[1] and the present Pope,[2] not to mention bishops, arch-deacons and men of learning. And this honour was not a tribute to wealth, which even now I neither possess nor desire; nor to ambition, a failing to which I have ever been a stranger; but solely to learning, which our countrymen ridicule, while the Italians worship it. In England there is no bishop who is not glad to be greeted by me, who does not desire my company, who does not want me in his home. The King himself, a little before his father's death, when I was in Italy, wrote a most affectionate letter to me with his own hand, and now too speaks often of me in the most honourable and affectionate terms; and whenever I greet him he welcomes me most courteously and looks at me in a most friendly fashion, making it plain that his feelings for me are as friendly as his speeches. And he has often commissioned his Almoner[3] to find a benefice for me. The Queen sought to take me as her tutor. Everyone knows that, if I were prepared to live even a few months at Court, he would heap on me as many benefices as I cared for; but I put my leisure and my learned labours before everything. The Archbishop of Canterbury, the Primate of all England and Chancellor of the Realm, a good and learned man, could not treat me with more affection were I his father or brother. And that you may understand that he is sincere in this, he gave me a living of nearly 100 nobles, which afterwards at my wish he changed into a pension of 100 crowns on my resignation; in addition he has given me more than 400 nobles during the last few years, although I never asked for anything. He gave me 150 nobles in one day. I received more than 100 nobles from other bishops in freely offered gifts. Mountjoy, a baron of the realm, formerly my pupil, gives me annually a pension of 100 crowns. The King and the Bishop of Lincoln, who has great influence through the King, make many splendid promises. There are two universities in England, Oxford and Cambridge, and both of them want me; at Cambridge I taught Greek and sacred literature for several months, for nothing, and have resolved always to do this. There are colleges here so religious, and of such modesty in living, that you would spurn any other religious life, could you see them. In London there is John Colet, Dean of St. Paul's, who has combined great learning with a marvellous piety, a man greatly respected by all.

[1] Robert Guibé (c. 1456–1513), Cardinal of St. Anastasia and Bishop of Nantes (1507).

[2] Leo X.

[3] Wolsey.

He is so fond of me, as all know, that he prefers my company above all others'; I do not mention many others, lest I doubly vex you with my loquacity as well as my boasting.

Now to say something of my works—I think you have read the *Enchiridion*,[1] through which not a few confess themselves inspired to the study of piety; I make no claim for myself, but give thanks to Christ for any good which has come to pass through me by His giving. I do not know whether you have seen the *Adagia*,[2] printed by Aldus. It is not a theological work, but most useful for every branch of learning; at least it cost me countless labours and sleepless nights. I have published a work *De rerum verborumque copia*,[3] dedicated to my friend Colet, very useful for those who desire to speak in public; but all these are despised by those who despise all good learning. During the last two years, apart from much else, I have emended the *Letters* of St. Jerome, obelizing what was false and spurious and explaining the obscure passages with notes. I have corrected the whole of the New Testament from collations of the Greek and ancient manuscripts, and have annotated more than a thousand passages, not without some benefit to theologians. I have begun commentaries on the *Epistles* of St. Paul, which I shall complete when I have published these. For I have resolved to live and die in the study of the Scriptures. I make these my work and my leisure. Men of consequence say that I can do what others cannot in this field; in your mode of life I shall be able to do nothing. Although I have been intimate with so many grave and learned men, here and in Italy and France, I have not yet found anyone who advised me to return to you or thought this the better course. Nay, even Nicholas Werner of blessed memory, your predecessor, would always dissuade me from this, advising me to attach myself rather to some bishop; he would add that he knew my mind and his little brothers' ways: those were the words he used, in the vernacular. In the life I live now I see what I should avoid, but do not see what would be a better course.

It now remains to satisfy you on the question of my dress. I have always up to now worn the canon's dress, and when I was at Louvain I obtained permission from the Bishop of Utrecht to wear a linen scapular instead of a complete linen garment, and a black capuce

---

[1] *Enchiridion militis Christiani*, printed in *Lucubratiunculae*, 1503.

[2] A new and enlarged edition under the title *Adagiorum Chiliades*, printed by Aldus in 1508.

[3] *De duplici copia verborum ac rerum commentarii duo*, Paris, Badius, 1512.

instead of a black cloak, after the Parisian custom. But on my journey to Italy, seeing the monks all along the way wearing a black garment with a scapular, I there took to wearing black, with a scapular, to avoid giving offence by any unusual dress. Afterwards the plague broke out at Bologna, and there those who nurse the sick of the plague customarily wear a white linen cloth depending from the shoulder—these avoid contact with people. Consequently when one day I went to call on a learned friend some rascals drew their swords and were preparing to set about me, and would have done so, had not a certain matron warned them that I was an ecclesiastic. Again the next day, when I was on my way to visit the Treasurer's sons, they rushed at me with bludgeons from all directions and attacked me with horrible cries. So on the advice of good men I concealed my scapular, and obtained a dispensation from Pope Julius II allowing me to wear the religious dress or not, as seemed good, provided that I wore clerical garb; and in this document he condoned any previous offences in the matter. In Italy I continued to wear clerical garb, lest the change cause offence to anyone. On my return to England I decided to wear my usual dress, and I invited to my lodging a friend of excellent repute for his learning and mode of life and showed him the dress I had decided to wear; I asked him whether this was suitable in England. He approved, so I appeared in public in this dress. I was at once warned by other friends that this dress could not be tolerated in England, that I had better conceal it. I did so; and as it cannot be concealed without causing scandal if it is eventually discovered, I stored it away in a box, and up to now have taken advantage of the Papal dispensation received formerly. Ecclesiastical law excommunicates anyone who casts off the religious habit so as to move more freely in secular society. I put it off under compulsion in Italy, to escape being killed; and likewise under compulsion in England, because it was not tolerated there, although myself I should much prefer to have worn it. To adopt it again now would cause more scandal than did the change itself.

There you have an account of my whole life, there you have my plans. I should like to change even this present mode of life, if I see a better. But I do not see what I am to do in Holland. I know that the climate and way of living will not agree with me; I shall have everyone looking at me. I shall return a white-haired old man, having gone away as a youth—I shall return a valetudinarian; I shall be exposed to the contempt of the lowest, used as I am to the respect of the highest.

I shall exchange my studies for drinking-parties. As to your promising me your help in finding me a place where I can live with an excellent income, as you write, I cannot conjecture what this can be, unless perhaps you intend to place me among some community of nuns, to serve women—I who have never been willing to serve kings nor archbishops. I want no pay; I have no desire for riches, if only I have money enough to provide for my health and my literary leisure, to enable me to live without burdening anyone. I wish we could discuss these things together face to face; it cannot be done in a letter conveniently or safely. Your letter, although it was sent by most reliable persons, went so far astray that if I had not accidentally come to this castle I should never have seen it; and many people had looked at it before I received it. So do not mention anything secret unless you know for certain where I am and have a very trustworthy messenger. I am now on my way to Germany, that is, Basle, to have my works published, and this winter I shall perhaps be in Rome. On my return journey I shall see to it that we meet and talk somewhere. But now the summer is nearly over and it is a long journey. Farewell, once my sweetest comrade, now my esteemed father.

XI. TO WOLFGANG FABRICIUS CAPITO[1]

Antwerp, 26 February 1516/17

To the distinguished theologian Wolfgang Fabricius Capito of Hagenau, skilled in the three languages, greetings:

Now that I see that the mightiest princes of the earth, King Francis of France, Charles the Catholic King, King Henry of England and the Emperor Maximilian have drastically cut down all warlike preparations and concluded a firm and, I hope, unbreakable treaty of peace, I feel entitled to hope with confidence that not only the moral virtues and Christian piety but also the true learning, purified of corruption, and the fine disciplines will revive and blossom forth; particularly as this aim is being prosecuted with equal zeal in different parts of the world, in Rome by Pope Leo, in Spain by the Cardinal of Toledo,[2] in England by King Henry VIII, himself no mean scholar, here by King Charles, a young man admirably gifted, in France by King

---

[1] The Hebrew scholar, who adhered to the Reformation, 1523.

[2] F. Ximenes (1436–1517), confessor of Queen Isabella, Archbishop of Toledo, 1495, founded Alcalá University, 1500; he promoted the Polyglot Bible.

Francis, a man as it were born for this task, who besides offers splendid rewards to attract and entice men distinguished for virtue and learning from all parts, in Germany by many excellent princes and bishops and above all by the Emperor Maximilian, who, wearied in his old age of all these wars, has resolved to find rest in the arts of peace: a resolve at once more becoming to himself at his age and more fortunate for Christendom. It is to these men's piety then that we owe it that all over the world, as if on a given signal, splendid talents are stirring and awakening and conspiring together to revive the best learning. For what else is this but a conspiracy, when all these great scholars from different lands share out the work among themselves and set about this noble task, not merely with enthusiasm but with a fair measure of success, so that we have an almost certain prospect of seeing all disciplines emerge once more into the light of day in a far purer and more genuine form? In the first place polite letters, for long reduced almost to extinction, are being taken up and cultivated by the Scots, the Danes and the Irish. As for medicine, how many champions has she found! Nicholas Leonicenus[1] in Rome, Ambrose Leo of Nola[2] at Venice, William Cop[3] and John Ruell[4] in France, and Thomas Linacre in England. Roman law is being revived in Paris by William Budaeus[5] and in Germany by Ulrich Zasius,[6] mathematics at Basle by Henry Glareanus.[7]

In theology there was more to do, for up till now its professors have almost always been men with an ingrained loathing for good learning, men who conceal their ignorance the more successfully as they do this on what they call a religious pretext, so that the ignorant herd is persuaded by them to believe it a violation of religion if anyone proceeds to attack their barbarism; for they prefer to wail for

[1] (1428–1524), taught medicine at Ferrara and made translations from Aristotle, Dio Cassius, Galen and Hippocrates.

[2] (d. 1525) Professor of Medicine at Naples, and from 1507 at Venice; physician to Aldus's household, where he met Erasmus.

[3] (1466–1532), physician, astronomer and humanist; learned Greek with Erasmus in Paris. He was physician to the Court of Francis I.

[4] (1479–1537), Dean of the Medical Faculty at Paris, 1508–9, and Physician to Francis I.

[5] (1467/8–1540), the Parisian humanist, whose *Annotationes in xxiv Pandectarum libros* were published by Badius in 1508.

[6] Ulrich Zäsi or Zasius (1461–1535) Lector Ordinarius in Laws at Freiburg from 1506 until his death.

[7] Henry Loriti of canton Glarus, usually known as Glareanus (1488–1563), had an academy at Basle where he took in thirty boarders.

help to the uneducated mob and incite it to stone-throwing if they see any danger of their ignorance on any point coming to light. But I am confident that here, too, all will go well as soon as the knowledge of the three languages [Greek, Latin and Hebrew] becomes accepted publicly in the schools, as it has begun to be . . . The humblest share in this work has fallen on me, as is fitting; I know not whether I have contributed anything of value; at all events I have infuriated those who do not want the world to come to its senses, so that it seems as if my poor efforts also have not been ineffective: although I have not undertaken the work in the belief that I could teach anything magnificent, but I wanted to open a road for others, destined to attempt greater things, that they might with greater ease ascend the shining heights without running into so many rough and quaggy places. Yet this humble diligence of mine is not disdained by the honest and learned, and none complain of it but a few so stupid that they are hissed off the stage by even ordinary persons of any intelligence. Here not long ago someone complained tearfully before the people, in a sermon of course, that it was all over with the Scriptures and the theologians who had hitherto upheld the Christian faith on their shoulders, now that men had arisen to emend the Holy Gospel and the very words of Our Lord: just as if I was rebuking Matthew or Luke instead of those whose ignorance or negligence had corrupted what they wrote correctly. In England one or two persons complain loudly that it is a shameful thing that I should dare to teach a great man like St. Jerome: as if I had changed what St. Jerome wrote, instead of restoring it!

Yet those who snarl out suchlike dirges, which any laundryman with a little sense would scoff at, think themselves great theologians . . . Not that I want the kind of theology which is customary in the schools nowadays consigned to oblivion; I wish it to be rendered more trustworthy and more correct by the accession of the old, true learning. It will not weaken the authority of the Scriptures or theologians if certain passages hitherto considered corrupt are henceforth read in an emended form, or if passages are more correctly understood on which up till now the mass of theologians have entertained delusions: no, it will give greater weight to their authority, the more genuine their understanding of the Scriptures. I have sustained the shock of the first meeting, which Terence calls the sharpest . . . One doubt still troubles me; I fear that under cover of the rebirth of ancient learning paganism may seek to rear its head, as even among Christians there are those who acknowledge Christ in name only, but in their hearts are Gentiles; or that with the renascence of Hebrew studies Judaism may seek to use this opportunity of revival; and there can be nothing more contrary or more hostile to the teaching of Christ than this plague. This is the nature of human affairs—nothing good has ever so flourished but some evil has attempted to use it as a pretext for insinuating itself. I could wish that those dreary quibblings could be either done away with or at least cease to be the sole activity of theologians, and that the simplicity and purity of Christ could penetrate deeply into the minds of men; and this I think can best be brought to pass if with the help provided by the three languages we exercise our minds in the actual sources. But I pray that we may avoid this evil without falling into another perhaps graver error. Recently several pamphlets have been published reeking of unadulterated Judaism. . . . Farewell.

XII. TO THOMAS MORE

Louvain, 5 March 1518

To his friend More, greeting:

First of all I ask you to entrust to the bearer, my servant John, any letters of mine or yours which you consider fit for publication with the alteration of some passages; I am simply compelled to publish my letters whether I like it or not. Send off the lad so that he returns here as quickly as possible. If you discover that Urswick is ill-disposed towards me perhaps he should not be troubled; otherwise, help me in the matter of a horse—I shall need one just now when I am about to go to Basle or Venice, chiefly for the purpose of bringing out the New Testament.[1] Such is my fate, dear More. I shall enact this part of my play also. Afterwards, I almost feel inclined to sing 'for myself and the Muses'; my age and my health, which grows daily worse, almost require this. Over here scoundrels in disguise are so all-powerful, and no one here makes money but innkeepers, advocates, and begging friars. It is unendurable when many speak ill and none do good.

At Basle they make the elegant preface added by Budaeus the excuse for the delay over your Utopia. They have now received it and have started on the work. Then Froben's father-in-law Lachner died. But Froben's press will be sweating over our studies none the less. I have not yet had a chance of seeing Linacre's *Therapeutice*,[2]

---

[1] Published at Basle, March 1519.

[2] A translation of Galen's *Methodus medendi*, not printed until June 1519. Lupset supervised the printing.

through some conspiracy of the Parisians against me. Inquire courteously of Lupset on the Appendix[1] to my *Copia* and send it.

The Pope and the princes are up to some new tricks on the pretext of the savagery of the war against the Turks. Wretched Turks! May we Christians not be too cruel! Even wives are affected. All married men between the ages of twenty-six and fifty will be compelled to take up arms. Meanwhile the Pope forbids the wives of men absent at the war to indulge in pleasure at home; they are to eschew elegant apparel, must not wear silk, gold or any jewellery, must not touch rouge or drink wine, and must fast every other day, that God may favour their husbands engaged in this cruel war. If there are men tied at home by necessary business, their wives must none the less observe the same rules as they would have had to observe if their husbands had gone to the war. They are to sleep in the same room but in different beds; and not a kiss is to be given meanwhile until this terrible war reaches a successful conclusion under Christ's favour. I know that these enactments will irritate wives who do not sufficiently ponder the importance of the business; though I know that your wife, sensible as she is, and obedient in regard to a matter of Christian observance, will even be glad to obey.

I send Pace's pamphlet, the *Conclusions on Papal Indulgences*,[2] and the *Proposal for Undertaking a War against the Turks*,[3] as I suspect that they have not yet reached England. They write from Cologne that some pamphlet about an argument between Julius and Peter at the gates of Paradise[4] has now been printed; they do not add the author's name. The German presses will not cease from their mad pranks until their rashness is restrained by some law; this does me much harm, who am endeavouring to help the world . . .

I beg you to let my servant sleep one or two nights with yours, to prevent his chancing on an infected house, and to afford him anything he may need, although I have supplied him with travelling money myself. I have at last seen the *Utopia* at Paris printed, but with many

---

[1] This may be the *De pueris statim ac liberaliter instituendis*, composed in Italy. More writes to Erasmus in 1516 (Allen 502) that he has received part of the MS. from Lupset, but it was not published until 1529.

[2] Luther's *Theses*, posted 31 October 1517 and printed shortly afterwards at Wittenberg.

[3] The proposals for a crusade drawn up at Rome, 16 November 1517.

[4] The *Julius Exclusus*, an attack on Pope Julius II, who died 1513. Erasmus never directly denied his authorship, and More speaks of a copy in Erasmus's hand (Allen 502).

misprints. It is now in the press at Basle; I had threatened to break with them unless they took more trouble with that business than with mine. Farewell, most sincere of friends.

XIII. TO BEATUS RHENANUS[1]

Louvain [c. 15 October] 1518

To his friend Rhenanus, greetings:

Let me describe to you, my dear Beatus, the whole tragi-comedy of my journey. I was still weak and listless, as you know, when I left Basle, not having come to terms with the climate, after skulking at home so long, and occupied in uninterrupted labours at that. The river voyage was not unpleasant, but that around midday the heat of the sun was somewhat trying. We had a meal at Breisach, the most unpleasant meal I have ever had. The smell of food nearly finished me, and then the flies, worse than the smell. We sat at table doing nothing for more than half an hour, waiting for them to produce their banquet, if you please. In the end nothing fit to eat was served; filthy porridge with lumps in it and salt fish reheated not for the first time, enough to make one sick. I did not call on Gallinarius. The man who brought word that he was suffering from a slight fever also told me a pretty story; that Minorite theologian with whom I had disputed about *heceitas*[2] had taken it on himself to pawn the church chalices. Scotist ingenuity! Just before nightfall we were put out at a dull village; I did not feel like discovering its name, and if I knew I should not care to tell you it. I nearly perished there. We had supper in a small room like a sweating-chamber, more than sixty of us, I should say, an indiscriminate collection of rapscallions, and this went on till nearly ten o'clock; oh, the stench, and the noise, particularly after they had become intoxicated! Yet we had to remain sitting to suit their clocks.

In the morning while it was still quite dark we were driven from bed by the shouting of the sailors. I went on board without having either supped or slept. We reached Strasbourg before lunch, at about

---

[1] Beat Bild (1485–1547), whose family came from Rheinau near Schlettstadt, became M.A., Paris, in 1505. He worked as a corrector at Henry Stephanus's press in Paris, with Schürer in Strasbourg, and from 1511 for fifteen years with Amerbach and Froben in Basle, where he edited and superintended the publication of numerous books.

[2] Haecceity, 'thisness', 'individuality', t.t. of Scotistic philosophy, cf. quiddity, 'essence'.

nine o'clock; there we had a more comfortable reception, particularly as Schürer produced some wine. Some of the Society[1] were there, and afterwards they all came to greet me, Gerbel outdoing all the rest in politeness. Gebwiler and Rudolfingen did not want me to pay, no new thing with them. Thence we proceeded on horseback as far as Speyer; we saw no sign of soldiers anywhere, although there had been alarming rumours. The English horse completely collapsed and hardly got to Speyer; that criminal smith had handled him so badly that he ought to have both his ears branded with red-hot iron. At Speyer I slipped away from the inn and took myself to my neighbour Maternus. There Decanus, a learned and cultivated man, entertained me courteously and agreeably for two days. Here I accidentally found Hermann Busch.

From Speyer I travelled by carriage to Worms, and from there again to Mainz. There was an Imperial secretary, Ulrich Varnbüler,[2] travelling by chance in the same carriage. He devoted himself to me with incredible assiduity over the whole journey, and at Mainz would not allow me to go into the inn but took me to the house of a canon; on my departure he accompanied me to the boat. The voyage was not unpleasant as the weather was fine, excepting that the crew took care to make it somewhat long; in addition to this the stench of the horses incommoded me. For the first day John Langenfeld, who formerly taught at Louvain, and a lawyer friend of his came with me as a mark of politeness. There was also a Westphalian, John, a canon at St. Victor's outside Mainz, a most agreeable and entertaining man.

After arriving at Boppard, as I was taking a walk along the bank while a boat was being procured, someone recognized me and betrayed me to the customs officer, 'That is the man'. The customs officer's name is, if I mistake not, Christopher Cinicampius, in the common speech Eschenfelder. You would not believe how the man jumped for joy. He dragged me into his house. Books by Erasmus were lying on a small table amongst the customs agreements. He exclaimed at his good fortune and called in his wife and children and all his friends. Meanwhile he sent out to the sailors who were calling for me two tankards of wine, and another two when they called out again, promising that when he came back he would remit the toll to

---

[1] i.e. the Literary Society of Strasbourg. A letter survives, addressed to Erasmus in the name of this Society, dated 1 September 1514, in which occur all the names mentioned here, with the exception of Gerbel's.

[2] A portrait drawing of Varnbüler by Albrecht Dürer is in the Albertina, Vienna; Dürer made also a woodcut from it.

the man who had brought him a man like myself. From Boppard John Flaminius, chaplain to the nuns there, a man of angelic purity, of sane and sober judgement and no common learning, accompanied me as far as Coblenz. At Coblenz Matthias, Chancellor to the Bishop, swept us off to his house—he is a young man but of staid manners, and has an accurate knowledge of Latin, besides being a skilled lawyer. There we supped merrily.

At Bonn the canon left us, to avoid Cologne: I wanted to avoid Cologne myself, but the servant had preceded me thither with the horses, and there was no reliable person in the boat whom I could have charged with the business of calling back my servant; I did not trust the sailors. So we docked at Cologne before six o'clock in the morning on a Sunday, the weather being by now pestilential. I went into an inn and gave orders to the ostlers to hire me a carriage and pair, ordering a meal to be made ready by ten o'clock. I attended Divine Service, the lunch was delayed. I had no luck with the carriage and pair. I tried to hire a horse; my own were useless. Everything failed. I realized what was up; they were trying to make me stop there. I immediately ordered my horses to be harnessed, and one bag to be loaded; the other bag I entrusted to the innkeeper, and on my lame horse rode quickly to the Count of Neuenahr's[1]—a five-hour journey. He was staying at Bedburg.

With the Count I stayed five days very pleasantly, in such peace and quiet that while staying with him I completed a good part of the revision I had taken that part of the New Testament with me. Would that you knew him, my dear Beatus! He is a young man but of rare good sense, more than you would find in an old man; he speaks little, but as Homer says of Menelaus, he speaks 'in clear tones', and intelligently too; he is learned without pretentiousness in more than one branch of study, wholly sincere and a good friend. By now I was strong and lusty, and well pleased with myself, and was hoping to be in a good state when I visited the Bishop of Liége and to return hale and hearty to my friends in Brabant. What dinner-parties, what felicitations, what discussions I promised myself! But ah, deceptive human hopes! ah, the sudden and unexpected vicissitudes of human affairs! From these high dreams of happiness I was hurled to the depths of misfortune.

[1] Hermann, Count of Neuenahr (1492–1530), a pupil of Caesarius, with whom he visited Italy in 1508–9. In 1517 he lectured in Cologne on Greek and Hebrew, and became later Chancellor of the University. Among his works is a letter in defence of Erasmus.

I had hired a carriage and pair for the next day. My companion, not wanting to say goodbye before night, announced that he would see me in the morning before my departure. That night a wild hurricane sprang up, which had passed before the next morning. Nevertheless I rose after midnight, to make some notes for the Count: when it was already seven o'clock and the Count did not emerge, I asked for him to be waked. He came, and in his customary shy and modest way asked me whether I meant to leave in such bad weather, saying he was afraid for me. At that point, my dear Beatus, some god or bad angel deprived me, not of the half of my senses, as Hesiod says, but of the whole: for he had deprived me of half my senses when I risked going to Cologne. I wish that either my friend had warned me more sharply or that I had paid more attention to his most affectionate re-monstrances! I was seized by the power of fate: what else am I to say? I climbed into an uncovered carriage, the wind blowing 'strong as when in the high mountains it shivers the trembling holm-oaks'. It was a south wind and blowing like the very pest. I thought I was well protected by my wrappings, but it went through everything with its violence. Towards nightfall a light rain came on, more noxious than the wind that preceded it: I arrived at Aachen exhausted from the shaking of the carriage, which was so trying to me on the stone-paved road that I should have preferred sitting on my horse, lame as he was. Here I was carried off from the inn by a canon, to whom the Count had recommended me, to Suderman's house. There several canons were holding their usual drinking-party. My appetite had been sharpened by a very light lunch; but at the time they had nothing by them but carp, and cold carp at that. I ate to repletion. The drinking went on well into the night. I excused myself and went to bed, as I had had very little sleep the night before.

On the following day I was taken to the Vice-Provost's house; it was his turn to offer hospitality. As there was no fish there apart from eel (this was certainly the fault of the storm, as he is a magnificent host otherwise) I lunched off a fish dried in the open air, which the Germans call *Stockfisch*, from the rod used to beat it—it is a fish which I enjoy at other times: but I discovered that part of this one had not been properly cured. After lunch, as the weather was appalling, I took myself off to the inn and ordered a fire to be lit. The canon whom I mentioned, a most cultured man, stayed talking with me for about an hour and a half. Meanwhile I began to feel very uncomfortable inside; as this continued, I sent him away and went to the privy. As this gave

my stomach no relief I inserted my finger into my mouth, and the
uncured fish came up, but that was all. I lay down afterwards, not so
much sleeping as resting, without any pain in my head or body; then,
having struck a bargain with the coachman over the bags, I received
an invitation to the evening compotation. I excused myself, without
success. I knew that my stomach would not stand anything but a few
sups of warmed liquor . . . On this occasion there was a magnificent
spread, but it was wasted on me. After comforting my stomach with
a sup of wine, I went home; I was sleeping at Suderman's house. As
soon as I went out of doors my empty body shivered fearfully in the
night air.

On the morning of the next day, after taking a little warmed ale
and a few morsels of bread, I mounted my horse, who was lame and
ailing, which made riding more uncomfortable. By now I was in such
a state that I would have been better keeping warm in bed than
mounted on horseback. But that district is the most countrified,
roughest, barren and unattractive imaginable, the inhabitants are so
idle; so that I preferred to run away. The danger of brigands—it was
very great in those parts—or at least my fear of them, was driven out
of my mind by the discomfort of my illness . . . After covering four
miles on this ride I reached Maastricht. There after a drink to soothe
my stomach I remounted and came to Tongres, about three miles
away. This last ride was by far the most painful to me. The awkward
gait of the horse gave me excruciating pains in the kidneys. It would
have been easier to walk, but I was afraid of sweating, and there was a
danger of the night catching us still out in the country. So I reached
Tongres with my whole body in a state of unbelievable agony. By
now, owing to lack of food and the exertion in addition, all my
muscles had given way, so that I could not stand or walk steadily. I
concealed the severity of my illness by my tongue—that was still
working. Here I took a sup of ale to soothe my stomach and retired
to bed.

In the morning I ordered them to hire a carriage. I decided to go
on horseback, on account of the paving stones, until we reached an
unpaved road. I mounted the bigger horse, thinking that he would go
better on the paving and be more sure-footed. I had hardly mounted
when I felt my eyes clouding over as I met the cold air, and asked for
a cloak. But soon after this I fainted; I could be roused by a touch.
Then my servant John and the others standing by let me come to
myself naturally, still sitting on the horse. After coming to myself I

got into the carriage . . . By now we were approaching the town of
St. Trond. I mounted once more, not to appear an invalid, riding in
a carriage. Once again the evening air made me feel sick, but I did not
faint. I offered the coachman double the fare if he would take me the
next day as far as Tirlemont, a town six miles from Tongres. He
accepted the terms. Here a guest whom I knew told me how ill the
Bishop of Liége had taken my leaving for Basle without calling on
him. After soothing my stomach with a drink I went to bed, and had
a very bad night . . . Here by chance I found a coach going to
Louvain, six miles away, and threw myself into it. I made the journey
in incredible and almost unendurable discomfort; however we reached
Louvain by seven o'clock on that day.

I had no intention of going to my own room, whether because I
had a suspicion that all would be cold there, or that I did not want to
run the risk of interfering with the amenities of the College in any
way, if I started a rumour of the plague. I went to Theodoric the
printer's . . . During the night a large ulcer broke without my feeling
it, and the pain had died down. The next day I called a surgeon. He
applied poultices. A third ulcer had appeared on my back, caused by
a servant at Tongres when he was anointing me with oil of roses for
the pain in the kidneys and rubbed one of my ribs too hard with a
horny finger . . . The surgeon on his way out told Theodoric and his
servant secretly that it was the plague; he would send poultices, but
would not come to see me himself . . . When the surgeon failed to
return after a day or two, I asked Theodoric the reason. He made
some excuse. But I, suspecting what the matter was, said 'What, does
he think it is the plague?' 'Precisely,' said he, 'he insists that you have
three plague-sores.' I laughed, and did not allow myself even to
imagine that I had the plague. After some days the surgeon's father
came, examined me, and assured me that it was the true plague. Even
so, I could not be convinced. I secretly sent for another doctor who
had a great reputation. He examined me, and being something of a
clown said, 'I should not be afraid to sleep with you—and make love
to you too, if you were a woman.' . . . [Still another doctor is summoned but does not return as promised, sending his servant instead.]
I dismissed the man and losing my temper with the doctors, commended myself to Christ as my doctor.

My appetite came back within three days . . . I then immediately
returned to my studies and completed what was still wanting to my
New Testament . . . I had given orders as soon as I arrived that no

one was to visit me unless summoned by name, lest I should frighten anyone or suffer inconvenience from anyone's assiduity; but Dorp forced his way in first of all, then Ath. Mark Laurin and Paschasius Berselius, who came every day, did much to make me well with their delightful company.

My dear Beatus, who would have believed that this meagre delicate body of mine, weakened now by age also, could have succeeded, after all the troubles of travel and all my studious exertions, in standing up to all these physical ills as well? You know how ill I was not long ago at Basle, more than once. I was beginning to suspect that that year would be fatal to me: illness followed illness, always more severe. But, at the very time when this illness was at its height, I felt no torturing desire to live and no trepidation at the fear of death. My whole hope was in Christ alone, and I prayed only that he would give me what he judged most salutary for me. In my youth long ago, as I remember, I would shiver at the very name of death. This at least I have achieved as I have grown older, that I do not greatly fear death, and I do not measure man's happiness by number of days. I have passed my fiftieth year; as so few out of so many reach this age, I cannot rightly complain that I have not lived long enough. And then, if this has any relevance, I have by now already prepared a monument to bear witness to posterity that I have lived. And perhaps if, as the poets tell, jealousy falls silent after death, fame will shine out the more brightly: although it ill becomes a Christian heart to be moved by human glory; may I have the glory of pleasing Christ! Farewell, my dearest Beatus. The rest you will learn from my letter to Capito.

XIV. TO MARTIN LUTHER

Louvain, 30 May 1519

Best greetings, most beloved brother in Christ. Your letter was most welcome to me, displaying a shrewd wit and breathing a Christian spirit.

I could never find words to express what commotions your books have brought about here. They cannot even now eradicate from their minds the most false suspicion that your works were composed with my aid, and that I am the standard-bearer of this party, as they call it. They thought that they had found a handle wherewith to crush good learning—which they mortally detest as threatening to dim the majesty of theology, a thing they value far above Christ—and at the same time to crush me, whom they consider as having some influence on the revival of studies. The whole affair was conducted with such clamourings, wild talk, trickery, detraction and cunning that, had I not been present and witnessed, nay, *felt* all this, I should never have taken any man's word for it that theologians could act so madly. You would have thought it some mortal plague. And yet the poison of this evil beginning with a few has spread so far abroad that a great part of this University was running mad with the infection of this not uncommon disease.

I declared that you were quite unknown to me, that I had not yet read your books, and accordingly neither approved nor disapproved of anything in them. I only warned them not to clamour before the populace in so hateful a manner without having yet read your books: this matter was *their* concern, whose judgement should carry the greatest weight. Further I begged them to consider also whether it were expedient to traduce before a mixed multitude views which were more properly refuted in books or discussed between educated persons, particularly as the author's way of life was extolled by one and all. I failed miserably; up to this day they continue to rave in their insinuating, nay, slanderous disputations. How often have we agreed to make peace! How often have they stirred up new commotions from some rashly conceived shred of suspicion! And these men think themselves theologians! Theologians are not liked in Court circles here; this too they put down to me. The bishops all favour me greatly. These men put no trust in books, their hope of victory is based on cunning alone. I disdain them, relying on my knowledge that I am in the right. They are becoming a little milder towards yourself. They fear my pen, because of their bad conscience; and I would indeed paint them in their true colours, as they deserve, did not Christ's teaching and example summon me elsewhere. Wild beasts can be tamed by kindness, which makes these men wild.

There are persons in England, and they in the highest positions, who think very well of your writings. Here, too, there are people, among them the Bishop of Liége, who favour your followers. As for me, I keep myself as far as possible neutral, the better to assist the new flowering of good learning; and it seems to me that more can be done by unassuming courteousness than by violence. It was thus that Christ brought the world under His sway, and thus that Paul made away with the Jewish Law, by interpreting all things allegorically. It is wiser to cry out against those who abuse the Popes' authority than against the Popes themselves: and I think that we should act in the same way with the Kings. As for the schools, we should not so much reject them as recall them to more reasonable studies. Where things are too generally accepted to be suddenly eradicated from men's minds, we must argue with repeated and efficacious proofs and not make positive assertions. The poisonous contentions of certain persons are better ignored than refuted. We must everywhere take care never to speak or act arrogantly or in a party spirit: this I believe is pleasing to the spirit of Christ. Meanwhile we must preserve our minds from being seduced by anger, hatred or ambition; these feelings are apt to lie in wait for us in the midst of our strivings after piety.

I am not advising you to do this, but only to continue doing what you are doing. I have looked into your Commentaries on the Psalms;[1] I am delighted with them, and hope that they will do much good. At Antwerp we have the Prior of the Monastery,[2] a Christian without spot, who loves you exceedingly, an old pupil of yours as he says. He is almost alone of them all in preaching Christ: the others preach human trivialities or their own gain.

I have written to Melanchthon. The Lord Jesus impart you His spirit each day more bountifully, to His own glory and the good of all. I had not your letter at hand when writing this.

XV. TO ULRICH HUTTEN[3]

Antwerp, 23 July 1519

To the illustrious knight Ulrich Hutten, greetings:

. . . As to your demand for a complete portrait, as it were, of More, would that I could execute it with a perfection to match the intensity of your desire! It will be a pleasure, for me as well, to dwell for a space on the contemplation of by far the sweetest friend of all. But in the first place, it is not given to every man to explore all More's gifts. And then I wonder whether he will tolerate being depicted by an indifferent artist; for I think it no less a task to portray More than it would be to portray Alexander the Great or Achilles, and they were no more deserving of immortality than he is. Such a subject requires in short the pencil of an Apelles; but I fear that I am more like

---

[1] *Operationes in Psalmos.* Wittenberg, 1519.
[2] James Probst or Proost (Praepositus) of Ypres (1486–1562).
[3] Ulrich Hutten (1488–1523), the German knight and humanist.

Horace's gladiators[1] than Apelles. Nevertheless, I shall try to sketch you an image rather than a full portrait of the whole man, so far as my observation or recollection from long association with him in his home has made this possible. If ever you meet him on some embassy you will then for the first time understand how unskilled an artist you have chosen for this commission; and I am downright afraid of your accusing me of jealousy or blindness, that out of so many excellences so few have been perceived by my poor sight or recorded by my jealousy.

But to begin with that side of More of which you know nothing, in height and stature he is not tall, nor again noticeably short, but there is such symmetry in all his limbs as leaves nothing to be desired here. He has a fair skin, his complexion glowing rather than pale, though far from ruddy, but for a very faint rosiness shining through. His hair is of a darkish blond, or if you will, a lightish brown, his beard scanty, his eyes bluish grey, with flecks here and there: this usually denotes a happy nature and is also thought attractive by the English, whereas we are more taken by dark eyes. It is said that no type of eyes is less subject to defects. His expression corresponds to his character, always showing a pleasant and friendly gaiety, and rather set in a smiling look; and, to speak honestly, better suited to merriment than to seriousness and solemnity, though far removed from silliness or buffoonery. His right shoulder seems a little higher than the left, particularly when he is walking: this is not natural to him but due to force of habit, like many of the little habits which we pick up. There is nothing to strike one in the rest of his body; only his hands are somewhat clumsy, but only when compared with the rest of his appearance. He has always from a boy been very careless of everything to do with personal adornment, to the point of not greatly caring for those things which according to Ovid's teaching should be the sole care of men. One can tell even now, from his appearance in maturity, how handsome he must have been as a young man: although when I first came to know him he was not more than three and twenty years old, for he is now barely forty.[2]

His health is not so much robust as satisfactory, but equal to all tasks becoming an honourable citizen, subject to no, or at least very few, diseases: there is every prospect of his living long, as he has a

---

[1] Satires 2, vii. 96 (where however the gladiators are the subject, and not the artists, of a crude charcoal sketch).

[2] Sir Thomas More's portrait at the age of fifty was painted by Hans Holbein; it is now in the Frick Collection, New York. Two portrait drawings of him by Holbein are in the Royal Library at Windsor Castle. See also p. 236, note 4.

father of great age[1]—but a wondrously fresh and green old age. I have never yet seen anyone less fastidious in his choice of food. Until he grew up he liked water to drink; in this he took after his father. But so as to avoid irritating anyone over this, he would deceive his comrades by drinking from a pewter pot ale that was very nearly all water, often pure water. Wine—the custom in England is to invite each other to drink from the same goblet—he would often sip with his lips, not to give the appearance of disliking it, and at the same time to accustom himself to common ways. He preferred beef, salt fish, and bread of the second quality, well risen, to the foods commonly regarded as delicacies: otherwise he was by no means averse to all sources of innocent pleasure, even to the appetite. He has always had a great liking for milk foods and fruit: he enjoys eating eggs. His voice is neither strong nor at all weak, but easily audible, by no means soft or melodious, but the voice of a clear speaker; for he seems to have no natural gift for vocal music, although he delights in every kind of music. His speech is wonderfully clear and distinct, with no trace of haste or hesitation.

He likes to dress simply and does not wear silk or purple or gold chains, excepting where it would not be decent not to wear them. It is strange how careless he is of the formalities by which the vulgar judge good manners. He neither insists on these from any, nor does he anxiously force them on others whether at meetings or at entertainments, although he knows them well enough, should he choose to indulge in them; but he considers it effeminate and not becoming masculine dignity to waste a good part of one's time in suchlike inanities.

Formerly he disliked Court life and the company of princes, for the reason that he has always had a peculiar loathing for tyranny, just as he has always loved equality. (Now you will hardly find any court so modest that has not about it much noisy ostentation, dissimulation and luxury, while yet being quite free of any kind of tyranny.) Indeed it was only with great difficulty that he could be dragged into the Court of Henry VIII, although nothing more courteous and unassuming than this prince could be desired. He is by nature somewhat greedy of independence and leisure; but while he gladly takes advantage of leisure when it comes his way, none is more careful or patient whenever business demands it.

[1] John More (1453?–1530), at this time a Judge of Common Pleas, promoted to the King's Bench in 1523.

He seems born and created for friendship, which he cultivates most sincerely and fosters most steadfastly. He is not one to be afraid of the 'abundance of friends' which Hesiod does not approve; he is ready to enter into friendly relations with any. He is in no way fastidious in choosing friends, accommodating in maintaining them, constant in keeping them. If he chances on anyone whose defects he cannot mend, he dismisses him when the opportunity offers, not breaking but gradually dissolving the friendship. Whenever he finds any sincere and suited to his disposition he so delights in their company and conversation that he appears to make this his chief pleasure in life. He loathes ball-games, cards and gambling, and the other games with which the ordinary run of men of rank are used to kill time. Furthermore, while he is somewhat careless of his own affairs, there is none more diligent in looking after his friends' affairs. Need I continue? Should anyone want a finished example of true friendship he could not do better than seek it in More.

In social intercourse he is of so rare a courtesy and charm of manners that there is no man so melancholy that he does not gladden, no subject so forbidding that he does not dispel the tedium of it. From his boyhood he has loved joking, so that he might seem born for this, but in his jokes he has never descended to buffoonery, and has never loved the biting jest. As a youth he both composed and acted in little comedies. Any witty remark he would still enjoy, even were it directed against himself, such is his delight in clever sallies of ingenious flavour. As a result he wrote epigrams as a young man, and delighted particularly in Lucian; indeed he was responsible for my writing the *Praise of Folly*, that is for making the camel dance.

In human relations he looks for pleasure in everything he comes across, even in the gravest matters. If he has to do with intelligent and educated men, he takes pleasure in their brilliance; if with the ignorant and foolish, he enjoys their folly. He is not put out by perfect fools, and suits himself with marvellous dexterity to all men's feelings. For women generally, even for his wife, he has nothing but jests and merriment. You could say he was a second Democritus, or better, that Pythagorean philosopher who saunters through the market-place with a tranquil mind gazing on the uproar of buyers and sellers. None is less guided by the opinion of the herd, but again none is less remote from the common feelings of humanity.

He takes an especial pleasure in watching the appearance, characters and behaviour of various creatures; accordingly there is almost no kind of bird which he does not keep at his home, and various other animals not commonly found, such as apes, foxes, ferrets, weasels and their like. Added to this, he eagerly buys anything foreign or otherwise worth looking at which comes his way, and he has the whole house stocked with these objects, so that wherever the visitor looks there is something to detain him; and his own pleasure is renewed whenever he sees others enjoying these sights.

When he was of an age for it, he was not averse to love-affairs with young women, but kept them honourable, preferring the love that was offered to that which he must chase after, and was more drawn by spiritual than by physical intercourse.

He had devoured classical literature from his earliest years. As a lad he applied himself to the study of Greek literature and philosophy; his father, so far from helping him (although he is otherwise a good and sensible man), deprived him of all support in this endeavour; and he was almost regarded as disowned, because he seemed to be deserting his father's studies—the father's profession is English jurisprudence. This profession is quite unconnected with true learning, but in Britain those who have made themselves authorities in it are particularly highly regarded, and this is there considered the most suitable road to fame, since most of the nobility of that island owe their origin to this branch of study. It is said that none can become perfect in it without many years of hard work. So, although the young man's mind born for better things not unreasonably revolted from it, nevertheless, after sampling the scholastic disciplines he worked at the law with such success that none was more gladly consulted by litigants, and he made a better living at it than any of those who did nothing else, so quick and powerful was his intellect.

He also devoted much strenuous attention to studying the ecclesiastical writers. He lectured publicly to a crowded audience on Augustine's *City of God* while still little more than a lad; and priests and elderly men were neither sorry nor ashamed to learn sacred matters from a youthful layman. For a time he gave his whole mind to the study of piety, practising himself for the priesthood in watchings, fastings and prayer, and other like preliminary exercises; in which matter he was far more sensible than most of those who rashly hurl themselves into this arduous calling without having previously made any trial of themselves. The only obstacle to his devoting himself to this mode of life was his inability to shake off his longing for a wife. He therefore chose to be a chaste husband rather than an unchaste priest.

Still, he married a girl,[1] as yet very young, of good family, but still untrained—she had always lived in the country with her parents and sisters—so that he could better fashion her to his own ways. He had her taught literature and made her skilled in all kinds of music; and he had really almost made her such as he would have cared to spend all his life with, had not an untimely death carried her off while still a girl, but after she had borne him several children: of whom there survive three girls, Margaret, Alice[2] and Cecily, and one boy, John. He would not endure to live long a widower, although his friends counselled otherwise. Within a few months of his wife's death he married a widow,[3] more for the care of the household than for his pleasure, as she was not precisely beautiful nor, as he jokingly says himself, a girl, but a keen and watchful housewife;[4] with whom he yet lives as pleasantly and agreeably as if she were a most charming young girl. Hardly any husband gets so much obedience from his wife by stern orders as he does by jests and cajolery. How could he fail to do so, after having induced a woman on the verge of old age, also by no means a docile character, and lastly most attentive to her business, to learn to play the cithern, the lute, the monochord and the recorders, and perform a daily prescribed exercise in this at her husband's wish?

He rules his whole household as agreeably, no quarrels or disturbances arise there. If any quarrel does arise he at once heals or settles the difference; and he has never let anyone leave his house in anger. His house seems blest indeed with a lucky fate, for none has lived there without rising to better fortune, and none has ever acquired a stain on his reputation there. One would be hard put to it to find any agree as well with their mothers as he with his stepmother—his father had already given him two, and he loved both of them as truly as he loved his mother. Recently his father gave him a third stepmother: More swears his Bible oath he has never seen a better. Moreover, he is so disposed towards his parents and children as to be neither tiresomely affectionate nor ever failing in any family duty.

He has a mind altogether opposed to sordid gain. He has put aside from his fortune for his children an amount which he considers sufficient

[1] Jane Colt (c. 1487–1511).

[2] More's second daughter was Elizabeth; Alice was the name of his stepdaughter.

[3] Alice Middleton.

[4] A group portrait of Sir Thomas More with his entire family was painted by Hans Holbein about 1527–8 at More's house in Chelsea. It was commissioned from the artist at the recommendation of Erasmus. The original has been lost; see Plate XXIX and p. 260.

for them; the rest he gives away lavishly. While he still made his living at the Bar he gave sincere and friendly counsel to all, considering his clients' interests rather than his own; he would persuade most of them to settle their differences—this would be cheaper. If he failed to achieve this, he would then show them a method of going to law at the least possible expense—some people here are so minded that they actually enjoy litigation. In the City of London, where he was born, he acted for some years as a judge in civil causes.[1] This office is not at all onerous—the court sits only on Thursday mornings—but is regarded as one of the most honourable. None dealt with so many cases as he, nor behaved with such integrity; he usually remitted the charge customarily due from litigants (as before the formal entering of the suit the plaintiff pays into court three shillings, the defendant likewise, and it is incorrect to demand more). By this behaviour he won the deep affection of the City.

He had made up his mind to rest content with this position, which was sufficiently influential and yet not exposed to grave dangers. Twice he was forced into embassies; as he acted in these with great sagacity, King Henry VIII would not rest until he could drag More to Court. Why not call it 'drag'? No man ever worked so assiduously to gain admission to the Court as he studied to escape it. But when the King decided to fill his household with men of weight, learning, sagacity and integrity, More was one of the first among many summoned by him: he regards More so much as one of his intimate circle that he never lets him depart from him. If serious matters are to be discussed, there is none more skilled than he; or if the King decides to relax in pleasant gossiping, there is no merrier companion. Often difficult affairs require a weighty and sagacious arbitrator; More solves these matters with such success that both parties are grateful. Yet no one has ever succeeded in persuading him to accept a present from anyone. How happy the states would be if the ruler everywhere put magistrates like More in office! Meanwhile he has acquired no trace of haughtiness.

Amid all these official burdens he does not forget his old friends and from time to time returns to his beloved literature. All the authority of his office, all his influence with the King, is devoted to the service of the State and of his friends. His mind, eager to serve all and wondrously prone to pity, has ever been present to help: he will now be better able to help others, as he has greater power. Some he assists

[1] More was elected Under-Sheriff, 1510.

with money, some he protects with his authority, others he advances by introductions; those whom he cannot help otherwise he aids with counsel, and he has never sent anyone away disappointed. You might call More the common advocate of all those in need. He regards himself as greatly enriched when he assists the oppressed, extricates the perplexed and involved, or reconciles the estranged. None confers a benefit so gladly, none is so slow to upbraid. And although he is fortunate on so many counts, and good fortune is often associated with boastfulness, it has never yet been my lot to meet any man so far removed from this vice.

But I must return to recounting his studies—it was these which chiefly brought More and myself together. In his youth he chiefly practised verse composition, afterwards he worked hard and long to polish his prose, practising his style in all kinds of composition. What that style is like, I need not describe—particularly not to you, who always have his books in your hands. He especially delighted in composing declamations, and in these liked paradoxical themes, for the reason that this offers keener practice to the wits. This caused him, while still a youth, to compose a dialogue in which he defended Plato's Communism, even to the community of wives. He wrote a rejoinder to Lucian's *Tyrannicide*; in this theme he desired to have me as his antagonist, to make a surer trial of his progress in this branch of letters. His *Utopia* was published with the aim of showing the causes of the bad condition of states; but was chiefly a portrait of the British State, which he has thoroughly studied and explored. He had written the second book first in his leisure hours, and added the first book on the spur of the moment later, when the occasion offered. Some of the unevenness of the style is due to this.

One could hardly find a better *ex tempore* speaker: a happy talent has complete command of a happy turn of speech. He has a present wit, always flying ahead, and a ready memory; and having all this ready to hand, he can promptly and unhesitatingly produce whatever the subject or occasion requires. In arguments he is unimaginably acute, so that he often puzzles the best theologians on their own ground. John Colet, a man of keen and exact judgement, often observes in intimate conversation that Britain has only one genius: although this island is rich in so many fine talents.

He diligently cultivates true piety, while being remote from all superstitious observance. He has set hours in which he offers to God not the customary prayers but prayers from the heart. With his

XXIX. SIR THOMAS MORE AND HIS FAMILY, 1527

XXX. ERASMUS AT THE AGE OF 54

friends he talks of the life of the world to come so that one sees that he speaks sincerely and not without firm hope. Such is More even in the Court. And then there are those who think that Christians are to be found only in monasteries! . . . There you have a portrait not very well drawn by a very bad artist from a most excellent model. You will like it less if you happen to come to know More better. But for the time being I have prevented your being able to cast in my teeth my failure to obey you, and always accusing me of writing too short letters. Still, this did not seem long to me as I was writing it, and I know that you will not find it long drawn out as you read it: our friend More's charm will see to that. Farewell.

XVI. TO WILLIBALD PIRCKHEIMER[1]

Basle, 14 March 1525

To the illustrious Willibald Pirckheimer, greetings:

I received safely the very pretty ring which you desired me to have as a memento of you. I know that gems are prized as bringing safety when one has a fall. But they say too, that if the fall was likely to be fatal, the evil is diverted on to the gem, so that it is seen to be broken after the accident. Once in Britain I fell with my horse from a fairly high bank: no damage was found to me or my horse, yet the gem I was wearing was whole. It was a present from Alexander, Archbishop of St. Andrews,[2] whom I think you know from my writings. When I left him at Siena, he drew it off his finger and handing it to me said: 'Take this as a pledge of our friendship that will never die'. And I kept my pledged faith with him even after his death, celebrating my friend's memory in my writings. There is no part of life into which magical superstition has not insinuated itself: if gems have some great virtue, I could have wished in these days for a ring with an efficacious remedy against 'slander's tooth'. As to the belief about falls, I shall follow your advice—I shall prefer to believe rather than risk myself.

Portraits are less precious than jewels—I have received from you a medallic and a painted portrait—but at least they bring my Willibald more vividly before me. Alexander the Great would only allow himself to be painted by Apelles's hand. You have found your Apelles in

---

[1] W. Pirckheimer (1470–1530), humanist. After studying law and Greek in Italy he settled at Nuremberg. Some of his works were illustrated by Dürer.

[2] Alexander Stewart (c. 1493–1513), natural son of James IV of Scotland, fell at Flodden. Erasmus was his tutor in Italy in 1508–9. For details of this ring see p. 247 f.

Albrecht Dürer,[1] an artist of the first rank and no less to be admired for his remarkable good sense. If only you had likewise found some Lysippus[2] to cast the medal! I have the medal of you on the right-hand wall of my bedroom, the painting on the left; whether writing or walking up and down, I have Willibald before my eyes, so that if I wanted to forget you I could not. Though I have a more retentive memory for friends than for anything else. Certainly Willibald could not be forgotten by me, even were there no memento, no portraits, no letters to refresh my memory of him. There is another very pleasant thing—the portraits often occasion a talk about you when my friends come to visit me. If only our letters travelled safely, how little we should miss of each other! You have a medal of me. I should not object to having my portrait painted by Dürer,[3] that great artist; but how this can be done I do not see. Once at Brussels he sketched me, but after a start had been made the work was interrupted by callers from the Court. Though I have long been a sad model for painters, and am likely to become a sadder one still as the days go on.[4] I read with pleasure what you write, as witty as it is wise, on the agitations of certain persons who are destroying the evangelical movement, to which they imagine themselves to be doing splendid service: and I have much to tell you in my turn about this. But this will be another time, when I have more leisure. Farewell.

XVII. TO MARTIN LUTHER

Basle, 11 April 1526

To Martin Luther, greetings:

Your letter has been delivered too late;[5] but had it arrived in the best of time, it would not have moved me one whit. I am not so

[1] Dürer made three portraits of him, two drawings (now in Berlin and in Brunswick) and an engraving.

[2] The Greek sculptor, c. 350 B.C. In a letter to Pirckheimer dated 8 January 1523–4 (Allen 1408, 29 n.) Erasmus appears dissatisfied with the reverse of the medal cast by Metsys in 1519. Extant examples all show a reverse revised in accordance with his suggestions.

[3] A drawing of Erasmus was made by Dürer in 1520 (now in the Louvre), and an engraving in 1526.

[4] Erasmus had his portrait painted by Holbein several times in 1523–4 and 1530–1. A number of originals and copies are still extant.

[5] Luther's letter, in which he evidently attempted to mitigate Erasmus's indignation against his De Servo Arbitrio (The Will not free), which was a reply to Erasmus's De Libero Arbitrio (On free Will), 1524. Luther's letter came 'too late' because Erasmus had already composed the Hyperaspistes Diatribe adversus Servum Arbitrium Martini Lutheri, Basle, Froben, 1526.

simple as to be appeased by one or two pleasantries or soothed by flattery after receiving so many more than mortal wounds. Your nature is by now known to all the world, but you have so tempered your pen that never have you written against anyone so frenziedly, nay, what is more abominable, so maliciously. Now it occurs to you that you are a weak sinner, whereas at other times you insist almost on being taken for God. You are a man, as you write, of violent temperament, and you take pleasure in this remarkable argument. Why then did you not pour forth this marvellous piece of invective on the Bishop of Rochester[1] or on Cochleus?[2] They attack you personally and provoke you with insults, while my *Diatribe*[3] was a courteous disputation. And what has all this to do with the subject—all this facetious abuse, these slanderous lies, charging me with atheism, Epicureanism, scepticism in articles of the Christian profession, blasphemy, and what not—besides many other points on which I[4] am silent? I take these charges the less hardly, because in all this there is nothing to make my conscience disturb me. If I did not think as a Christian of God and the Holy Scriptures, I could not wish my life prolonged even until tomorrow. If you had conducted your case with your usual vehemence, without frenzied abuse, you would have provoked fewer men against you: as things are, you have been pleased to fill more than a third part of the volume with such abuse, giving free rein to your feelings. How far you have given way to me the facts themselves show—so many palpable crimes do you fasten on me; while my *Diatribe* was not even intended to stir up those matters which the world itself knows of.

You imagine, I suppose, that Erasmus has no supporters. More than you think. But it does not matter what happens to us two, least of all to myself who must shortly go hence, even if the whole world were applauding us: it is *this* that distresses me, and all the best spirits with me, that with that arrogant, impudent, seditious temperament of yours you are shattering the whole globe in ruinous discord, exposing good men and lovers of good learning to certain frenzied Pharisees, arming for revolt the wicked and the revolutionary, and in short so carrying on the cause of the Gospel as to throw all things sacred and profane into chaos; as if you were eager to prevent this

[1] John Fisher (1459?-1535).
[2] John Dobeneck of Wendelstein.
[3] i.e., the *De Libero Arbitrio.*
[4] Reading *reticeo* for *retices.*

storm from turning at last to a happy issue; I have ever striven towards such an opportunity. What you owe me, and in what coin you have repaid me—I do not go into that. All that is a private matter; it is the public disaster which distresses me, and the irremediable confusion of everything, for which we have to thank only your uncontrolled nature, that will not be guided by the wise counsel of friends, but easily turns to any excess at the prompting of certain inconstant swindlers. I know not whom you have saved from the power of darkness; but you should have drawn the sword of your pen against those ungrateful wretches and not against a temperate disputation. I would have wished you a better mind, were you not so delighted with your own. Wish me what you will, only not your mind, unless God has changed it for you.

XVIII. TO THEOPHRASTUS PARACELSUS[1]

[Basle, c. March 1527]

To the most skilled physician Theophrastus of Einsiedeln, etc., greetings:

It is not incongruous to wish continued spiritual health to the medical man through whom God gives us physical health. I wonder how you know me so thoroughly, having seen me once only. I recognize how very true are your dark sayings, not by the art of medicine, which I have never learned, but from my own wretched sensations. I have felt pains in the region of the liver in the past, and could not divine the source of the trouble. I have seen the fat from the kidneys in my water many years ago. Your third point[2] I do not quite understand, nevertheless it appears to be convincing.

As I told you, I have no time for the next few days to be doctored, or to be ill, or to die, so overwhelmed am I with scholarly work. But if there is anything which can alleviate the trouble without weakening the body, I beg you to inform me. If you will be so good as to explain at greater length your very concise and more than laconic notes, and prescribe other remedies which I can take until I am free, I cannot promise you a fee to match your art or the trouble you have taken, but I do at least promise you a grateful heart.

[1] Theophrastus Bombast of Einsiedeln (also known as Theophrastus of Hohenheim, whence his ancestors came), 1493–1541. The name Paracelsus may be a translation of Hohenheim, or may signify a claim to be greater than Celsus, the Roman physician. Appointed *physicus et ordinarius Basiliensis* in 1527.

[2] Paracelsus had diagnosed the stone, from which Erasmus suffered, as being due to crystallization of salt in the kidneys.

Erasmus 1466-1536

You have resurrected Froben,[1] that is, my other half: if you restore me also, you will have restored both of us by treating each of us singly. May we have the good fortune to keep you in Basle!

I fear you may not be able to read this letter dashed off immediately [after receiving yours]. Farewell.

Erasmus of Rotterdam, by his own hand.

XIX. TO MARTIN BUCER[2]

Best greetings: Basle, 11 November 1527

You plead the cause of Capito with some rhetorical skill; but I see that, eloquent advocate as you are otherwise, you are not sufficiently well equipped to undertake his defence. Were I to advance my battle-line of conjectures and proofs, you would realize that you had to devise a different speech. But I have had too much of squabbling, and do not easily bestir myself against men whom I once sincerely loved. What the Knight of Eppendorff[3] ventures or does not venture to do is his concern; only that he returns too frequently to this game. I shall not involve Capito in the drama unless he involves himself again; let him not think me such a fool as not to know what is in question. But I have written myself on these matters. Furthermore, as to your pleading your own cause and that of your church, I think it better not to give any answer, because this matter would require a very lengthy oration, even if it were not a matter of controversy. This is merely a brief answer on scattered points.

The person who informed me about 'languages'[4] is one whose trustworthiness not even you would have esteemed lightly, and he thinks no ill of you. Indeed I have never disliked you as far as concerns private feelings. There are persons living in your town who were chattering here about 'all the disciplines having been invented by

[1] Froben died before the year was out.

[2] Martin Butzer (c. 1491–1551), later Bucer, a Dominican, who obtained dispensation from his vows in 1521 and adhered to the Reformation. At this time he was a member of the Strasbourg party, and this letter is probably an answer to a request for an interview for Bucer and other Strasbourg delegates on their way through Basle to Berne. He eventually became Regius Professor of Divinity at Cambridge under Edward VI.

[3] Henry of Eppendorff, a former friend who followed Hutten on his quarrel with Erasmus.

[4] Erasmus stated in the Responsio of 1 August 1530, that in the Reformed schools little was taught beyond dogmata et linguae and it may be some such criticism, based on what he had heard from a reliable source (perhaps Pirckheimer at Nuremberg), to which Bucer had taken exception in his letter.

godforsaken wretches'. Certainly persons of this description, whatever name must be given them, are in the ascendancy everywhere, all studies are neglected and come to a standstill. At Nuremberg the City Treasury has hired lecturers, but there is no one to attend their lectures.

You assemble a number of conjectures as to why I have not joined your church. But you must know that the first and most important of all the reasons which withheld me from associating myself with it was my conscience: if my conscience could have been persuaded that this movement proceeded from God, I should have been now long since a soldier in your camp. The second reason is that I see many in your group who are strangers to all Evangelical soundness. I make no mention of rumours and suspicions, I speak of things learned from experience, nay, learned to my own injury; things experienced not merely from the mob, but from men who appear to be of some worth, not to mention the leading men. It is not for me to judge of what I know not; the world is wide. I know some as excellent men before they became devotees of your faith, what they are now like I do not know: at all events I have learned that several of them have become worse and none better, so far as human judgement can discern.

The third thing which deterred me is the intense discord between the leaders of the movement. Not to mention the Prophets and the Anabaptists, what embittered pamphlets Zwingli, Luther and Osiander write against each other! I have never approved the ferocity of the leaders, but it is provoked by the behaviour of certain persons; when they ought to have made the Gospel acceptable by holy and forbearing conduct, if you really had what you boast of. Not to speak of the others, of what use was it for Luther to indulge in buffoonery in that fashion against the King of England, when he had undertaken a task so arduous with the general approval? Was he not reflecting as to the role he was sustaining? Did he not realize that the whole world had its eyes turned on him alone? And this is the chief of this movement; I am not particularly angry with him for treating me so scurrilously: but his betrayal of the cause of the Gospel, his letting loose princes, bishops, pseudo-monks and pseudo-theologians against good men, his having made doubly hard our slavery, which is already intolerable—that is what tortures my mind. And I seem to see a cruel and bloody century ahead, if the provoked section gets its breath again, which it is certainly now doing. You will say that there is no crowd without an admixture of wicked men. Certainly it was the duty of the principal men to exercise special care in matters of conduct, and not be even on speaking terms with liars, perjurors, drunkards and fornicators. As it is I hear and almost *see*, that things are far otherwise. If the husband had found his wife more amenable, the teacher his pupil more obedient, the magistrate the citizen more tractable, the employer his workman more trustworthy, the buyer the seller less deceitful, it would have been great recommendation for the Gospels. As things are, the behaviour of certain persons has had the effect of cooling the zeal of those who at first, owing to their love of piety and abhorrence of Pharisaism, looked with favour on this movement; and the princes, seeing a disorderly host springing up in its wake made up of vagabonds, fugitives, bankrupts, naked, wretched and for the most part even wicked men, are cursing, even those who in the beginning had been hopeful.

It is not without deep sorrow that I speak of all this, not only because I foresee that a business wrongly handled will go from bad to worse, but also because at last I shall myself have to suffer for it. Certain rascals say that my writings are to blame for the fact that the scholastic theologians and monks are in several places becoming less esteemed than they would like, that ceremonies are neglected, and that the supremacy of the Roman Pontiff is disregarded; when it is quite clear from what source this evil has sprung. They were stretching too tight the rope which is now breaking. They almost set the Pope's authority above Christ's, they measured all piety by ceremonies, and tightened the hold of the confession to an enormous extent, while the monks lorded it without fear of punishment, by now meditating open tyranny. As a result 'the stretched string snapped', as the proverb has it; it could not be otherwise. But I sorely fear that the same will happen one day to the princes, if they too continue to stretch *their* rope too tightly. Again, the other side having commenced the action of their drama as they did, no different ending was possible. May we not live to see worse horrors!

However it was the duty of the leaders of this movement, if Christ was their goal, to refrain not only from vice, but even from every appearance of evil; and to offer not the slightest stumbling block to the Gospel, studiously avoiding even practices which, although allowed, are yet not expedient. Above all they should have guarded against all sedition. If they had handled the matter with sincerity and moderation, they would have won the support of the princes and bishops: for they have not all been given up for lost. And they should not have heedlessly wrecked anything without having something better ready to put in its place. As it is, those who have abandoned the Hours do not pray at all. Many who have put off pharisaical clothing are worse in other matters than they were before. Those who disdain the episcopal regulations do not even obey the commandments of God. Those who disregard the careful choice of foods indulge in greed and gluttony. It is a long-drawn-out tragedy, which every day we partly hear ourselves and partly learn of from others. I never approved of the abolition of the Mass, even though I have always disliked these mean and money-grabbing mass-priests. There were other things also which could have been altered without causing riots. As things are, certain persons are not satisfied with any of the accepted practices; as if a new world could be built of a sudden. There will always be things which the pious must endure. If anyone thinks that Mass ought to be abolished because many misuse it, then the Sermon should be abolished also, which is almost the only custom accepted by your party. I feel the same about the invocation of the saints and about images.

Your letter demanded a lengthy reply, but even this letter is very long, with all that I have to do. I am told that you have a splendid gift for preaching the Word of the Gospel, and that you conduct yourself more courteously than do many. So I could wish that with your good sense you would strive to the end that this movement, however it began, may through firmness and moderation in doctrine and integrity of conduct be brought to a conclusion worthy of the Gospel. To this end I shall help you to the best of my ability. As it is, although the host of monks and certain theologians assail me with all their artifices, nothing will induce me wittingly to cast away my soul. You will have the good sense not to circulate this letter, lest it cause any disturbance. We would have more discussions if we could meet. Farewell. I had no time to read this over.

Erasmus of Rotterdam, by my own hand.

XX. TO ALFONSO VALDES[1]

Basle, 1 August 1528

To the most illustrious Alfonso Valdes, Secretary to His Imperial Majesty, greetings:

I have learned very plainly from other men's letters what you indicate very discreetly, as is your way—that there are some who seek to

---

[1] Alfonso Valdes (1490?–1532), a devoted admirer of Erasmus, was from 1522 onwards one of Charles V's secretaries. He wrote two dialogues in defence of the Emperor.

XXXI. ERASMUS AT THE AGE OF 60

XXXII. ERASMUS'S DEVICE

make Terminus,[1] the seal on my ring, an occasion for slander, protesting that the addition of the device Concedo nulli [I yield to none] shows intolerable arrogance. What is this but some fatal malady, consisting in misrepresenting everything? Momus[2] is ridiculed for criticizing Venus's slipper; but these men outdo Momus himself, finding something to carp at in a ring. I would have called them Momuses, but Momus carps at nothing but what he has first carefully inspected. These fault-finders, or rather false accusers, criticize with their eyes shut what they neither see nor understand: so violent is the disease. And meanwhile they think themselves pillars of the Church, whereas all they do is to expose their stupidity combined with a malice no less extreme, when they are already more notorious than they should be. They are dreaming if they think it is Erasmus who says Concedo nulli. But if they read my writings they would see that there is none so humble that I rank myself above him, being more liable to yield to all than to none.

Now those who know me intimately from close association will attribute any vice to me sooner than arrogance, and will acknowledge that I am closer to the Socratic utterance, 'This alone I know, that I know nothing', than to this, 'I yield to none'. But if they imagine that I have so insolent a mind as to put myself before all others, do they also think me such a fool as to profess this in a device? If they had any Christian feeling they would understand those words either as not mine or as bearing another meaning. They see there a sculptured figure, in its lower part a stone, in its upper part a youth with flying hair. Does this look like Erasmus in any respect? If this is not enough, they see written on the stone itself Terminus; if one takes this as the last word, that will make an iambic dimeter acatalectic, Concedo nulli Terminus; if one begins with this word, it will be a trochaic dimeter acatalectic, Terminus concedo nulli. What if I had painted a lion and added as a device 'Flee, unless you prefer to be torn to pieces'? Would they attribute these words to me instead of the lion? But what they are doing now is just as foolish; for if I mistake not, I am more like a lion than a stone.

They will argue, 'We did not notice that it was verse, and we know nothing about Terminus'. Is it then to be a crime henceforward to have written verse, because they have not learned the theory of

[1] On this gem see Edgar Wind, 'Aenigma Termini', in Journ. of the Warburg Institute, 1 (1937–8), p. 66.

[2] Greek god of ridicule.

metre? At least, as they knew that in devices of this kind one actually aims at a certain degree of obscurity in order to exercise the guessing powers of those who look at them, if they did not know of Terminus —although they could have learned of him from the books of Augustine or Ambrose—they should have inquired of experts in this kind of matter. In former times field boundaries were marked with some sign. This was a stone projecting above the earth, which the laws of the ancients ordered never to be moved; here belongs the Platonic utterance, 'Remove not what thou hast not planted'. The law was reinforced by a religious awe, the better to deter the ignorant multitude from daring to remove the stone, by making it believe that to violate the stone was to violate a god in it, whom the Romans call Terminus, and to him there was also dedicated a shrine and a festival, the Terminalia. This god Terminus, as the Roman historian has it, was alone in refusing to yield to Jupiter because 'while the birds allowed the deconsecration of all the other sanctuaries, in the shrine of Terminus alone they were unpropitious'.[1] Livy tells this story in the first book of his *History*, and again in Book 5 he narrates how 'when after the taking of auguries the Capitol was being cleared, Juventas [Youth] and Terminus would not allow themselves to be moved'.[2] This omen was welcomed with universal rejoicing, for they believed that it portended an eternal empire. The *youth* is useful for war, and *Terminus* is fixed.

Here they will exclaim perchance, 'What have *you* to do with a mythical god?' He came to me, I did not adopt him. When I was called to Rome, and Alexander, titular Archbishop of St. Andrews,[3] was summoned home from Siena by his father King James of Scotland, as a grateful and affectionate pupil he gave me several rings for a memento of our time together. Among these was one which had *Terminus* engraved on the jewel; an Italian interested in antiquities had pointed this out, which I had not known before. I seized on the omen and interpreted it as a warning that the term of my existence was not far off—at that time I was in about my fortieth year. To keep this thought in my mind I began to seal my letters with this

[1] Livy, 1, 55, 3. Livy refers to the clearing of the Tarpeian rock by Tarquinius Superbus (534–510 B.C.), involving the deconsecration of existing shrines, as a preliminary to the building of the temple of Juppiter Capitolinus. The auguries allowed the evacuation of the other gods, Terminus and Juventas alone refusing to depart.

[2] Livy, 5, 54, 7.

[3] See p. 66.

sign. I added the verse, as I said before. And so from a heathen god I made myself a device, exhorting me to correct my life. For Death is truly a boundary which knows no yielding to any. But in the medal there is added in Greek, Ὅρα τέλος μακροῦ βίου, that is, 'Consider the end of a long life', in Latin *Mors ultima linea rerum*. They will say, 'You could have carved on it a dead man's skull'. Perhaps I should have accepted that, if it had come my way: but this pleased me, because it came to me by chance, and then because it had a double charm for me; from the allusion to an ancient and famous story, and from its obscurity, a quality specially belonging to devices.

There is my defence on *Terminus*, or better say on hair-splitting. And if only they would at last set a *term* to their misrepresentations! I will gladly come to an agreement with them to change my device, if they will change their malady. Indeed by so doing they would be doing more for their own authority, which they complain is being undermined by the lovers of good learning. I myself am assuredly so far from desiring to injure their reputation that I am deeply pained at their delivering themselves over to the ridicule of the whole world by these stupid tricks, and not blushing to find themselves confuted with mockery on every occasion. The Lord keep you safe in body and soul, my beloved friend in Christ.

XXI. TO CHARLES BLOUNT[1]

Freiburg im Breisgau, 1 March 1531

To the noble youth Charles Mountjoy, greetings:

. . . I have determined to dedicate to you Livy, the prince of Latin history, already many times printed, but never before in such a magnificent or accurate edition: and if this is not enough, augmented by five books recently discovered; these were found by some good genius in the library of the monastery at Lorsch by Simon Grynaeus,[2] a man at once learned without arrogance in all branches of literature and at the same time born for the advancement of liberal studies. Now this monastery was built opposite Worms, or Berbethomagium, by Charlemagne seven hundred years and more ago, and equipped with great store of books; for this was formerly the special care of princes,

[1] Preface to *T. Livii . . . historiae*, Basle, Froben, 1531. Charles Blount (b. 1518), eldest son of William Blount, Lord Mountjoy.

[2] c. 1495–1541, Professor of Greek at Basle, 1529. He found the MS. containing Livy, Bks. 41–5, in 1527.

and this is usually the most precious treasure of the monasteries. The original manuscript was one of marvellous antiquity, painted[1] in the antique fashion with the letters in a continuous series, so that it has proved very difficult to separate word from word, unless one is knowledgeable, careful and trained for this very task. This caused much trouble in preparing a copy to be handed to the printer's men for their use; a careful and faithful watch was kept to prevent any departure from the original in making the copy. So if the poor fragment which came to us recently from Mainz was justly welcomed by scholars with great rejoicing,[2] what acclamation should greet this large addition to Livy's *History*?

Would to God that this author could be restored to us complete and entire. There are rumours flying round that give some hope of this: men boast of unpublished Liviana existing, now in Denmark, now in Poland, now in Germany. At least now that fortune has given us these remnants against all men's expectations, I do not see why we should despair of the possibility of finding still more. And here, in my opinion at least, the princes would be acting worthily if they offered rewards and attracted scholars to the search for such a treasure, or prevailed upon them to publish—if there are perchance any who are suppressing and hiding away to the great detriment of studies something in a fit state to be of public utility. For it seems perfectly absurd that men will dig through the bowels of the earth almost down to Hades at vast peril and expense in order to find a little gold or silver: and yet will utterly disregard treasures of this kind, as far above those others in value as the soul excels the body, and not consider them worth searching for. This is the spirit of Midases, not of princes; and as I know that your character is utterly at variance with this spirit, I doubt not that you will most eagerly welcome this great gain. Now, there are chiefly two considerations which remove all possible doubt as to this half-decade's being genuinely by Livy: in the first place that of the diction itself, which in all features recalls its author: secondly that of the arguments or epitomes of Florus, which correspond exactly with these books.

And so, knowing that there is no kind of reading more fitting for men of note than that of the historians, of whom Livy is easily the

[1] Not 'illuminated'. Erasmus refers elsewhere (Allen 919. 55) to a codex as *non scripto sed picto*.

[2] The MS., now lost, containing Bks. 33, 17–49 and 40, 37–59, found in the cathedral library at Mainz, published in Mainz, J. Schoeffer, November 1518.

chief (I speak of the Roman historians), particularly as we have nothing of Sallust beyond two fragments, and bearing in mind what an insatiable glutton, so to speak, your father has always been for history (and I doubt not that you resemble him in this also): I thought I should not be acting incongruously in publishing these five books with a special dedication to you. Although in this point I should not wish you to resemble your father too closely. He is in the way of poring over his books every day from dinner until midnight, which is wearisome to his wife and attendants and a cause of much grumbling among the servants; so far he has been able to do this without loss of health; still, I do not think it wise for you to take the same risk, which may not turn out as successfully. Certainly when your father was studying along with the present king while still a young man, they read chiefly history, with the strong approval of his father Henry VII, a king of remarkable judgement and good sense.

Joined to this edition is the Chronology of Henry Glareanus, a man of exquisite and many-sided learning, whose indefatigable industry refines, adorns and enriches with the liberal disciplines not the renowned Gymnasium at Freiburg alone, but this whole region as well. The Chronology shows the order of events, the details of the wars, and the names of persons, in which up till now there has reigned astonishing confusion, brought about through the fault of the scribes and dabblers in learning. Yet this was the sole guiding light of history! Without this Pole star our navigation on the ocean of history is completely blind: and without this thread to help him, the reader becomes involved in an inextricable maze, learned though he be, in these labyrinths of events. If you consider your letter well repaid by this gift, it will now be your turn to write me a letter. Farewell.

XXII. TO BARTHOLOMEW LATOMUS[1]

To Bartholomew Latomus, greetings: Basle, 24 August 1535

. . . In apologizing for your silence you are wasting your time, believe me; I am not in the habit of judging tried friends by this common courtesy. It would be impudent of me to charge you with an omission which you have an equal right to accuse me of in turn . . . The heads of the colleges are not doing anything new. They are afraid

---

[1] (1498?–1570). Taught Latin and Greek at Freiburg and became head of a college there; in 1534 became the first Professor of Latin in the Collège de France. Retired to Coblenz in 1542.

of their own revenues suffering, this being the sole aim of most of them. You would scarcely believe to what machinations they stooped at Louvain in their efforts to prevent a trilingual college being established. I worked strenuously in the matter, and have made myself accordingly very unpopular. There was an attempt to set up a chair of languages at Tournai, but the University of Louvain and the Franciscans at Tournai did not rest until the project was abandoned. The house erected for this purpose overlooked the Franciscans' garden—that was the cause of the trouble . . .

I have had a long life, counting in years; but were I to calculate the time spent in wrestling with fever, the stone and the gout, I have not lived long. But we must patiently bear whatever the Lord has sent upon us, Whose will no one can resist, and Who alone knows what is good for us . . . The glory [of an immortal name] moves me not at all, I am not anxious over the applause of posterity. My one concern and desire is to depart hence with Christ's favour.

Many French nobles have fled here for fear of the winter storm, after having been recalled.[1] 'The lion shall roar, who shall not fear?' says the Prophet.[2] A like terror has seized the English, from an unlike cause. Certain monks have been beheaded and among them a monk of the Order of St. Bridget[3] was dragged along the ground, then hanged, and finally drawn and quartered. There is a firm and probable rumour here that the news of the Bishop of Rochester having been co-opted by Paul III as a cardinal caused the King to hasten his being dragged out of prison and beheaded—his method of conferring the scarlet hat. It is all too true that Thomas More has been long in prison and his fortune confiscated. It was being said that he too had been executed, but I have no certain news as yet.[4] Would that he had never embroiled himself in this perilous business and had left the theological cause to the theologians. The other friends who from time to time honoured me with letters and gifts now send nothing and write nothing from fear, and accept nothing from anyone, as if under every stone there slept a scorpion.

It seems that the Pope is seriously thinking of a Council here. But I do not see how it is to meet in the midst of such dissension between princes and lands. The whole of Lower Germany is astonishingly

---

[1] By the Edict of Courcy.

[2] Amos iii. 8.

[3] Richard Reynolds of the Bridgettine Syon College at Isleworth.

[4] More had been executed 6 July 1535.

infected with Anabaptists: in Upper Germany they pretend not to notice them. They are pouring in here in droves; some are on their way to Italy. The Emperor is besieging Goletta; in my opinion there is more danger from the Anabaptists.

I do not think that France is entirely free of this plague; but they are silent there for fear of the cudgel . . .

Now I must tell you something about my position which will amuse you. I had written to Paul III at the instance of Louis Ber, the distinguished theologian. Before unsealing the letter he spoke of me with great respect. And as he had to make several scholars cardinals for the coming Council, the name of Erasmus was proposed among others. But obstacles were mentioned, my health, not strong enough for the duties, and my low income; for they say there is a decree which excludes from this office those whose annual income is less than 3,000 ducats. Now they are busy heaping benefices on me, so that I can acquire the proper income from these and receive the red hat. The proverbial cat in court-dress. I have a friend in Rome who is particularly active in the business; in vain have I warned him more than once by letter that I want no cures or pensions, that I am a man who lives from day to day, and every day expecting death, often longing for it, so horrible sometimes are the pains. It is hardly safe for me to put a foot outside my bedroom, and even the merest trifle upsets me.[1] With my peculiar, emaciated body I can only stand warm air. And in this condition they want to push me forward as a candidate for benefices and cardinals' hats! But meanwhile I am gratified by the Supreme Pontiff's delusions about me and his feelings towards me. But I am being more wordy than I intended. I should easily forgive your somewhat lengthy letter, if you were to repeat that fault often . . . Farewell.

[1] Lit. 'not even the peeping of an ass is safe'. This Greek proverb, used of those who go to law about trifles, refers to the story of a potter whose wares were smashed by a donkey in the workshop going to look out of the window. In court the potter, asked of what he complained, replied: 'Of the peeping of an ass'. See Apuleius, *Met.* IX, 42.

LIST OF ILLUSTRATIONS
AND INDEX OF NAMES

LIST OF ILLUSTRATIONS

I. PORTRAIT OF ERASMUS. By Quentin Metsys. 1517. Rome, Galleria Corsini. *Facing p. 14*

One half of a diptych, the pendant being a portrait of Erasmus's friend, Pierre Gilles (Petrus Aegidius), town clerk of Antwerp. The diptych was sent to Sir Thomas More in London; the portrait of Gilles is now in the collection of the Earl of Radnor at Longford Castle.

II. VIEW OF ROTTERDAM at the beginning of the sixteenth century. Contemporary engraving, hand-coloured. *Facing p. 15*

III. PORTRAIT BUST OF JOHN COLET, Dean of St. Paul's (1467–1519). By Pietro Torrigiano. St. Paul's School, Hammersmith, London. *Facing p. 30*

John Colet, a close friend of Erasmus (see pp. 30–1), founded St. Paul's School. The artist, a Florentine sculptor, was active in London for many years and is best known for his effigies on some of the royal tombs in Westminster Abbey. The attribution of this bust is due to F. Grossmann (*Journal of the Warburg and Courtauld Institutes*, XIII, July 1950), who identified it as a cast from Torrigiano's original bust on Colet's tomb (destroyed in the Great Fire of 1666) and also pointed out that Holbein's drawing of Colet in the Royal Library at Windsor Castle (No. 12199) was made from the lost monument after Colet's death.

IV. PORTRAIT OF SIR THOMAS MORE (1477–1535). Dated 1527. By Hans Holbein. New York, Frick Collection. *Facing p. 31*

See also Holbein's drawing of Thomas More with his family, Pl. XXIX.

V. Pen and ink sketches by Erasmus. 1514. Basle, University Library (MS A. IX. 56). *Facing p. 46*

These drawings of grotesque heads and other scribbles are found in Erasmus's manuscript copy of the *Scholia to the Letters of St. Jerome*, preserved in the Library of Basle University and published by Emil Major (*Handzeichnungen des Erasmus von Rotterdam*, Basle, 1933). Erasmus worked on this manuscript shortly after his arrival in Basle in August 1514. His edition of the *Letters of Jerome* was published by Froben in 1516 (see p. 90).

VI. A Manuscript Page of Erasmus. Basle, University Library. *Facing p. 47*

See note on Pl. V.

VII. Title-page of the *Adagia*, printed by Aldus Manutius in 1508. *Facing p. 62*

The printing of this edition was supervised by Erasmus during his visit to Venice (see pp. 64–5). On this title-page is the emblem of the Aldine Press, which is found again on the reverse of Aldus's portrait medal (Pl. IX).

VIII. VIEW OF VENICE, 1493. Woodcut. *After p. 62*

From Schedel's *Weltchronik*, Nuremberg, 1493.

'The portrait, probably commissioned on the occasion of the scholar's fiftieth birthday, shows him surrounded by his large family. It is the first example of an intimate group portrait not of devotional or ceremonial character painted this side of the Alps. At that time Thomas More was living in his country house at Chelsea with his second wife, Alice, his father, his only son and his son's fiancée, three married daughters, eleven grandchildren and a relative, Margaret Giggs. The artist, who had been recommended to him by his friend Erasmus, was also enjoying his hospitality.' (P. Ganz, op. cit., Cat. No. 175).

The original painting is lost; a copy by Richard Locky, dated 1530, is at Nostell Priory. The drawing was sent by More to Erasmus at Basle so as to introduce his family, for which purpose the names and ages were inscribed. In two letters to Sir Thomas and his daughter, dated 5 and 6 September 1530, Erasmus sent his enthusiastic thanks: 'I cannot put into words the deep pleasure I felt when the painter Holbein gave me the picture of your whole family, which is so completely successful that I should scarcely be able to see you better if I were with you.' (Allen, vol. 8, Nos. 2211–2).

Compare also Erasmus's pen portrait of Sir Thomas More in his letter to Hutten, pp. 231–9.

Drawn at Antwerp, during Dürer's journey to the Netherlands. When he received the false news of the murder of Luther at Whitsuntide 1521, Dürer wrote in his diary: 'O Erasmus of Rotterdam, where art thou? Listen, thou Knight of Christ, ride out with the Lord Christ, defend the truth and earn for thyself the martyr's crown!'

In his *Diary of a Journey to the Netherlands*, Dürer noted in late August 1520: 'I have taken Erasmus of Rotterdam's portrait once more', but he does not say when he took his first portrait. The earlier work is assumed to have been done one month before, and to be identical with the drawing in the Louvre (Pl. xxx). This drawing is mentioned by Erasmus himself in a letter to Pirckheimer of 1525 (p. 240); in an earlier letter to the same friend (1522) he says that Dürer had started to paint him in 1520. The second portrait drawing is lost; hence it cannot be proved that this second portrait was made in metal point—as is usually assumed—and not in charcoal, or that the engraving here reproduced was based on it.

Frontispiece: DECORATIVE PORTRAIT OF ERASMUS WITH HIS DEVICE, TERMINUS. Engraving by Hans Holbein, 1535.

ACKNOWLEDGEMENTS

For help in the collection of illustrations we are specially indebted to M. Daniel van Damme, Curator of the Erasmus Museum at Anderlecht and author of the *Éphéméride illustrée de la Vie d'Erasme*, published in 1936 on the occasion of the fourth centenary of Erasmus's death. For photographs and permission to reproduce we have to thank also the Frick Collection, New York (Pl. IV), the Öffentliche Kunstsammlung, Basle (Pl. X–XI, XIV, XXV, XXIX, XXXII), the Library of Basle University (Pl. V–VI), and the Warburg Institute, University of London (Pl. III). The photographs for Pl. II, VII, XVIII–XX and XXVI are by M. Mauhin, Anderlecht, those for Plates VIII and XVII by Dr. F. Stoedtner, Düsseldorf, and that for Plate IX by Fiorentini, Venice.

INDEX OF NAMES

71 72 73   12 11

Revised January, 1970

harper ✦ torchbooks

American Studies: General

HENRY ADAMS Degradation of the Democratic Dogma. ‡ *Introduction by Charles Hirschfeld.* TB/1450

LOUIS D. BRANDEIS: Other People's Money, *and How the Bankers Use It. Ed. with Intro. by Richard M. Abrams* TB/3081

HENRY STEELE COMMAGER, Ed.: The Struggle for Racial Equality TB/1300

CARL N. DEGLER: Out of Our Past: *The Forces that Shaped Modern America* CN/2

CARL N. DEGLER, Ed.: Pivotal Interpretations of American History
Vol. I TB/1240; Vol. II TB/1241

A. S. EISENSTADT, Ed.: The Craft of American History: *Selected Essays*
Vol. I TB/1255; Vol. II TB/1256

LAWRENCE H. FUCHS, Ed.: American Ethnic Politics TB/1368

MARCUS LEE HANSEN: The Atlantic Migration: 1607-1860. *Edited by Arthur M. Schlesinger. Introduction by Oscar Handlin* TB/1052

MARCUS LEE HANSEN: The Immigrant in American History. *Edited with a Foreword by Arthur M. Schlesinger* TB/1120

ROBERT L. HEILBRONER: The Limits of American Capitalism TB/1305

JOHN HIGHAM, Ed.: The Reconstruction of American History TB/1068

ROBERT H. JACKSON: The Supreme Court in the American System of Government TB/1106

JOHN F. KENNEDY: A Nation of Immigrants. *Illus. Revised and Enlarged. Introduction by Robert F. Kennedy* TB/1118

LEONARD W. LEVY, Ed.: American Constitutional Law: *Historical Essays* TB/1285

LEONARD W. LEVY, Ed.: Judicial Review and the Supreme Court 1B/1296

LEONARD W. LEVY: The Law of the Commonwealth and Chief Justice Shaw: *The Evolution of American Law, 1830-1860* TB/1309

GORDON K. LEWIS: Puerto Rico: *Freedom and Power in the Caribbean. Abridged edition* TB/1371

RICHARD B. MORRIS: Fair Trial: *Fourteen Who Stood Accused, from Anne Hutchinson to Alger Hiss* TB/1335

GUNNAR MYRDAL: An American Dilemma: *The Negro Problem and Modern Democracy. Introduction by the Author.*
Vol. I TB/1443; Vol. II TB/1444

GILBERT OSOFSKY, Ed.: The Burden of Race: *A Documentary History of Negro-White Relations in America* TB/1405

CONYERS READ, Ed.: The Constitution Reconsidered. *Revised Edition. Preface by Richrd B. Morris* TB/1384

ARNOLD ROSE: The Negro in America: *The Condensed Version of Gunnar Myrdal's* An American Dilemma. *Second Edition* TB/3048

JOHN E. SMITH: Themes in American Philosophy: *Purpose, Experience and Community* TB/1466

WILLIAM R. TAYLOR: Cavalier and Yankee: *The Old South and American National Character* TB/1474

American Studies: Colonial

BERNARD BAILYN: The New England Merchants in the Seventeenth Century TB/1149

ROBERT E. BROWN: Middle-Class Democracy and Revolution in Massachusetts, 1691-1780. *New Introduction by Author* TB/1413

JOSEPH CHARLES: The Origins of the American Party System TB/1049

HENRY STEELE COMMAGER & ELMO GIORDANETTI, Eds.: Was America a Mistake? *An Eighteenth Century Controversy* TB/1329

WESLEY FRANK CRAVEN: The Colonies in Transition: 1660-1712† TB/3084

CHARLES GIBSON: Spain in America † TB/3077

CHARLES GIBSON, Ed.: The Spanish Tradition in America + HR/1351

LAWRENCE HENRY GIPSON: The Coming of the Revolution: 1763-1775. † *Illus.* TB/3007

JACK P. GREENE, Ed.: Great Britain and the American Colonies: 1606-1763. + *Introduction by the Author* HR/1477

AUBREY C. LAND, Ed.: Bases of the Plantation Society + HR/1429

JOHN LANKFORD, Ed.: Captain John Smith's America: *Selections* from his Writings ‡ TB/3078

LEONARD W. LEVY: Freedom of Speech and Press in Early American History: *Legacy of Suppression* TB/1109

PERRY MILLER: Errand Into the Wilderness TB/1139

PERRY MILLER T. H. JOHNSON, Eds.: The Puritans: *A Sourcebook of Their Writings*
Vol. I TB/1093; Vol. II TB/1094

† The New American Nation Series, edited by Henry Steele Commager and Richard B. Morris.
‡ American Perspectives series, edited by Bernard Wishy and William E. Leuchtenburg.
a History of Europe series, edited by J. H. Plumb.
§ The Library of Religion and Culture, edited by Benjamin Nelson.
‖ Researches in the Social, Cultural, and Behavioral Sciences, edited by Benjamin Nelson.
° Harper Modern Science Series, edited by James A. Newman.
Not for sale in Canada.
+ Documentary History of the United States series, edited by Richard B. Morris.
# Documentary History of Western Civilization series, edited by Eugene C. Black and Leonard W. Levy.
Λ The Economic History of the United States series, edited by Henry David et al.
¶ European Perspectives series, edited by Eugene C. Black.
** Contemporary Essays series, edited by Leonard W. Levy.
* The Stratum Series, edited by John Hale.

1

EDMUND S. MORGAN: The Puritan Family: *Religion and Domestic Relations in Seventeenth Century New England* TB/1227
RICHARD B. MORRIS: Government and Labor in Early America TB/1244
WALLACE NOTESTEIN: The English People on the Eve of Colonization: 1603-1630. † *Illus.* TB/3006
FRANCIS PARKMAN: The Seven Years War: *A Narrative Taken from Montcalm and Wolfe, The Conspiracy of Pontiac, and A Half-Century of Conflict. Edited by John H. McCallum* TB/3083
LOUIS B. WRIGHT: The Cultural Life of the American Colonies: 1607-1763. † *Illus.* TB/3005
YVES F. ZOLTVANY, Ed.: The French Tradition in America + HR/1425

American Studies: The Revolution to 1860

JOHN R. ALDEN: The American Revolution: 1775-1783. † *Illus.* TB/3011
MAX BELOFF, Ed.: The Debate on the American Revolution, 1761-1783: *A Sourcebook* TB/1225
RAY A. BILLINGTON: The Far Western Frontier: 1830-1860. † *Illus.* TB/3012
STUART BRUCHEY: The Roots of American Economic Growth, 1607-1861: *An Essay in Social Causation. New Introduction by the Author.* TB/1350
WHITNEY R. CROSS: The Burned-Over District: *The Social and Intellectual History of Enthusiastic Religion in Western New York, 1800-1850* TB/1242
NOBLE E. CUNNINGHAM, JR., Ed.: The Early Republic, 1789-1828 + HR/1394
GEORGE DANGERFIELD: The Awakening of American Nationalism, 1815-1828. † *Illus.* TB/3061
CLEMENT EATON: The Freedom-of-Thought Struggle in the Old South. *Revised and Enlarged. Illus.* TB/1150
CLEMENT EATON: The Growth of Southern Civilization, 1790-1860. † *Illus.* TB/3040
ROBERT H. FERRELL, Ed.: Foundations of American Diplomacy, 1775-1872 HR/1393
LOUIS FILLER: The Crusade against Slavery: 1830-1860. † *Illus.* TB/3029
DAVID H. FISCHER: The Revolution of American Conservatism: *The Federalist Party in the Era of Jeffersonian Democracy* TB/1449
WILLIAM W. FREEHLING, Ed.: The Nullification Era: *A Documentary Record* ‡ TB/3079
WILLIM W. FREEHLING: Prelude to Civil War: *The Nullification Controversy in South Carolina, 1816-1836* TB/1359
PAUL W. GATES: The Farmer's Age: *Agriculture, 1815-1860* Δ TB/1398
FELIX GILBERT: The Beginnings of American Foreign Policy: *To the Farewell Address* TB/1200
ALEXANDER HAMILTON: The Reports of Alexander Hamilton. ‡ *Edited by Jacob E. Cooke* TB/3060
THOMAS JEFFERSON: Notes on the State of Virginia. ‡ *Edited by Thomas P. Abernethy* TB/3052
FORREST MCDONALD, Ed.: Confederation and Constitution, 1781-1789 + HR/1396
BERNARD MAYO: Myths and Men: *Patrick Henry, George Washington, Thomas Jefferson* TB/1108
JOHN C. MILLER: Alexander Hamilton and the Growth of the New Nation TB/3057
JOHN C. MILLER: The Federalist Era: 1789-1801. † *Illus.* TB/3027

RICHARD B. MORRIS, Ed.: Alexander Hamilton and the Founding of the Nation. *New Introduction by the Editor* TB/1448
RICHARD B. MORRIS: The American Revolution Reconsidered TB/1363
CURTIS P. NETTELS: The Emergence of a National Economy, 1775-1815 Δ TB/1438
DOUGLASS C. NORTH & ROBERT PAUL THOMAS, Eds.: *The Growth of the American Economy to 1860* + HR/1352
R. B. NYE: The Cultural Life of the New Nation: 1776-1830. † *Illus.* TB/3026
GILBERT OSOFSKY, Ed.: Puttin' On Ole Massa: *The Slave Narratives of Henry Bibb, William Wells Brown, and Solomon Northup* ‡ TB/1432
JAMES PARTON: The Presidency of Andrew Jackson. *From Volume III of the* Life of Andrew Jackson. *Ed. with Intro. by Robert V. Remini* TB/3080
FRANCIS S. PHILBRICK: The Rise of the West, 1754-1830. † *Illus.* TB/3067
MARSHALL SMELSER: The Democratic Republic, 1801-1815 † TB/1406
TIMOTHY L. SMITH: Revivalism and Social Reform: *American Protestantism on the Eve of the Civil War* TB/1229
JACK M. SOSIN, Ed.: The Opening of the West + HR/1424
GEORGE ROGERS TAYLOR: The Transportation Revolution, 1815-1860 Δ TB/1347
A. F. TYLER: Freedom's Ferment: *Phases of American Social History from the Revolution to the Outbreak of the Civil War. Illus.* TB/1074
GLYNDON G. VAN DEUSEN: The Jacksonian Era: 1828-1848. † *Illus.* TB/3028
LOUIS B. WRIGHT: Culture on the Moving Frontier TB/1053

American Studies: The Civil War to 1900

W. R. BROCK: An American Crisis: *Congress and Reconstruction, 1865-67* ° TB/1283
T. C. COCHRAN & WILLIAM MILLER: The Age of Enterprise: *A Social History of Industrial America* TB/1054
W. A. DUNNING: Reconstruction, Political and Economic: 1865-1877 TB/1073
HAROLD U. FAULKNER: Politics, Reform and Expansion: 1890-1900. † *Illus.* TB/3020
GEORGE M. FREDRICKSON: The Inner Civil War: *Northern Intellectuals and the Crisis of the Union* TB/1358
JOHN A. GARRATY: The New Commonwealth, 1877-1890 † TB/1410
JOHN A. GARRATY, Ed.: The Transformation of American Society, 1870-1890 + HR/1395
HELEN HUNT JACKSON: A Century of Dishonor: *The Early Crusade for Indian Reform.* † *Edited by Andrew F. Rolle* TB/3063
ALBERT D. KIRWAN: Revolt of the Rednecks: *Mississippi Politics, 1876-1925* TB/1199
ARTHUR MANN: Yankee Reforms in the Urban Age: *Social Reform in Boston, 1800-1900* TB/1247
ARNOLD M. PAUL: Conservative Crisis and the Rule of Law: *Attitudes of Bar and Bench, 1887-1895. New Introduction by Author* TB/1415
JAMES S. PIKE: The Prostrate State: *South Carolina under Negro Government.* ‡ *Intro. by Robert F. Durden* TB/3085
WHITELAW REID: After the War: *A Tour of the Southern States, 1865-1866.* ‡ *Edited by C. Vann Woodward* TB/3066
FRED A. SHANNON: The Farmer's Last Frontier: *Agriculture, 1860-1897* TB/1348

2

VERNON LANE WHARTON: The Negro in Mississippi, 1865-1890   TB/1178

American Studies: The Twentieth Century

RICHARD M. ABRAMS, Ed.: The Issues of the Populist and Progressive Eras, 1892-1912 +   HR/1428
RAY STANNARD BAKER: Following the Color Line: American Negro Citizenship in Progressive Era. ‡ Edited by Dewey W. Grantham, Jr. Illus.   TB/3053
RANDOLPH S. BOURNE: War and the Intellectuals: Collected Essays, 1915-1919. ‡ Edited by Carl Resek   TB/3043
A. RUSSELL BUCHANAN: The United States and World War II. † Illus.
     Vol. I TB/3044; Vol. II TB/3045
THOMAS C. COCHRAN: The American Business System: A Historical Perspective, 1900-1955   TB/1080
FOSTER RHEA DULLES: America's Rise to World Power: 1898-1954. † Illus.   TB/3021
JEAN-BAPTISTE DUROSELLE: From Wilson to Roosevelt: Foreign Policy of the United States, 1913-1945. Trans. by Nancy Lyman Roelker   TB/1370
HAROLD U. FAULKNER: The Decline of Laissez Faire, 1897-1917   TB/1397
JOHN D. HICKS: Republican Ascendancy: 1921-1933. † Illus.   TB/3041
ROBERT HUNTER: Poverty: Social Conscience in the Progressive Era. ‡ Edited by Peter d'A. Jones   TB/3065
WILLIAM E. LEUCHTENBURG: Franklin D. Roosevelt and the New Deal: 1932-1940. † Illus.   TB/3025
WILLIAM E. LEUCHTENBURG, Ed.: The New Deal: A Documentary History +   HR/1354
ARTHUR S. LINK: Woodrow Wilson and the Progressive Era: 1910-1917. † Illus. TB/3023
BROADUS MITCHELL: Depression Decade: From New Era through New Deal, 1929-1941 ∆   TB/1439
GEORGE E. MOWRY: The Era of Theodore Roosevelt and the Birth of Modern America: 1900-1912. † Illus.   TB/3022
WILLIAM PRESTON, JR.: Aliens and Dissenters: Federal Suppression of Radicals, 1903-1933   TB/1287
WALTER RAUSCHENBUSCH: Christianity and the Social Crisis. ‡ Edited by Robert D. Cross   TB/3059
GEORGE SOULE: Prosperity Decade: From War to Depression, 1917-1929 ∆   TB/1349
GEORGE B. TINDALL, Ed.: A Populist Reader: Selections from the Works of American Populist Leaders   TB/3069
TWELVE SOUTHERNERS: I'll Take My Stand: The South and the Agrarian Tradition. Intro. by Louis D. Rubin, Jr.; Biographical Essays by Virginia Rock   TB/1072

Art, Art History, Aesthetics

CREIGHTON GILBERT, Ed.: Renaissance Art ** Illus.   TB/1465
EMILE MALE: The Gothic Image: Religious Art in France of the Thirteenth Century. § 190 illus.   TB/344
MILLARD MEISS: Painting in Florence and Siena After the Black Death: The Arts, Religion and Society in the Mid-Fourteenth Century. 169 illus.   TB/1148
ERWIN PANOFSKY: Renaissance and Renascences in Western Art. Illus.   TB/1447
ERWIN PANOFSKY: Studies in Iconology: Humanistic Themes in the Art of the Renaissance. 180 illus.   TB/1077

JEAN SEZNEC: The Survival of the Pagan Gods: The Mythological Tradition and Its Place in Renaissance Humanism and Art. 108 illus.   TB/2004
OTTO VON SIMSON: The Gothic Cathedral: Origins of Gothic Architecture and the Medieval Concept of Order. 58 illus.   TB/2018
HEINRICH ZIMMER: Myths and Symbols in Indian Art and Civilization. 70 illus. TB/2005

Asian Studies

WOLFGANG FRANKE: China and the West: The Cultural Encounter, 13th to 20th Centuries. Trans. by R. A. Wilson   TB/1326
L. CARRINGTON GOODRICH: A Short History of the Chinese People. Illus.   TB/3015
DAN N. JACOBS, Ed.: The New Communist Manifesto and Related Documents. 3rd revised edn.   TB/1078
DAN N. JACOBS & HANS H. BAERWALD, Eds.: Chinese Communism: Selected Documents   TB/3031
BENJAMIN I. SCHWARTZ: Chinese Communism and the Rise of Mao   TB/1308
BENJAMIN I. SCHWARTZ: In Search of Wealth and Power: Yen Fu and the West   TB/1422

Economics & Economic History

C. E. BLACK: The Dynamics of Modernization: A Study in Comparative History   TB/1321
STUART BRUCHEY: The Roots of American Economic Growth, 1607-1861: An Essay in Social Causation. New Introduction by the Author.   TB/1350
GILBERT BURCK & EDITORS OF Fortune: The Computer Age: And its Potential for Management   TB/1179
JOHN ELLIOTT CAIRNES: The Slave Power. ‡ Edited with Introduction by Harold D. Woodman   TB/1433
SHEPARD B. CLOUGH, THOMAS MOODIE & CAROL MOODIE, Eds.: Economic History of Europe: Twentieth Century #   HR/1388
THOMAS C. COCHRAN: The American Business System: A Historical Perspective, 1900-1955   TB/1180
ROBERT A. DAHL & CHARLES E. LINDBLOM: Politics, Economics, and Welfare: Planning and Politico-Economic Systems Resolved into Basic Social Processes   TB/3037
PETER F. DRUCKER: The New Society: The Anatomy of Industrial Order   TB/1082
HAROLD U. FAULKNER: The Decline of Laissez Faire, 1897-1917 ∆   TB/1397
PAUL W. GATES: The Farmer's Age: Agriculture, 1815-1860 ∆   TB/1398
WILLIAM GREENLEAF, Ed.: American Economic Development Since 1860 +   HR/1353
J. L. & BARBARA HAMMOND: The Rise of Modern Industry. || Introduction by R. M. Hartwell   TB/1417
ROBERT L. HEILBRONER: The Future as History: The Historic Currents of Our Time and the Direction in Which They Are Taking America   TB/1386
ROBERT L. HEILBRONER: The Great Ascent: The Struggle for Economic Development in Our Time   TB/3030
FRANK H. KNIGHT: The Economic Organization   TB/1214
DAVID S. LANDES: Bankers and Pashas: International Finance and Economic Imperialism in Egypt. New Preface by the Author TB/1412
ROBERT LATOUCHE: The Birth of Western Economy: Economic Aspects of the Dark Ages   TB/1290

Literature & Literary Criticism

Philosophy

ERNST CASSIRER: Rousseau, Kant and Goethe. *Intro. by Peter Gay* TB/1092
FREDERICK COPLESTON, S. J.: Medieval Philosophy TB/376
F. M. CORNFORD: From Religion to Philosophy: *A Study in the Origins of Western Speculation* § TB/20
WILFRID DESAN: The Tragic Finale: *An Essay on the Philosophy of Jean-Paul Sartre* TB/1030
MARVIN FARBER: The Aims of Phenomenology: *The Motives, Methods, and Impact of Husserl's Thought* TB/1291
MARVIN FARBER: Basic Issues of Philosophy: *Experience, Reality, and Human Values* TB/1344
MARVIN FARBERS: Phenomenology and Existence: *Towards a Philosophy within Nature* TB/1295
PAUL FRIEDLANDER: `Plato: An Introduction TB/2017
MICHAEL GELVEN: A Commentary on Heidegger's "Being and Time" TB/1464
J. GLENN GRAY: Hegel and Greek Thought TB/1409
W. K. C. GUTHRIE: The Greek Philosophers: *From Thales to Aristotle* ° TB/1008
G. W. F. HEGEL: On Art, Religion Philosophy: *Introductory Lectures to the Realm of Absolute Spirit.* || *Edited with an Introduction by J. Glenn Gray* TB/1463
G. W. F. HEGEL: Phenomenology of Mind. ° || *Introduction by George Lichtheim* TB/1303
MARTIN HEIDEGGER: Discourse on Thinking. *Translated with a Preface by John M. Anderson and E. Hans Freund. Introduction by John M. Anderson* TB/1459
F. H. HEINEMANN: Existentialism and the Modern Predicament TB/28
WERER HEISENBERG: Physics and Philosophy: *The Revolution in Modern Science. Intro. by F. S. C. Northrop* TB/549
EDMUND HUSSERL: Phenomenology and the Crisis of Philosophy. § *Translated with an Introduction by Quentin Lauer* TB/1170
IMMANUEL KANT: Groundwork of the Metaphysic of Morals. *Translated and Analyzed by H. J. Paton* TB/1159
IMMANUEL KANT: Lectures on Ethics. § *Introduction by Lewis White Beck* TB/105
WALTER KAUFMANN, Ed.: Religion From Tolstoy to Camus: *Basic Writings on Religious Truth and Morals* TB/123
QUENTIN LAUER: Phenomenology: *Its Genesis and Prospect. Preface by Aron Gurwitsch* TB/1169
MAURICE MANDELBAUM: The Problem of Historical Knowledge: *An Answer to Relativism* TB/1198
H. J. PATON: The Categorical Imperative: *A Study in Kant's Moral Philosophy* TB/1325
MICHAEL POLANYI: Personal Knowledge: *Towards a Post-Critical Philosophy* TB/1158
KARL R. POPPER: Conjectures and Refutations: *The Growth of Scientific Knowledge* TB/1376
WILLARD VAN ORMAN QUINE: Elementary Logic *Revised Edition* TB/577
WILLARD VAN ORMAN QUINE: From a Logical Point of View: *Logico-Philosophical Essays* TB/566
JOHN E. SMITH: Themes in American Philosophy: *Purpose, Experience and Community* TB/1466
MORTON WHITE: Foundations of Historical Knowledge TB/1440
WILHELM WINDELBAND: A History of Philosophy *Vol. I: Greek, Roman, Medieval* TB/38
Vol. II: Renaissance, Enlightenment, Modern TB/39

LUDWIG WITTGENSTEIN: The Blue and Brown Books ° TB/1211
LUDWIG WITTGENSTEIN: Notebooks, 1914-1916 TB/1441

Political Science & Government

C. E. BLACK: The Dynamics of Modernization: *A Study in Comparative History* TB/1321
DENIS W. BROGAN: Politics in America. *New Introduction by the Author* TB/1469
CRANE BRINTON: English Political Thought in the Nineteenth Century TB/1071
ROBERT CONQUEST: Power and Policy in the USSR: *The Study of Soviet Dynastics* ° TB/1307
ROBERT A. DAHL & CHARLES E. LINDBLOM: Politics, Economics, and Welfare: *Planning and Politico-Economic Systems Resolved into Basic Social Processes* TB/1277
HANS KOHN: Political Ideologies of the 20th Century TB/1277
ROY C. MACRIDIS, Ed.: Political Parties: *Contemporary Trends and Ideas* ** TB/1322
ROBERT GREEN MC CLOSKEY: American Conservatism in the Age of Enterprise, 1865-1910 TB/1137
MARSILIUS OF PADUA: The Defender of Peace. *The Defensor Pacis. Translated with an Introduction by Alan Gewirth* TB/1310
KINGSLEY MARTIN: French Liberal Thought in the Eighteenth Century: *A Study of Political Ideas from Bayle to Condorcet* TB/1114
BARRINGTON MOORE, JR.: Political Power and Social Theory: *Seven Studies* || TB/1221
BARRINGTON MOORE, JR.: Soviet Politics—The Dilemma of Power: *The Role of Ideas in Social Change* || TB/1222
BARRINGTON MOORE, JR.: Terror and Progress—USSR: *Some Sources of Change and Stability* TB/558
JOHN B. MORRALL: Political Thought in Medieval Times TB/1076
KARL R. POPPER: The Open Society and Its Enemies *Vol. I: The Spell of Plato* TB/1101
Vol. II: The High Tide of Prophecy: Hegel, Marx, and the Aftermath TB/1102
CONYERS READ, Ed.: The Constitution Reconsidered. *Revised Edition, Preface by Richard B. Morris* TB/1384
JOHN P. ROCHE, Ed.: Origins of American Political Thought: *Selected Readings* TB/1301
JOHN P. ROCHE, Ed.: American Political Thought: *From Jefferson to Progressivism* TB/1332
HENRI DE SAINT-SIMON: Social Organization, The Science of Man, and Other Writings. || *Edited and Translated with an Introduction by Felix Markham* TB/1152
CHARLES SCHOTTLAND, Ed.: The Welfare State ** TB/1323
JOSEPH A. SCHUMPETER: Capitalism, Socialism and Democracy TB/3008

Psychology

ALFRED ADLER: The Individual Psychology of Alfred Adler: *A Systematic Presentation in Selections from His Writings. Edited by Heinz L. & Rowena R. Ansbacher* TB/1154
LUDWIG BINSWANGER: Being-in-the-World: *Selected Papers.* || *Trans. with Intro. by Jacob Needleman* TB/1365
HADLEY CANTRIL: The Invasion from Mars: *A Study in the Psychology of Panic* || TB/1282
MIRCEA ELIADE: Cosmos and History: *The Myth of the Eternal Return* § TB/2050
MIRCEA ELIADE: Myth and Reality TB/1369

MIRCEA ELIADE: Myths, Dreams and Mysteries: *The Encounter Between Contemporary Faiths and Archaic Realities* §   TB/1320
MIRCEA ELIADE: Rites and Symbols of Initiation: *The Mysteries of Birth and Rebirth* §   TB/1236
HERBERT FINGARETTE: The Self in Transformation: *Psychoanalysis, Philosophy and the Life of the Spirit* || TB/1177
SIGMUND FREUD: On Creativity and the Unconscious: *Papers on the Psychology of Art, Literature, Love, Religion.* § *Intro. by Benjamin Nelson*   TB/45
J. GLENN GRAY: The Warriors: *Reflections on Men in Battle. Introduction by Hannah Arendt*   TB/1294
WILLIAM JAMES: Psychology: *The Briefer Course. Edited with an Intro. by Gordon Allport*   TB/1034
C. G. JUNG: Psychological Reflections. *Ed. by J. Jacobi*   TB/2001
KARL MENNINGER, M.D.: Theory of Psychoanalytic Technique   TB/1144
JOHN H. SCHAAR: Escape from Authority: *The Perspectives of Erich Fromm*   TB/1155
MUZAFER SHERIF: The Psychology of Social Norms. *Introduction by Gardner Murphy*   TB/3072
HELLMUT WILHELM: Change: *Eight Lectures on the I Ching*   TB/2019

Religion: Ancient and Classical, Biblical and Judaic Traditions

W. F. ALBRIGHT: The Biblical Period from Abraham to Ezra   TB/102
SALO W. BARON: Modern Nationalism and Religion   TB/818
C. K. BARRETT, Ed.: The New Testament Background: *Selected Documents*   TB/86
MARTIN BUBER: Eclipse of God: *Studies in the Relation Between Religion and Philosophy*   TB/12
MARTIN BUBER: Hasidism and Modern Man. *Edited and Translated by Maurice Friedman*   TB/839
MARTIN BUBER: The Knowledge of Man. *Edited with an Introduction by Maurice Friedman. Translated by Maurice Friedman and Ronald Gregor Smith*   TB/135
MARTIN BUBER: Moses. *The Revelation and the Covenant*   TB/837
MARTIN BUBER: The Origin and Meaning of Hasidism. *Edited and Translated by Maurice Friedman*   TB/835
MARTIN BUBER: The Prophetic Faith   TB/73
MARTIN BUBER: Two Types of Faith: *Interpenetration of Judaism and Christianity* °   TB/75
MALCOLM L. DIAMOND: Martin Buber: *Jewish Existentialist*   TB/840
M. S. ENSLIN: Christian Beginnings   TB/5
M. S. ENSLIN: The Literature of the Christian Movement   TB/6
ERNST LUDWIG EHRLICH: A Concise History of Israel: *From the Earliest Times to the Destruction of the Temple in A.D. 70* °   TB/128
HENRI FRANKFORT: Ancient Egyptian Religion: *An Interpretation*   TB/77
ABRAHAM HESCHEL: The Earth Is the Lord's & The Sabbath. *Two Essays*   TB/828
ABRAHAM HESCHEL: God in Search of Man: *A Philosophy of Judaism*   TB/807
ABRAHAM HESCHEL: Man Is not Alone: *A Philosophy of Religion*   TB/838
ABRAHAM HESCHEL: The Prophets: *An Introduction*   TB/1421

T. J. MEEK: Hebrew Origins   TB/69
JAMES MUILENBURG: The Way of Israel: *Biblical Faith and Ethics*   TB/133
H. J. ROSE: Religion in Greece and Rome   TB/55
H. H. ROWLEY: The Growth of the Old Testament   TB/107
D. WINTON THOMAS, Ed.: Documents from Old Testament Times   TB/85

Religion: General Christianity

ROLAND H. BAINTON: Christendom: *A Short History of Christianity and Its Impact on Western Civilization. Illus.*   Vol. I TB/131; Vol. II TB/132
JOHN T. MCNEILL: Modern Christian Movements. *Revised Edition*   TB/1402
ERNST TROELTSCH: The Social Teaching of the Christian Churches. *Intro. by H. Richard Niebuhr*   Vol. TB/71; Vol. II TB/72

Religion: Early Christianity Through Reformation

ANSELM OF CANTERBURY: Truth, Freedom, and Evil: *Three Philosophical Dialogues. Edited and Translated by Jasper Hopkins and Herbert Richardson*   TB/317
MARSHALL W. BALDWIN, Ed.: Christianity through the 13th Century #   HR/1468
W. D. DAVIES: Paul and Rabbinic Judaism: *Some Rabbinic Elements in Pauline Theology. Revised Edition* °   TB/146
ADOLF DEISSMANN: Paul: *A Study in Social and Religious History*   TB/15
JOHANNES ECKHART: Meister Eckhart: *A Modern Translation by R. Blakney*   TB/8
EDGAR J. GOODSPEED: A Life of Jesus   TB/1
ROBERT M. GRANT: Gnosticism and Early Christianity   TB/136
WILLIAM HALLER: The Rise of Puritanism   TB/22
GERHART B. LADNER: The Idea of Reform: *Its Impact on the Christian Thought and Action in the Age of the Fathers*   TB/149
ARTHUR DARBY NOCK: Early Gentile Christianity and Its Hellenistic Background   TB/111
ARTHUR DARBY NOCK: St. Paul °   TR/104
GORDON RUPP: Luther's Progress to the Diet of Worms °   TB/120

Religion: The Protestant Tradition

KARL BARTH: Church Dogmatics: *A Selection. Intro. by H. Gollwitzer. Ed. by G. W. Bromiley*   TB/95
KARL BARTH: Dogmatics in Outline   TB/56
KARL BARTH: The Word of God and the Word of Man   TB/13
HERBERT BRAUN, et al.: God and Christ: *Existence and Province. Volume 5 of Journal for Theology and the Church, edited by Robert W. Funk and Gerhard Ebeling*   TB/255
WHITNEY R. CROSS: The Burned-Over District: *The Social and Intellectual History of Enthusiastic Religion in Western New York, 1800-1850*   TB/1242
NELS F. S. FERRE: Swedish Contributions to Modern Theology. *New Chapter by William A. Johnson*   TB/147
WILLIAM R. HUTCHISON, Ed.: American Protestant Thought: *The Liberal Era* ‡   TB/1385
ERNST KASEMANN, et al.: Distinctive Protestant and Catholic Themes Reconsidered. *Volume 3 of Journal for Theology and the Church,*